A DOCTOR'S LIFE IN HONG KONG

John Mackay

A Doctor's Life in Hong Kong
By John Mackay

ISBN-13: 978-988-8843-28-2

© 2024 John Mackay

BIOGRAPHY & AUTOBIOGRAPHY

EB198

All rights reserved. No part of this book may be reproduced in material form, by any means, whether graphic, electronic, mechanical or other, including photocopying or information storage, in whole or in part. May not be used to prepare other publications without written permission from the publisher except in the case of brief quotations embodied in critical articles or reviews. For information contact info@earnshawbooks.com

Published in Hong Kong by Earnshaw Books Ltd.

Contents

Foreword		3
Chapter One:	Proud to be a Mackay	5
Chapter Two:	1896–1935 From Buckie to Bombay	11
Chapter Three:	1935–1945 An Indian Childhood	31
Chapter Four:	1945–1961 School and University in Scotland	47
Chapter Five:	1955–1961 Crossing the World – Travels as a Student	77
Chapter Six:	1961–1963 and beyond – The Bahamas	103
Chapter Seven:	A New Life in Hong Kong	129
Chapter Eight:	A Partner in Practice	147
Chapter Nine:	1976–2016 Exploring China	185
Chapter Ten:	A Happy Retirement – Family, Gardens, Golf and Travel	237
Chapter Eleven:	India Revisited – A Nostalgic Journey of Rediscovery	265
My Family		313
Epilogue		323
Acknowledgements		327
About The Author		329

Foreword

Winston Churchill was reported once to have said of Clement Atlee, "He is a modest man. Indeed, he has a lot to be modest about."

I have written this memoir to record a long life in interesting times. This first volume concerns my Scottish background, early childhood in India in the days of the Raj, my education back in Scotland, and my career as a doctor in Hong Kong from 1963 during a time of remarkable development in this unique territory.

The second part tells of my love of mountains and my travel to many countries to climb their highest mountains.

I hope that reading my story gives everyone some interest and pleasure, an insight into my life, and fires their desire for a more adventurous life of their own.

Chapter One
Proud to be a Mackay

The Mackay Clan is one of the oldest families in Scotland. The name is derived from the Gaelic MacAodh, or Mackay in its English form.

More recent historical research traces the origins of the Clan to Iye Mackay, first chief of the Clan Mackay, who was born in about 1210. His family had been Mormears, or Kings, of Moray, until they were driven out by King Malcolm IV of Scotland, who ruled from 1153 to 1165. The Clan fled to Strathnaver in the far north of Scotland in what is now Caithness and Sutherland; they were welcomed by the Norse Harald Maddadsson, Mormaer of Caithness, an enemy of the king at that time.

Family Bible and church records show that my Mackay ancestors came from those who remained in the Moray area, on the Moray Firth. The male Mackays and Flemings — the family of my mother — joined the professions, such as the law, medicine, church, education, accountancy and the Army; others became landowners and farmers — the county set. The women taught in school, nursed and married — they produced large families. My strongest claim to royal blood is through Margaret Young,

Manu Forti

the wife of my great, great grandfather James Mackay; they married in the 1830s. Her family tree goes all the way back to King David 1, King of Scotland, 1124-1153.

One important fact about my clan is that they were Protestant, not Catholic. In 1560, the Scottish Reformation Parliament approved a Protestant confession of faith and rejected the jurisdiction of the Pope and the Catholic Mass. Scotland became a largely Protestant and Presbyterian country. A minority of the population remained Catholic. This split became the most important division in the country for the next 400 years, more than the divide between England and Scotland. The Mackays became Presbyterian, the faith of my family.

In 1715 and 1745, Jacobite forces that wanted to put a Stuart king back on the throne of England started rebellions in Scotland. On both occasions, the Clan Mackay fought on the British side. During the 1745 uprising, Mackay soldiers intercepted and captured gold sent from France to the Jacobite leader Charles Edward Stuart, grandson of King James II of Britain. Bonny Prince Charlie was the final hope of restoring a Stuart monarchy to the British throne. After leaving France, he arrived in Scotland in July 1745 and raised an army from some Scottish clans, but not the Mackays. After early success, he and his troops were defeated by a British army lead by William, Lord Cumberland, the son of George II, at the Battle of Culloden on April 16, 1746, near Inverness in the Scottish Highlands. It was the last pitched battle on British soil. Prince Charles fled to France and never returned to Britain. Both Prince Charles and Lord Cumberland were aged 24 at the time of Culloden. Ever since, Britain has been ruled by a Protestant king or queen.

British Military
The Mackays have a long history of distinguished service in the British military, including at the Battle of Waterloo in 1815 against Napoleon Bonaparte. They served in the British Army in India, including during the Indian Mutiny in 1857. That year, Private David Mackay of the 93rd Sutherland Highlanders won the Victoria Cross—the highest British medal for bravery—during an attack by the 2nd Battalion of Punjabis, the only Sikh regiment to mutiny, on November 16, 1857. They attacked a fortification at Secundrabagh, Lucknow, in northern India. After intense fighting, Mackay took the colours of the rebel Punjabis. Later that same day, he was injured during an attack on a second fort in Lucknow; he had to return to Britain for treatment. My father also served as a soldier in India, as an officer in the British Indian Army; I will describe his history in a later chapter.

In 1900, another Mackay, John Frederick, won a Victoria Cross during the Boer War. Serving with the Gordon Highlanders, he fought at the Battle of Crow's Nest Hill, North Johannesburg on May 29th. The official citation read: "Corporal McKay repeatedly rushed forward, under a withering fire at short ranges, to attend to wounded comrades, dressing their wounds whilst he himself was without shelter, and in one instance, he carried a wounded man from the open, under a heavy fire, to the shelter of a boulder."

Many Mackays served in colonial administrations around the world. Donald Mackay, the then head of the clan, was Governor of

Bombay from 1885 to 1890 and Under Secretary of State for India from 1894 to 1895. He was also the first President of the British Academy from 1902 to 1907. According to historical records, the Clan Mackay had its first chief in the 13th Century, based in Sutherland and Caithness, in the far north of Scotland. He was designated 'of Strathnaver', a town in the county. In ancient times, Strathnaver also meant 'the Mackay Country', referring to an area extending over most of northwest Sutherland. The clan seat was Castle Varrich, near the village of Tongue. In the 17th Century, the seat moved to Tongue House, built in 1678. In 1829, the Mackay clan had to sell the house and the majority of their estate to pay debts owed to the Sutherland family. Today it is the Scottish home of the Countess of Sutherland.

In the 17th Century, the chief of the clan was given the additional title of Lord Reay. The current chief is Aeneas Simon Mackay, the 15th Lord Reay, who was born on March 20, 1965. He succeeded his father to the title in 2013. Since January 2019, he has been a Conservative member of the British House of Lords. He works in corporate finance. In 2009, my wife, Judith, and I marched up the Royal Mile with the Chieftain in the Scottish Homecoming Parade in Edinburgh.

The Flemings
My mother was a Fleming. This name was derived from the French, le Fleming. The family originated in the 8th Century, county of Flanders, until it was annexed by the French Republic in the 1790s. This once-powerful medieval principality is now split between the Netherlands and France. The earliest Fleming in Scotland was Baldwin of Biggar, grandson of Erkenbald Flandrensis, who died in 1100. In 1155, Henry II passed a decree expelling all Flemish people from England; this increased the number of Flemings in Scotland. In addition, King Malcolm IV

invited others to come. The adoption of the hereditary surname Fleming by the descendants of Erkenbald Flandrensis in various parts of Britain, including Scotland, is well documented. His descendants are likely to account for a large number of Flemings alive today.

The family tree of the Fleming family to which my mother belonged goes back to a John Fleming of Deskie in Moray, who married in 1772.

Chapter Two
1896–1935
From Buckie to Bombay

My father, Richard Johnstone Mackay, was born on October 21, 1896, in Buckie in the county of Banff, on the Moray Firth in the northeast of Scotland. He was the third son in a family of seven children. Buckie had a population of about 4,000 who lived off farming, forestry, fishing and shipbuilding. Its industrial centre was Cluny Harbour, built in 1877; it was a thriving fishing and shipbuilding port. In 1913, Buckie had the largest steam drifter fleet in Scotland. Around the harbour were large factories and smoke houses that processed the fishermen's catches. In the 1880s, the town was connected to the Great North of Scotland Railway, with trains via Aberdeen to London and to Inverness to transport the fish to market.

The residents of Buckie are hardy people—between October and March, the average temperature is about five degrees Celsius and it is dark by 4 p.m.

My grandfather, Robert Young Mackay, was a lawyer. He had a successful practice in Buckie until about 1920 when he was appointed the Procurator Fiscal for the county of Dumfries in southwest Scotland. He died in office in 1929. In the Scottish justice system, the Procurator Fiscal is the Crown prosecutor who decides whether or not to pursue cases brought to him by the police; he is a pivotal figure in the criminal system. His wife, Edith, died in 1948 at Lockerbie, at the house of her son, Rob. She was the only one of my grandparents I ever met.

The fathers of both of my parents were lawyers. Their positions as senior lawyers made both men leading figures in the community. My mother's father was John Grant Fleming, a partner in the firm Thurburn and Fleming, in the nearby town of Keith.

My two grandfathers married daughters of the same wealthy local family, the Culbards. William Culbard owned the biggest leather business in the north of Scotland. He bought hides from local suppliers and from Russia and Denmark; he sold them in Edinburgh, Scotland's capital, in London and on the continent. The family owned Old Mills, a large estate outside Elgin, the county town of Moray. Culbard was a Lieutenant Colonel in the Third Emergency Rendezvous (ERV), a reserve unit of the British Army. Between 1875 and 1881, he was also Provost (Mayor) of Elgin. He and his wife had five daughters. After World War II, my family and I returned to Britain from India, where my father served in the British Indian Army. We went to live in Old Mills; two of the five daughters, Amelia and Christina, both spinsters, were living there at that time. They were my great-aunts.

In a letter to my sister Eleanore in February 1968, my father described his childhood and how he could have lost his life when he was only one year old. This was the start of an autobiography, never completed.

> My two elder brothers were supposed to be looking after me when I was lying in my pram outside our

house (now the Commercial Hotel) in the sloping High Street of Buckie. They must have got a bit bored with it for they conceived the brilliant idea of taking the pram for a walk. Of course, the slope of the road proved too much for them and the heavy pram, with me in it, careered down the hill and ended upside down in the gutter. Apart from that and the usual childhood illnesses, including scarlet fever, my childhood was uneventful.

Shortly after his birth, his father built a house at Benreay, Buckie, for his growing family; it had a garden. Like other families of their social status, the Mackays had domestic servants.

My father attended a kindergarten with more than 50 children. Then he went to the local Cluny Primary School; before he arrived at school, he took off his shoes so that he would not be conspicuous at school amongst the sons of the local fisher folk who had no shoes. On his way home, he put his shoes on again. Next was the Buckie Higher Grade School, with a class of 40 boys and girls. Their teacher was James Moir. "He taught mainly with the strap, which we all felt from time to time for one reason or another, mainly minor," my father wrote in a letter. "To supplement my education, such as it was, I was given extra tuition by Miss Lyall, whom I chiefly remember for her beautifully kept hands and wax-like skin. The idea was that I should qualify for a scholarship at Fettes, where my brothers Norris and Alastair had already gone."

Alastair was five years older than my own father. Fettes College, in Edinburgh, was one of Scotland's most prestigious schools. Founded in 1870 on a 350 acres estate, it was a fee-paying private institution; two thirds of the students boarded at the school and the other third came during the day. It followed

A DOCTOR'S LIFE IN HONG KONG

Great Grandfather Culbard

Grandfather Mackay and wife

JOHN MACKAY

Grandfather Fleming and wife

Father and mother

the English, not the Scottish, educational curriculum.

> I eventually took the exam but failed, possibly due to its being my first visit to Edinburgh with so much to see, and the glimmer of the Edinburgh Exhibition in what is now the Slateford Gardens and, more probably due to Alastair meeting me at the school just before the exam and threatening all sorts of calamities if I passed. He didn't want me there.

Like his classmates, my father received pocket money of a penny a week; he liked sports, especially soccer.

> We always seemed to have a ball and we played till all hours, often to the wrath of Mother when I was late for meals, in the Public Park and what is now the Victoria Park, the home of Buckie Thistle (Football Club). We attended most of the Buckie Thistle games, the most memorable being a match against the Black Watch, a Scottish Regiment, who against anticipation turned out to be white not black, against Elgin City, always a good game, and particularly against Keith when we shouted against the Ciards. I remember one match against Keith when a Buckie loon (young boy) — Imlach — played goal for Keith and we all barracked him and shouted with joy when he was beaten by our local hero, butcher and centre forward, Jock Mackenzie. But he was good — they both were.
>
> After soccer, my interests centred on the harbour where I had a lot of pals among the fishermen and often went out with them on trial trips, etc, and once for four days. I have never been so seasick — in fact, I

have never been seasick since—in the 'Protect', a steam drifter, in which my father had an interest. We landed our catch at Fraserburgh, and I caught a huge coal fish, a pollock, which one of the crew had to help me haul in—I thought it was a whale when it ran away with my line and I had shouted for help. Actually, there were whales all around us when the drift nets were being hauled in—my first and last sighting of whales alongside and rather frightening.

This is how my father described his daily life.

We made our own amusements and, without radio and television, spent much time reading and, better still, being read to—at which my mother was adept. Our normal day started with breakfast at 8 a.m. of porridge, tea and toast (my father had bacon and eggs every day). On Sundays, breakfast was at 9 a.m. and we all had a cooked course, usually sausages. Lunch was a solid meal, three courses. Tea consisted of bread and butter followed by bread and jam and then whatever was going in the way of buns, with a gingerbread cake on Sundays. Supper was porridge again, though the parents and bigger ones had a two-course meal.
    On Sunday after breakfast, all the maids (cook, table maid, housemaid and nurse) joined us for family prayers (a reading and prayer) and then we all rushed to get ready for church at 11 a.m.—filling in any spare time by memorising psalm verses, etc., set for the afternoon Sunday school. After church, in fine weather, we would troop down to the harbour and out to the pier, coming back via the top of the sea wall

normally (and especially if Mother wasn't with us). Then a huge lunch and, while father relaxed with his British Weekly and Spectator, we went off to Sunday school, followed by a walk into the country till teatime.

Then evening service, to which Father always went but which was optional for the rest of us. Dad usually brought home someone for supper, most often the organist, Emslie, and, after supper — which was always cold (the only let-off for the maids during the week) — we were joined by the Bank Manager, Anderson, and we sat in the drawing room chatting and listening to Dad (and anyone else that way inclined) singing. He had a fine voice and did quite a lot of concert singing, as well as helping out as required in the church choir. And so to bed.

The church minister was Dr Miller, a somewhat awesome character with a long beard who preached 45-minute sermons. He christened all the family and was often in the house.

Like many of their neighbours, the Mackays were devout Presbyterians. In the first half of the 20th Century, religion played an important role in the lives of Scottish people. In 1560, the Scottish Parliament voted to make the country Protestant. In 1690, the Church of Scotland became the Presbyterian Church; across the border, the Church of England was Anglican, with the monarch as head of the church. This constitutional order has continued in both countries until today. Members of the family did not abstain from smoking or drinking, but on Sunday no gambling or any sort of entertainment or sport was available in towns in Moray or Banff.

The regimen in the house was spartan.

Every day, my father started with a cold bath and mother with a tepid one into which we kids were thrust more often than not in spite of our loud protests. My father kept this habit all this life, in spite of doctors' advice. My Saturday night hot bath was much more to my liking. My father also was an adept and strong swimmer and diver and had swum out to the Mucks at Buckie and the Skerries at Lossiemouth, off-shore reefs.

He also saved my life later on when I was caught in a current on Banff Beach and did so in a manner that I was able to copy when saving Rob and Cubs similarly at Banff Beach. His hobby was bowling and he managed the Buckie Bowling Green from its inception till he left Buckie, and was presented with silver mounted bowls for his services, which I still use.

I had a friend who lived in the house of the local doctor, Dr Duguid. Unfortunately, one day I clambered over the doctor's wall rather carelessly and fell onto some broken glass, cutting my knee badly, and, when I got home across the cutting, the doctor had to be sent for and, with my mother (a trained nurse) holding my leg, the doctor stitched it up — this without any anaesthetic. My main worry was that I might miss the annual school prize-giving the following week at which I was to receive my very first prize — but I still bear the scars. My next and most painful experience was having teeth extracted, again without anaesthetic, by the local chemist, there being no real dentist. Then, on one occasion, I fell into the harbour, and, as when I returned from my four days in a drifter, I had to bathe and change in the washhouse before I was allowed into the house.

After my father failed the exam for Fettes, his parents sent him to a school in Lyon in southeast France for a year to learn French and to lose his strong Buckie accent. This must have been a most traumatic experience. His aunt Christina Culbard had agreed to take him to Lyon where he was to stay with the head of a school. Instead she saw him onto a train at Calais Railway Station with a message tied to his wrist giving his name, and the name and address of the school master in Lyon, while she herself went to Paris. He was eleven and only spoke broad Scots. He arrived in Lyons in early evening and he showed the label to passersby. After a couple of hours of wandering, he finally found the right house. He was tired, hungry, cold and wet. He rang the door. A large personage opened it, loomed over him, hairy bristles glinting in the lamplight. It was the headmaster's wife. After a year he spoke perfect French.

Back in Britain, the school he was sent to was Wellingborough School in Northamptonshire, one of the oldest schools in the country founded in 1595. It stood on a 45 acre site on the edge of the market town of Wellingborough in the east of the county. It was a fee-paying all-boys boarding school. My father enjoyed his time there, both in the classroom and on the sports field. He spent eight months of the year at the school, and the remaining four at home in Buckie. He became captain of the school soccer team; he had been playing the game since he was a young boy. He also joined the Officer Cadet Corps, an institution common in secondary schools in Britain to give students practice in the military life.

Wellingborough was one of dozens of such boarding schools in Britain; they educated the sons of the wealthy and the middle classes. Many were founded in the middle of the 19th Century, just as the British Empire was expanding around the world. The schools taught patriotism and the unfolding history of this empire, which became during my father's childhood the largest in history. By 1913, it ruled over 412 million people, 23 per cent of the world's population at that time; by 1920, it covered 35.5 million square kilometres, 24 per cent of the world's land area. Many students at these schools were sons of civil and military officials stationed in distant countries, which did not have the facilities needed to educate their children. The government paid the school fees for these students. This experience of living away from home and family prepared the students, in their turn, for work overseas; they became used to independence and the company of other men—skills they would need if they joined the army or the colonial service. The downside of these boarding schools was to separate children from their parents for most of their childhood and bring them up in an exclusively male environment.

My father completed schooling in the summer of 1914. He had to abandon any thoughts of going to university because of the outbreak of World War I on July 28 that year. He had been in the school Officer Cadet Corps and volunteered to join the army but was turned down because of his poor eyesight; he needed glasses. When the war broke out, the leaders of the warring countries and their peoples believed that the conflict would be over in several months, probably by Christmas. No one imagined that it would last for four years and three months and claim nearly 18 million lives, military and civilian. It was the most terrible war in human history at that time.

The war devastated the families of both my father and my mother. At the start of the war, Alastair, the eldest brother of my father, joined the Seaforth Highlanders; he was killed in action in 1916, aged just 25. The next brother, Norris, tried to enlist but was turned down because he was asthmatic; in March 1929, he died of asthma, aged 37.

A DOCTOR'S LIFE IN HONG KONG

Two of my mother's brothers, Ian and William, also joined the Seaforth Highlanders. Ian was killed at Ypres on July 31, 1917, aged just 25. William survived the fighting but died of the influenza epidemic in 1918; it killed about 50 million people worldwide, including many who were between 20 and 40 and in good health, as was William.

The war brought crippling losses to all combatant countries. As it went on and the casualties mounted, the British army relaxed the physical criteria for enlistment. My father applied again to join the infantry; again he was turned down, but was allowed to join the Northamptonshire Regiment as an officer. During WWI, the regiment served on the Western Front in France, at Gallipoli in Turkey, in Egypt and Palestine. My father was wounded in action in France and was invalided out to a hospital in London.

Later he served in Palestine with the Egyptian Expeditionary Force, under General Edmund Allenby, that drove the Ottoman/German army north from Egypt to Damascus and Aleppo, where the armistice ended fighting in October 1918. He was awarded the Military Cross during the fighting in Palestine. He did not tell us what he did to merit this prestigious award; in fact, he told us almost nothing about his army life, in World War I or in India. In this, he was like many soldiers. What they experienced was too traumatic and too personal to recount.

The official British Army website reads: "The Military Cross (M.C.) is granted in recognition of "an act or acts of exemplary gallantry during active operations against the enemy on land to all members, of any rank in Our Armed Forces ... Bars were awarded to the MC in recognition of the performance of further acts of gallantry meriting the award and recipients of a bar continue to use post nominal letters M.C."

In total, 181 fellow students and teachers from his school were killed in the war. According to official British War Records, the

JOHN MACKAY

Northamptonshire Regiment raised 13 Battalions and received 58 Battle Honours, four Victoria Crosses and lost 5,950 men during the the war.

Later I found, in the London Gazette, the official citation for his Military Cross:

First Name:
Richard Johnstone
Surname:
MacKay
Information:
Also attached to the 92nd Punjabis
Rank:
Lieutenant
Rank (2nd):
Acting Captain
Gazette Info:
Gazette issue 31480. Military Cross: For marked gallantry and initiative in action on September 19, 1918. During the attack on the Tabsor system, he led his company with great gallantry, capturing both its objectives, six machine guns and 50 prisoners. Later in the day, when the enemy were found to be occupying both sides of the Wady el Ayun, he displayed great skill in the disposal of his company, and by his quick grasp of the situation under very heavy fire, worked up the foothills, occupied the enemy in front, and eventually, by a flank attack, drove the enemy from his position, thus clearing the road to the mouth of the Wady. His gallantry and example throughout the day were an inspiration to all ranks.
Gazette Date:
29/07/1919
Gazette Page:
9752

A DOCTOR'S LIFE IN HONG KONG

Duty Location:
EGYPT
Service:
British Army
Regiment:
92nd Punjabis
Battalion:
2ND BATTALION
Collection:
Search Records of Soldiers Awards from the London Gazette

After the war, my father was demobilised. He wanted to train as an accountant, but his father could not finance him. So he had to decide what to do. He was 23. Like his brothers, he did not want to return to Buckie and make his life there. So he joined the British Indian Army (BIA). He had fought alongside Indian army units in World War I and might well have been impressed by the service.

His two younger brothers were too young to fight in World War I. Culbard became a banker and spent his career with the Chartered Bank in Malaya; he spent four years in a Japanese prison camp in Singapore in appalling conditions. He survived but did not work again. Rowand became an accountant, joined the Burmah Oil Company; he lost all his belongings in Burma when the Japanese invaded, but evaded capture. Johanna, the youngest of the family, became a nurse, married and lived in Dumfries.

The British Indian Army (BIA) was the military force of India, the most important country of the Empire, the Jewel in the Crown. Official military records show him as a Lieutenant of the 92nd in 1919. The BIA was both the final guarantor of British rule over this vast country and an essential source of soldiers for overseas wars, including World Wars I and II. It was made up of British officers and Indian soldiers. The BIA was founded in 1859, two years after the Indian Mutiny, in which local soldiers rebelled against their British officers of the East India Company. The mutiny lasted from May 1857 until June 1858 and resulted in the deaths of 6,000 British people and hundreds of thousands of Indians, in the fighting and famines and diseases which followed.

The mutiny was the nightmare of any imperial power – the local soldiers of its own army turning against it and aiming to inspire the population to join the rebellion. It caused a complete reorganisation in Britain's governance of India. The British Crown took over direct rule of India from the East India Company (EIC) and established its own unified army. Previously, the army had been under the control of the EIC. The EIC was dissolved in 1874. In 1903, Lord Kitchener was appointed Commander-in-Chief of the BIA and reorganised the army along British lines. He concentrated forces in the north of the country, especially to defend the North West Frontier against foreign attack. During World War I, 140,000 soldiers of the BIA fought on the Western Front in France and Belgium. Nearly 700,000 fought in the Middle East. During the conflict, 47,746 Indians were killed or went missing and 65,000 wounded.

This is how the British Military History website describes the BIA:

> The Indian Army was a separate organisation to the British Army, although there was a close relationship between the two. The majority of the officers in the BIA were British men who had joined the Army, trained at Sandhurst and then been admitted to the BIA.
>
> In addition, the BIA had Viceroy Commissioned Officers (VCOs). These were experienced Indian soldiers who had served as Other Ranks and, due

to their ability and leadership, were granted a commission by the Viceroy of India.

In the early 1920s, Indian men were permitted to attend the Royal Military College, Sandhurst. On commissioning, they became King's Commissioned Officers with the same status as their British colleagues... A process of 'Indianisation' commenced in the 1930s, with the intention of gradually replacing British officers with Indian personnel. World War II hastened this process... At the end of the war, the highest rank held by a British Indian was that of Brigadier.

The Indian soldiers were all volunteers, a situation that persisted throughout the Second World War. They were drawn from various races and religions, although there was a preference for the martial races from the Punjab. As a result of the Indian Mutiny, regiments did not consist of soldiers from only one race or religion, so Punjabi Muslims served in the Sikh regiment and Sikhs served in the Punjab regiments.

The main task of the Indian Army was to police the Indian Empire. As World War II loomed, the Indian government did sanction the possibility of Indian troops serving abroad... By the end of the war, the Indian Army had grown to a force of about 2.5 million men, making it the largest volunteer army ever raised. Indian troops served with distinction in France in 1940, Egypt, Libya, the Sudan, Abyssinia, Syria, Persia, Iraq, Malaya and Burma.

From his years in combat in World War I, my father had a good understanding of the British Army. But going to live and serve long-term in India was something else entirely. The 1921 census showed a population of 318 million living on 1.8 million square miles, of which 61 per cent was directly ruled by Britain and the remaining 39 per cent states ruled by nobles who had ceded the power of defence and foreign relations to Britain. Of the population, 68 per cent were Hindu, followed by 22 per cent Muslim, then Buddhist, Christian, Sikh and others. The Indians spoke 222 vernacular languages; of the men, 13.9 per cent were literate in English and, of the women, 2.1 per cent. It was a society divided not only by race, religion and language but also caste.

He joined the colonial system, which the British had painstakingly built up in India after the 1857 mutiny against the East India Company. There were compounds where officials, soldiers and other British people lived, offices where they worked and social and sporting clubs similar to those they had at home. The military establishment was even larger and more complicated; it involved sprawling garrisons and cantonments. The officers of the BIA, like my father, had one of the most important jobs in India; it fell to them to ensure the internal security of this enormous and diverse country, using for the great majority Indian volunteer soldiers. This became increasingly difficult after 1921, when Mohandas Gandhi, known as the Mahatma (Great Soul), became leader of the Indian National Congress (INC) and led non-violent national campaigns calling for self-rule. If nearly 50,000 Indians died for Britain in World War I, why did they not deserve their own government? On January 26, 1930, the INC declared the independence of India — the British government did not accept it.

Officers such as him were expected to learn the principal language of the soldiers they commanded. The British Indian Army had its own rules and norms of behaviour, different from those of the Northamptonshire Regiment.

On one occasion, during the 1920s, while he was in the BIA, he visited Hong Kong. He had been advised by the Regimental Medical Officer to take sick leave. He chose a steamer from India to Shanghai via Hong Kong and back. Later he told us that Hong Kong was a dull place, but he said Shanghai was wonderful.

At the time my father reached India, the question of marriage for officers like him was highly regulated. During the East India Company period up to 1858, intermarriage of British men and Indian ladies had been common. But the experience of the Mutiny and the establishment of direct rule—the Raj—changed all that. A military officer was not allowed to marry an Indian or Anglo-Indian, the descendant of an earlier mixed marriage. The BIA regarded early marriage as an impediment to a young man's career and did not pay a marriage allowance until he was 26. He also needed the permission of his Colonel to marry. In India itself, there was a serious imbalance between the number of British men and women; so the majority sought a bride among their friends at home or ladies who came during the summer for two or three months and joined a season of dances, balls, gymkhanas, tennis matches and other events that facilitated the meeting of men and women. This annual arrival of ladies from Britain was ironically called 'The Fishing Fleet'. The colonial system meant that both men and women had little time or opportunity for dating and to get to know each other. And how did a woman coming from Britain understand the life she would have in this strange and distant country?

My mother, Alix Thurburn Fleming, was born on August 21, 1900, four years after my father. Her birthplace was the family home, Reidhaven House in Keith, a small town also in Banffshire, 13 miles from Buckie. It is home to the Strathisla distillery, founded in 1876 and the oldest continuously operating distillery in the Scottish Highlands.

Her father was a lawyer and a partner in Thurburn and Fleming, one of the leading law firms in the area. When she was born, she had two elder brothers and one elder sister — Ian, aged eight, Lillias, aged seven and William, aged one. Six years later a young brother, Innes, arrived.

Reidhaven was a happy and prosperous house, filled with children and servants to look after them. My mother had a tutor until she was old enough to go to St Dennis, a private boarding school for girls in Edinburgh. She went to a 'finishing school', Heathfield School, an elite girls' boarding school on 36 acres in Ascot, Berkshire, west of London. It prepared its students to join high society.

My mother relates that her father, who had as one of his clients the Duke of Gordon in Banff, once asked the Duke if he would support him for Parliament. My grandfather had been for years the election agent for the official Liberal party candidates, landed gentry imposed from elsewhere onto the local party by head office. He was convinced that he could easily do better at the polls being widely known and respected in the county. The Duke turned him down with the observation that only 'gentlemen' were suitable to be MPs, not those who actually earned a living, even as a reputable lawyer.

Her other story, illustrating medicine of that time, concerned her mother, Edith. At a time when her mother was in her mid-forties she was unwell and called in the doctor. The doctor could not find anything physically wrong, suggesting the problem was psychological, and recommended to her and my grandfather that the best thing would be for her to have another baby! She did so. My mother blamed the doctor for her mother's early death. This family doctor in Keith was well regarded and up to date in terms of the early 1900s. For pernicious anaemia he prescribed raw liver for my grandmother Fleming, an excellent source of iron and Vitamin B12; and for my slim mother, a glass of Guinness Stout every day, which she hated.

After her graduation from Heathfield School in 1919, my mother had a busy life, as a woman of society. She did the Grand Tour of France, Italy and Germany and visited relatives in Orkney and the rest of Scotland; she travelled locally by bicycle, further afield by car and on the Highland Line railway. She was socially skilled, playing the piano, bridge, tennis and golf and taking part in amateur theatricals. In the era before television, you made your own entertainment at home. According to the mores of that time, a woman of her social class did not do paid work. My mother lost her father in 1925; he died at the age of 66.

For my parents, a major attraction of their marriage was that both came from the same area and had grown up together. Their families knew each other well. In addition, my mother knew much about living abroad. Many of her friends and acquaintances had left Britain to work and live overseas. So she knew what life as the wife of a military officer in India would be like. After my father received permission from his Colonel, he was given leave and returned to Scotland. The wedding took place in 1931 at St Gerardine's Church in Lossiemouth, in the county of Moray. A reception photograph showed 20 family members; it was taken at Ardival, the holiday seaside home of the Fleming family. They would have married earlier but my father was not allowed to do so while he was a junior officer.

After their marriage, they returned to India and lived in Lahore, where my father was serving with the 8th Punjab Regiment. In 1933, my elder brother Donald was born at Reidhaven House, home of the Fleming family, in Keith in Scotland. It was also the place where I was born two and a half years later.

Chapter Three
1935–1945
An Indian Childhood

I was born on May 31. 1935, during the reign of King George V, in Keith, a country town in Banff, Scotland, at Reidhaven House. This was the home of my mother's family, the Flemings. At the corner of Mid Street and the town square, it was a large mansion and grand establishment for one of the leading lawyers in the county, my grandfather John Grant Fleming. Next door was Malta House where he had his office in the firm of Thurburn and Fleming. My brother Donald had been born in the same house two and a half years earlier.

My mother, Alix, and my father had known each other since they were children. He joined the British Indian army at the age of 23 so she had to wait until he had risen to the rank of Captain and had the permission of his Colonel before they could get married. She accepted that she would have to lead an itinerant life as the wife of an army officer with the 8th Punjab Regiment, then based in Lahore, keeping the peace on the North-West Frontier.

Today, Lahore is one of the major cities of Pakistan, the country

1943 John and Donald in India

created for the Muslims of India after the Partition of 1947. Like most colonial wives, my mother preferred to bear her children at home in Britain, which provided a better quality of medical care and the support of her family that was not available abroad. This meant regular travel from Britain to India. Fortunately for us, this was by the 1930s a well-established route, with large and comfortable passenger boats travelling from Southampton to Bombay (now Mumbai). It was a journey of 6,900 nautical miles that took 30 days, passing through the Strait of Gibraltar, the Suez Canal, the Red Sea and the Arabian Sea. She had returned once to Reidhaven House for the birth of Donald. She returned a second time to prepare for my arrival. Both of my mother's parents had already died, her father when she was only 18, her mother in 1934. Living at Reidhaven House at that time was Betty Fleming, her sister-in-law. Betty was the wife of Innes, the youngest of my mother's four siblings. A graduate in law from

JOHN MACKAY

Edinburgh University, Innes was in line to take over the family law firm in Keith.

When I was just four months old, my mother returned to India in September 1935, taking me, Donald and a nanny. We went to Lahore, to join my father. I did not realise it, of course, but that first overseas journey set the pattern for the rest of my life. Like my father and mother, I would leave home after my studies and live away from my mother country. While they made journeys in large passenger ships, I have clocked up thousands of miles on aeroplanes; their speed and convenience have enabled me to visit countries all over the world, especially in Asia.

I remember nothing of that first visit. But my parents later told of the worst moment — being urinated on by a lion at the Lahore Zoo; apparently this was his well-known way of warning people from getting too close to him. In the spring of 1936, we returned to Scotland to avoid India's scorching summer. In the summer of 1938, we made my second overseas visit, this time to France. There were four of us this time — me, my mother, a teenage cousin Jill Thomson and my brother Donald.

During these early years, dramatic events were occurring around me. In December 1936, British King Edward VIII abdicated, in order to marry Wallis Simpson, an American divorcee. The British government and public could not accept such a marriage. So he chose to give up his throne after only 11 months. His brother succeeded him and took the name of George V1. In March 1938, Adolf Hitler annexed Austria to form a Greater Germany. In July, while we were visiting Paris, Hitler was negotiating to take over the Sudetenland, a region of Czechoslovakia with a substantial ethnic German population. On September 30, the leaders of Britain, France and Italy signed an agreement with Hitler to cede to him control of the region. The Czechs called it the Munich Betrayal. We returned from

France to Scotland in the late summer of 1938. We did not know it then, but it would be 30 years before my mother returned to continental Europe.

On September 1, 1939, the Nazi Wehrmacht invaded Poland. On September 3, Britain and France declared war on Germany. World War II had begun. At that moment, I was in Scotland with my mother and Donald. My mother had to make a major decision — where should we live? If we remained in Scotland and the war escalated, it might become impossible to rejoin my father in India. A journey through the Mediterranean would become too dangerous; with ships dedicated to transport soldiers and war materials, there would be none to carry civilians. To stay in Scotland, then, might result in separation from my father for several years, even until the end of the war. So my mother decided to return to India as soon as possible. I have a clear memory of our departure this time — stepping out onto the quayside and being overawed by the towering grey bow of the passenger ship that would take us through the Mediterranean and Suez Canal to Bombay. We did not return to Scotland until after the end of the European war, in July 1945, when I was 10. My mother made a very wise decision. Thanks to her, the family was united throughout the war and was never in physical danger.

Happy Memories
I have happy memories of my six childhood years in India. The war was far away. The closest it came was in March 1944 when the Japanese army invaded northeast India from Burma, a British colony that Japan had captured in 1942. At the major battles of Imphal and Kohima, British forces defeated the Japanese army and drove it back to Burma. The Battle of Imphal, capital of the state of Manipur, lasted from March until July 1944. The Japanese sustained heavy losses, with 55,000 killed and wounded. The

other threat came from the Indian National Army, a force made up of pro-independence Indians, expatriate Indians living in Malaya and Burma, and Indian POWs held by the Japanese. They were led by Rash Behari Bose.

They fought alongside the Japanese in Burma and at the Battle of Imphal. But the number never exceeded 50,000. The British Indian Army succeeded in retaining the loyalty of the vast majority of its Indian soldiers.

My family and I were able to spend the war without fear of the German bombing raids that devastated British cities and industrial and military sites. But, one morning in the summer of 1943, the war arrived suddenly in our home. We were in an army cantonment in Jutogh, near Simla in Northern India. That morning I found my mother crying; in her lap was a letter saying that her younger brother, Innes Fleming, had been killed during the invasion of Sicily. He was commanding a unit of the Gordon Highlanders. This tragedy left his widow Betty with two small children, John and George, and ended the possibility of Innes, a qualified lawyer, from taking over the family law firm in Keith. My mother adored Innes: he was an outgoing man who enjoyed shooting and fishing and was a well-liked member of the Banff community.

My father rarely spoke about his army life. One thing he told us was about an officer training course in India, also attended by a trainee named Bernard Montgomery. He went on to become Montgomery of El Alamein, the battle in Egypt in October to November 1942 in which he commanded the Eighth Army. He later led it during the Allied invasion of Sicily and Italy and commanded all Allied ground forces during the D-Day landings in Normandy from June 6, 1944. This is what my father said of him: "Montgomery knew more about the tactics of warfare than the trainers. He insisted that, in making a tactical decision,

NEVER compromise. Make decision A or B."

The most memorable event of my six childhood years in India was also related to the war. It was the Passing Out parade in Delhi in 1940 of the 8th Punjab Regiment, of which my father was the Colonel. Their training finished, the soldiers were going to fight in Italy. My father took the salute on a magnificent grey horse. After the parade was over, we left in a staff car, the soldiers running alongside, draping us with golden garlands of marigolds. Wounded in World War I, my father was not fit to go with the regiment to the front line. It must have been a wrench for him to part from a Regiment with which he had served for over 20 years. During World War II, the regiment fought on many fronts — in Singapore, the Burma campaign, the Dutch East Indies, French Indochina, Iran, Iraq and Italy. It suffered more than 4,500 casualties. Two of its men won the Victoria Cross, the highest medal for gallantry awarded by the British army — Havildar Parkash Singh in Burma and Sepoy Kamal Ram in Italy.

At Partition in 1947, the 8th Punjab Regiment was allocated to Pakistan. Ten years later, in 1957, my father was deeply touched when he was invited to meet officers and men of the that regiment when they came to perform at the Edinburgh Military Tattoo.

In India, we had the itinerant life common to families of those in colonial service. We spent the winters on the plains and the summer in the hills, to escape the heat. For the first three years, my father was still with the 8th Punjab Regiment; we lived in army married quarters in Old Delhi. My joy there was to explore the vicinity and climb over a railway engine abandoned by a Rajah; Donald and I sailed boats made from banana petals down a stream. Once, we were very upset to see the daughter of one of the servants during a writing lesson. Every time she made a mistake, she would have her hands slapped by a ruler held by the teacher. We consoled ourselves in the belief that as a female she was lucky to get an education at all.

In 1941, my father was promoted to a staff position in Army Headquarters in New Delhi; we moved into a large house in the city. Like other British families and those of rich and middle-class Indians, we had several servants, in rising order of caste and status, in the house; a cleaner, a cook, a nanny, a waiter, a butler, a head servant or Khitmatgar, and outside a gardener and a driver. New Delhi was the new capital built by the British between 1911 and 1931. Previously, the capital of British India was Calcutta, in the far east of the country. New Delhi, in the north, was a more central location. The two main designers were Edwin Lutyens and Herbert Baker, leading British architects of the time. The government inaugurated the capital on February 13, 1931. The scale and cost of the new city was a sign of Britain's ambition to remain ruler of the country for many decades. None of the British officials at that time could have imagined that, just 16 years later, they would leave and an independent India would take their place. It retained New Delhi as its capital, up to today.

In our new house, we were joined for some months by my aunt, Gwen Mackay, and her son Alastair; they had fled Burma just before the Japanese took over in 1942; they left everything behind. My uncle Rowand Mackay, an accountant with the Burmah Oil Company, was able to escape a little later. They buried the family silver in the garden; but, when they went to look for it after the war, they found that, of course, it had gone. Another uncle, Culbard Mackay, was not so fortunate. He worked for the Chartered Bank in Malaya. He was arrested by the Japanese in Singapore in 1942 and spent the next three years in the Changi Prisoner of War camp in the city. His wife and two children escaped on the last boat out and spent the rest of the war in Australia. The Japanese detained about 3,000 civilians in Changi Prison, five times the number for which it was built.

During their internment, about 850 POWs died, out of a total population of 11,700, a low number compared to the average death rate of 27 per cent in Japanese POW camps. Conditions in the camp were appalling. In 1945, Culbard was liberated but his health had suffered so severely that he was never able to work again. He returned with his family to live in a lovely old house in the Cotswolds in England.

New Delhi had much to offer a young boy. One attraction was its exotic wildlife. An animal was eating our vegetables, so we set a trap, and caught a huge porcupine. My father shot it and my mother kept its quills with which to write. The carcass was no doubt eaten by the servants.

Two events remain vivid in my memory. On one occasion, Donald and I were invited to a children's party at the Palace of the Viceroy, the most senior British official in India; at that time, it was Lord Linlithgow. This imposing building had 340 rooms and was surrounded by an estate of 130 hectares. After independence, it became the official residence of the President of India. In terms of area, it is the largest residence of any head of state in the world. Donald and I were shown an exciting film in which an army of red ants defeated an army of black ants; there were many things to eat and drink at the Palace. The second event I remember was when the family was given a front row seat to watch a splendid army parade at which three Victoria Crosses were awarded—one posthumously—to Gurkhas who had distinguished themselves in the war against Japan.

Houseboat on Dal Lake
In the years that followed, we spent the winters in Delhi. In the summers, while my father soldiered in the capital, the rest of us went up into the foothills of the Himalayas, firstly to Jutogh, Simla and then Kashmir.

JOHN MACKAY

In 1864, the colonial government proclaimed Simla as the summer capital, to enable the Viceroy and his officials to escape the sweltering heat of the plains. The Viceroys at the time I was there were Lord Linlithgow followed in 1943 by Viscount Wavell. Today it is the capital of the state of Himachal Pradesh.

The summer trip to Kashmir in 1944 was memorable. Because my father was with us, we drove from New Delhi in an official staff car. It was a journey of 500 miles that took two days. First, we crossed dry plains, then climbed for hours through arid, sun-baked mountainsides until we entered a tunnel leading to the Vale of Kashmir. Emerging on the northern side of the mountain, I was delighted to find the road banked by walls of snow, the first time I could remember being so close to it. We stayed in Srinagar, the summer capital of Kashmir. We spent time on a luxury houseboat on the Dal Lake, one of the natural treasures of the region. By then, there were three children; my sister, Eleanore, had been born in November 1942 in Delhi. Dal Lake covered 75 square kilometres, surrounded by royal gardens built during the Mughal era (1526-1857). By 2021, the lake had shrunk to twelve square kilometres. Sadly, Srinagar's tourist trade has collapsed since 2016, due to civil unrest and increasing violence between the majority Muslim population and the Indian security forces.

We spent the rest of the holiday in Gulmarg, in a log cabin at the Highland Hotel. In the winter, it was a ski resort and in the summer a place for hill walking and golf. It had three golf courses, one of them, at 2,650 metres, the highest in the world. There were difficult moments for my mother — both Donald and I contracted chicken pox. Another came after an ill-fated visit to the barber. Resplendent in golden curls, I was escorted there by a servant, and returned home with a military short back and sides. The golden curls had gone for good: my mother never forgave my escort. One near disaster came when Donald had rheumatic fever; somehow, he inhaled the oral thermometer — this set off a spasm of coughing. Fortunately, by leaning over the side of the bed, he managed to cough it out. Nearly two decades later, his rheumatic fever meant he was turned down for National Service in Britain.

My mother managed the household with the help of several staff; they included a head man, waiter, cook, wash amah and gardener. In her spare time, she played tennis and golf, wrote books for children, and poetry and did water colour sketches. One of our guests in the houseboat was well-known author Rumer Godden who portrayed my mother in a scene in her novel on Kashmir, *Kingfishers Catch Fire*, published in 1953.

Darjeeling: The Aroma of Drying Tea
By July 1944, the Japanese advance into India had been stalled by the epic battles of Imphal and Kohima. Allied forces prepared to retake Burma. My father was posted to Calcutta to organise the supply of arms and food to the army. To join him there, we took the train from Delhi along the historic Trunk Route, 900 miles down the valley of the Ganges, which took more than two days. We were comfortable having a family compartment to ourselves. I spent the time looking out of the window. I was fascinated by everything I saw — immense water-wheels lifting the water from the river to the fields, buffalos harnessed to wooden beams walking endlessly in circles to power the wheel; a glimpse of elephants drawing ploughs through the fields; and different river craft, ranging from small fishing boats to heavy barges and passenger ferries.

Because it was the heat of the summer, we stayed only a few days in Calcutta, before going on to Darjeeling, a city in the north of West Bengal in the Himalayas at an elevation of 2,000 metres (6,560 feet). The area was, and is, famous for the tea it grows in sprawling plantations. The journey by train took about 18 hours, first across the plains for 340 miles to Siliguri at 380 feet at the start of the Himalayan foothills. From there we travelled on a tiny train pulled by a steam-driven engine. The oldest station on the route, Siliguri opened in August 1880. Before then it had been the terminal for trains coming from Calcutta. Travellers had to ride horses or horse-drawn tongas to reach Darjeeling.

Ghoom is the highest point on the route at an altitude of 7,404 feet. This is the highest railway station in India and was the second highest in the world at that time. As the train has to ascend to such a height over a distance of 80 kilometres, there are sharp gradients, bends and curves on the way; the sharpest curve has a radius of just 69 feet. In 1896, Mark Twain went to Darjeeling. After his trip on the same train we took, he remarked, "It is the most enjoyable day I have spent on earth."

We spent our final summer in the mountains in 1945, in a small village called Takdah south of Darjeeling. It was a delightful spot set amid tea plantations. I started collecting butterflies, there were many gorgeous varieties. One day I found one very rarely caught swallowtail, newly hatched, standing on the ground in a patch of sunlight while its wings straightened out. I killed it, took it home and pinned it out ready to show it next morning to a man who had been sent out by the British Natural History Museum specifically to catch butterflies. Unfortunately, during the night, it was eaten by a mouse. On another occasion, we drove in an open car from Takdah to the confluence of the Teesta River and a tributary where there was a sand spit perfect for a picnic. We passed through clouds of butterflies — but, to my great disappointment, I had no net to catch any.

Below the house was the village of Rungli Rungliot; it consisted of two rows of native shop-housing on either side of the ridge. On one visit to the village square, I found a buffalo that had just been slaughtered by the village butcher; the head, lopped off by a kukri, was still hanging from the post to which it had been tied. In the local Paharia dialect, the name Rungli Rungliot means 'thus far and no further'. Legend has it that during a great flood, the waters of the Teesta River in north Bengal rose so high into the Himalayas that they reached the spurs nearest to the highest mountaintops. Trapped by the rising water, the local people went to the nearest lama who was praying in a temple. They asked for his aid and he told them to order the flood to stop. The people said the floods would not pay attention to them. The lama then said he himself must then give the order. He said, "Rungli Rungliot" — the floods stopped and the lama returned to prayer. The story is remembered by *Thus Far and No Further*, a memoir by Rumer Godden about her time there and in other hill stations. Altogether, she wrote 60 books, several were made into films.

The centre of social life in Takdah was the Tea Planters Club built in 1911; it had a dining room, billiards room, and a large balcony overlooking a cricket pitch and tennis courts. We got to know one of the planters who showed us round his drying shed with the wonderful aroma of drying tea. He also showed us his lake in which he kept the Golden Mahseer, a fish like the largest salmon, which he had caught in the Teesta River.

Scattered Schooling
This itinerant life of moving every six months from the plains to the hills meant that my education was fragmented. The first school I can remember was an army school at Jutogh, near Simla. I used to ride there on a pony led by the groom. There were about a dozen students, probably all army children like me, and two English school teachers. I was about five years old. The pony was a small round animal called Judy. Much to my surprise, one

night she produced a foal. We called him Punch.

Then in Delhi for the winter months, we had another school. I remember the first day of term there; it was a mixed school, boys and girls, British and Indian. It was held outdoors in a large grassy compound around a ruined castle. Donald and I went for only one day. At lunchtime, he went home, upset that it was a school with Indian pupils; it was the first time he had had that experience. The next morning, when the bus came to take me alone to the school, I created such a scene that the bus had to leave without me. My mother was most upset because the school had a good reputation and she had gone to some trouble to get us in. Our strong reaction reflected the fact that, during our five years in India, Donald and I lived in a British-only world. The children we studied and played with and the guests who came to our house were all British; the only Indians we met were servants. My father had a great regard for the Indian officers with whom he served. He remarked on the quandary for young Sikhs, whether to shave and have haircuts like the English officers, or to retain the tradition of their people in not shaving or cutting their hair.

I have clearer memories of the school at Takdah, near Darjeeling, which I attended when I was eight. It was small, with fewer than a dozen pupils of different ages. Down the road from our house was a larger establishment. This was St Paul's, a boarding school for boys mainly older than we were. It was run like a British Public School. I remember Donald and I were lying in the bushes on the hillside, watching fascinated as the boys did army cadet training; they rushed at stuffed sacks hanging from poles and plunged bayonets into them, shouting as they ran forward, "Kill the enemy." We must have been very still, because, on one occasion, a gorgeous cock pheasant walked right in front of us.

After that summer in 1945, we travelled from the mountains in Darjeeling to Calcutta by train, and then on a night sleeper train for a further 400 miles to Gopalpur, a resort in Odisha state on the Bay of Bengal. We arrived just before sunrise and ran excitedly across the sandy beach to the sea—the first time we had seen it for five years. We had a lot of fun, diving through the surf wearing little conical rattan hats to protect our heads as the local people did. We went out with the fishermen on their primitive boats made from tree-trunks tied together, the water washing in and out over us. Dad joined us for a while on leave from Calcutta.

In May 1945, the war in Europe ended and the war against Japan was close to its end, in August. My parents decided it was safe for my mother and us children to return to Britain. We travelled by train from Gopalpur, 745 miles across the country to Poona, a military transit station in the hills sixty miles from Bombay; there we waited to catch the next ship home from Bombay. I remember Poona because I spent a week in hospital suffering from amoebic dysentery; it was cured by medication and an unpleasant medicated enema. In Poona, I bought my first book, a western, *Gunsmoke McGonagall*, a grand story that I still have today. Donald enjoyed outings with the army's Poona Yacht Club. Today there is a revered organisation in Portsmouth, on the south coast of England, called The Imperial Poona Yacht Club. It must have had its origins in colonial India.

We returned to Britain on a troop carrier with thousands of servicemen. As the family of an officer, we had a cabin to ourselves. There was little to buy with my pocket money, so I chose two exotic sweets I had not tasted before—Turkish Delight, and chewing gum.

When I look back, I realise how fortunate Donald, Eleanore and I were to have spent the war in India. We were never in physical danger nor did we endure the shortages and rationing so many faced during that terrible period. We were able to visit and enjoy many places in an extraordinary country. And we were united as a family. It was indeed a blessing.

As a boy of ten enjoying the sea voyage, I did not realise I would never return to 'British' India, the country that had allowed me to spend such a joyful six years.

My early childhood in India, while it was under the British Raj, had a lasting effect on me. Through my young eyes, India was a fascinating, colourful, exciting place of dramatic contrasts. Exquisite ancient palaces and temples, and hovels lived in by coolies. Immaculate army officers in colourful uniforms with turbans, and beggars in loincloths. The aroma of mouth-watering spices, and the awful smell of the drains. Peacocks strutting on the plains, and gaunt vultures sitting, waiting for a meal. The music and the dancers. The man who came to the door with a large basket, from which he coaxed a large cobra with his flute. It gave me a wanderlust that has stayed with me, and a desire to return to India, which was fulfilled, with my brother Donald 50 years later.

Many years later I learned how important the British Indian Army had been. Field Marshall Sir Claude Auchinleck, Commander of British Forces in India, was reported as saying, the British "couldn't have come through both wars [World Wars I and II] if they hadn't had the Indian Army". Britain recruited more than two and a half million volunteer soldiers to fight under British command; more than 87,000 were killed. They fought in Europe, North Africa, Burma and South Asia, and helped to liberate Singapore and Hong Kong from the Japanese at the end of the war. India was also a major producer of armaments for the war effort.

By 1945, it was clear the Indian National Congress could no

longer be denied their wish for independence. Britain had been so severely weakened by the war that it was in no longer in a position to control the subcontinent of India.

CHAPTER FOUR
1945–1961
School and University in Scotland

My mother and we three children arrived in Southampton in July 1945. We took a train to London and from there a London North Eastern Railway train to Aberdeen where we transferred to a Highland Line train to Elgin. We stayed there at Old Mills, the Culbard family mansion, for several weeks until the tenants had moved out of Ardival, my mother's house in Lossiemouth, six miles north of Elgin.

Old Mills House was an imposing building surrounded by acres of garden. It had been in our family for generations; it was bought by my great, great grandfather William Culbard in 1889, a successful businessman and Lord Provost of Elgin. Still living there were two elderly great-aunts, Amy and Chrissie. For a young boy of 10, it was a fascinating house. Stone-flagged narrow corridors on the ground floor linked together three houses. Wooden stairways led to bedrooms on the first floor. One of the bedrooms was haunted. The dining room had twelve oil portraits of family ancestors; none was labelled, leading to endless speculation that continues to this day on who they were.

My cousin Margaret Miller, trained in dress design, helped to date them by their clothing. The corridors had prints of biblical scenes; one I remember depicted *The Deluge*—a dark craggy landscape under sheets of rain.

The estate included the water-powered grain mill known as King's Mill that had been working since before 1230, when it was granted to the Priory of Pluscarden by King Alexander II.

Lossiemouth is a fishing port on the Moray Firth and was once the third largest in Scotland for white fish landings. Like Buckie, it had a railway station next to the harbour so fish landed in the day could be auctioned off in the afternoon and delivered in London the following morning.

It is also home to an important base of the Royal Air Force. Built in 1939, it was bombed by the Luftwaffe in 1940, but continued as a base for Lancaster bombers. They sank the German battle cruiser *Tirpitz* in 1944. My memories of the airport are mixed. On the plus side, I learned to drive a car under my father's direction on an unused runway, and I was excited by the fighter planes with exotic names like Sabre, Mustang, Typhoon, Hawker Hunter practising take-offs and landings. The downside was the fact that the end of the runway was only a few feet from the golf course and the noise was deafening, particularly the Blackburn Buccaneers, that had an air-braking system that screamed like banshees.

Britain had won the war, but had it won the peace? It had spent close to £7 billion pounds, or a quarter of the national wealth, on the war effort. The country had suffered 264,000 military and 61,000 civilian deaths; one in three houses had been destroyed by bombing, as had many shops and factories. Two thirds of its navy and 177 merchant ships had been sunk. The country depended on loans from the United States to maintain living standards and rebuild the economy. Repayment of the

British war debt to the USA was not paid off till 2006.

Rationing had been introduced at the start of the war. After the victory, it remained in force for a further nine years. This covered many food items, as well as soap, petrol and clothing. In the far north of Scotland, we were fortunate, compared to other people in Britain. Bombing of the area had been limited and agriculture was one of its key industries, so we had access to better supplies of food than people in many other places.

For our family, especially my mother, it was an enormous change of lifestyle. Before and during the war, she had lost both parents and all her four siblings. In India, she had been the memsahib of a household of as many as five servants and enjoyed the freedom to socialise, play golf, play tennis and swim at an exclusive whites-only club in Delhi. Now she was living in what had been her mother's house in Lossiemouth. She had only one daily help and had to do the childcare and cooking herself; Donald and I did the washing-up. She had to cope with ration books for food and sweets and clothing and myriad government regulations. She also had to organise schooling for Donald and me, and later, for Eleanore, all on a modest army pension.

Another major issue was the future of my father, then only 50. He had been in the British Indian Army for 22 years and had reached the rank of Brigadier. He loved India and the men and officers who served under him. The new Labour government that came to power in July 1945 wanted to make India a fully independent dominion like Canada and Australia. But this was not enough for the Indian National Congress and All-India Muslim League, who wanted full independence; the Muslim League wanted a separate state for Muslims. Before World War II, Britain had the economic and military strength to control the country and communal violence. But, after the war, it no longer had that strength. In February 1947, the British government sent Lord Louis Mountbatten as the new Viceroy of India; his mandate was to oversee the British withdrawal.

For the autumn term of 1945, Donald went as a boarder to Merchiston Castle School in Edinburgh, a boys-only Public School with a high reputation. In Britain the term public school meant a private school rather than a state school. For that autumn term, I went to the village school in Lossiemouth. I had to learn the local dialect; for example a boy was a 'loon' and a girl a 'quine'. I was in a class of about 30 boys and girls, ruled by a female teacher trained in strict discipline before the war. She struck errant pupils on their hands with a thick leather belt, a tawse. I did not suffer that fate but did have my hair pulled once for homework not up to my usual standard. One boy in the class was different—quiet and friendly, and mentally sub-normal. He was allowed to spend his time in class drawing pictures. I saw him years after he left school, riding around with the milkman on a horse-drawn cart, delivering milk to the houses—he seemed to be as happy as anything.

In January 1946, my mother took me to a boarding school. This was Dalhousie Castle, a boys-only Preparatory school of sixty pupils, getting them ready to go on to a Public School. It was in a real castle a few miles south of Edinburgh and belonged to the Lords Dalhousie; there were portraits of the Noble Lords in the dining room. That first winter was the coldest on record, with snow lying for weeks; this made rugby impossible, but we could play soccer. Coming from India, I found the cold brutal; my fingers were chapped, but playing in the snow was fun.

For my first two terms, with no scholastic record to offer, I was placed in the most junior class. At the end of the academic year, I won three class prizes. For the next year, I was promoted two years ahead. Physical fitness was important. Before breakfast, the junior boys did half an hour of exercises led by

JOHN MACKAY

Dalhousie Castle School

the small and dynamic headmaster K.M. Mylne. The senior boys did more difficult exercises in the next half hour, again under the leadership of the Headmaster, the fittest person in school. The teaching staff was an odd collection of people — a man who had been exempted from war service because he had flat feet, an Irishman from neutral Eire and elderly ladies too old for military service even before the war started.

Every afternoon, we had sports — rugby was the important one. Three boys from the school went on to play for Scotland — Ian Donald and the McLung brothers, Tommy and Gilbert. I was lightly built and not very fast and played only once for the school. I was better at hockey, playing right half for the school. I was even better at cricket, for which I earned my 'colours' by taking five wickets more than once. After sports, we had hot showers, with an obligatory passage through a cold shower afterwards. There was always a master on duty to make sure we did not avoid the cold shower, even in the middle of winter.

I enjoyed reading the exciting books written by Sir H. Rider

Haggard and by G.A. Henty about brave British adventurers in the days when the British Empire was at its zenith. Very suitably, I was put in charge of the school library.

In my final year, I was in the second top class; the top class was taught Latin and Greek by the headmaster. One day during the final term, I was very moved when the headmaster walked up to the sports ground and told me, with tears in his eyes, that I had passed the Common Entrance exam necessary for me to get into a Public School. He complimented me for having a better mark in mathematics than a boy in the top class, who was the scorer for the cricket team.

Having placed Donald and me into Merchiston School in September, my mother, taking Eleanore with her, went back to India to rejoin my father; he was now posted to Madras as military area commander. During our school holidays at Christmas 1946, Donald and I stayed with my uncle Rob and his mother, our last living grandparent, in Lockerbie in Dumfries and Galloway in southwest Scotland; he was a solicitor in the town. During the Easter holiday, we stayed at the Linga Hotel at Gullane in East Lothian, 35 kilometres east of Edinburgh. The hotel was excellently situated looking over a golf course; the owner had two boys at the same school as Donald and me. I enjoyed the easy access to the golf course but did not like the riding lessons on very large horses at stables near North Berwick. I remember that the hotel owner often struggled with the starting handle to start his car; I was hoping he would fail and allow me onto the golf course rather than onto a horse.

It was in the early summer of 1947 that my father, aged 50, retired from the BIA with the rank of Brigadier. It was a few months before the Partition of India in August that year; after that, the army would no longer be led by British officers. If he had stayed in the army until India became independent, he would

JOHN MACKAY

Madras area Command 1945-1947 Brigadier Mackay in centre

have received a Golden Handshake — an end-of-service gratuity. For him, it was a very emotional period. He had devoted 26 years of his life to India and foresaw what would happen when it was divided into two separate countries. He did not want to be there for the violence he saw coming.

Lord Mountbatten had proposed to the Hindu and Muslim leaders a united, independent secular India, as had been the wish of Mahatma Gandhi. Most of the Congress Party accepted this, but the Muslim League did not. It insisted on its own state. The British government appointed Sir Cyril Radcliffe, a London barrister, to chair a commission to draw up the border between the two countries. It was mission impossible — Radcliffe had no prior knowledge of India and was given only weeks to complete such a complicated task. In the contested areas, Hindus, Muslims and Sikhs lived in the same towns. King Solomon could not have drawn a just border between them.

So India was formed out of the majority Hindu regions and Pakistan from the majority Muslim regions, one in the west and one in the east. Partition proved to be a human catastrophe — 7.2 million Muslims moved from their homes in India to Pakistan and 7.3 million Sikhs and Hindus went the other way. There was communal violence on an unprecedented scale, with estimates of the dead ranging from 200,000 to two million. The nightmare my father had predicted came to pass; he was wise to have left and not witnessed this tragedy in his second homeland.

My father returned with my mother and Eleanore to Britain in time to pick us up from school at the end of the summer term in 1947. For us children, his return meant that we could see much more of him. In India, as I remember, he was always in army uniform, going to or coming from work. Even when we were all in the same house, we saw little of him — and none at all when he was on duty in the plains and we were in the hills to escape from the summer heat. For the summer holidays in 1947, the family was able to stay together at our house, Ardival, at Lossiemouth. None of us went abroad again for the next three years. The government had limited the amount of money a person could take abroad for a holiday to £25 pounds; this was to conserve wealth that had been severely depleted by the war.

We did have one holiday in what felt like a foreign country — the island of Barra in the Outer Hebrides. We sailed there on a Macbrayne ferry from Oban, and found it a bleak, almost treeless, rocky and hilly island, where the children went to school to learn English; their mother tongue was Scots Gaelic. We stayed in a low stone house with a thatched roof, sheltered from the winds off the Atlantic, and were very well looked after by the mistress of the house. It was a great holiday of hill walking, exploration, fishing for trout in the streams and enjoying the space and clean air and crystal-clear water in the bays. We explored Kisimul Castle on an islet in Castlebay. The tower-house castle had been the stronghold of the MacNeils of Barra since the late 15th Century. It had been falling into ruin until the clan chieftainship passed on to a Canadian architect. Each summer he came to Barra to oversee the restoration of the castle. One morning he took us out in a boat to look over the castle, still largely a shell, and explained his dream of restoring it to a habitable condition. In 2001, he leased it to Historic Scotland for an annual fee of one pound and a bottle of whisky. For the rest of the time, we fished in the bay or a stream that came down from the hill behind the house. One day, we drove to the north of the island and identified the place where the excellent comedy *Whisky Galore* was filmed in 1948; it was the story of the SS Politician, a cargo ship loaded with whisky that had run aground during a storm in 1941, spilling crates of whisky into the sea that washed them ashore. At that time, rationing was still severe; nearly all the whisky produced in Scotland was shipped to the US to earn much-needed dollars.

Our hometown of Lossiemouth had much to offer — a huge beach where we built sand castles, dug for worms as bait for fishing from the rocks or harbour piers, hooking out crabs from below the rocks at low tide, collecting mushrooms in the fields, bicycling everywhere, taking expeditions to the sandstone cliffs at Covesea for picnics, and golf. We all played golf — it was my father who taught me the game. I have played it ever since, in courses all over the world. I started with wooden-shafted clubs such as a driver, fairway iron, mashie and putter. We received lessons from the Club Professional, George Smith; he had won the Scottish Northern Open but had been crippled by rheumatoid arthritis of the hands. I never swam in the sea because it was too cold, or went out in a boat. Donald and two school friends once went out on a deep-sea fishing boat; but they did not enjoy it and all were seasick.

Before the war, Lossiemouth was a thriving fishing village. Its harbour was at the mouth of the river Lossie, with houses tucked along the banks of the river and shielded from the west and north winds by a ridge of high ground. On the seaward side of the ridge, on the high ground, wealthy southerners had built houses with grand sea views, and played golf at the Moray Golf Club, a classic links course running along the shore. After the war, with limits on foreign travel, the pre-war pattern revived for a short while. I remember two parties for children of these grand houses. They were socially a nightmare for me who was happier on my own exploring the countryside. Expeditions further afield took us the six miles south to Elgin to visit Old Mills House, home of two elderly aunts of my father, Amelia and Christina Culbard. When they died, my father's brother Rowand bought the house, water mill and grounds.

More distant, 23 miles to the east was Keith, where I was born, and we visited Aunt Betty Fleming and her boys John and George at Reidhaven House; it was always a pleasure to go there because Betty was such a cheerful character, a good cook and the boys were just a little younger than Donald and me. An additional attraction was the billiard table where we learned to play billiards and 'slosh', an abbreviated type of snooker involving potting the coloured balls only. Visits often coincided with the Keith Show. This was one of the major agricultural shows in the north of Scotland, involving immense prize cattle, sheep and poultry, displays of farm machinery, baking, flowers and vegetables and athletic contests on foot, on bicycles, on round bales of straw and on horses. An additional attraction was a fair in the town square right next to Reidhaven House where travellers and gypsies brought all sorts of game booths, food stalls, fortune tellers and even an 'African Chief' who could walk barefoot over broken glass.

To the west was Forres, the home of other relatives, Innes Thomson and his children Keith, Jill and Barbara. Their mother Lillias, my mother's sister, had died during the war. These cousins were about ten years older than us and lived in a large house with a big garden. They took us down to Findhorn, a great tidal bay, to look at the sea birds and the seals.

Further west, just north of Inverness, lived Andrew Ross and his sister Joan. They were my father's cousins and owned a mixed arable and dairy farm. We enjoyed the day trip, driving to the farm, being given a splendid lunch and coming home with eggs, salted butter and crowdie cheese. In the days of rationing, these were real treats. Later we had our own hen coup, a steady supply of eggs and a roast chicken from time to time. Only Donald had the skill and nerve to kill a hen, as humanely as possible, by twisting its neck; we all did the plucking, and my mother prepared it for the table.

In the autumn of 1948, I joined Donald at Merchiston Castle School. I did not see much of him because the boys were segregated by age; they moved together each new academic year from one house to the next. This was done specifically to avoid the bullying and 'unnatural' relationships reported to occur in other schools with a system where boys of all ages stayed together in the same house throughout their schooling. Academically, I was put in the stream for sciences; another stream did languages and a third did the best they could.

At school, rugby was THE game. I was never heavy enough to cause damage to the opposition, nor fast enough to evade pursuit so I never progressed to the senior teams at Merchiston. During my first year, I did play for a school team against Prep Schools, picked because I was small for my years. I remember one game against St Mary's at Melrose, when I played Fly Half against a boy called Gordon Waddell. We lost. He went on to

Merchiston Castle School

play for Scotland's rugby team as Fly Half 18 times, five of them as captain. In my last year, I played no rugby because I had fractured my left femur the previous summer. We played rugby for the autumn and first half of the spring terms. We had half a term of athletics, with minimal coaching and only a grass running track. I remember when our best middle-distance runner ran a mile in just under five minutes—at a time when Roger Bannister was closing in on the historic first four-minute mile. The school captain, Colin Wilmshurst, excelled at athletics and captained the British team at the 1954 Commonwealth Games in Vancouver. In the summer, I happily played cricket, continuing to take wickets with my slow off-spins, and score some runs, too, but never in the first team. A pleasant option was golf, which I played sometimes on courses on the slopes of the Pentland hills; courses at Swanston and Torphin were the nearest to reach by bicycle.

In the summer of 1952, I had a serious accident which blighted my final year at Merchiston. With my cousin Alastair and a friend, I went on a cycling holiday in Brittany in northern France. On the second day, in heavy rain and my head down, I crashed into a car. I never saw it coming. I woke up a day or so later in Poitiers Hospital. I had suffered a fractured left femur, a fractured collar bone and concussion. My father came to France to escort me back; it was my first flight in an aeroplane. I was semiconscious with sedation and encased in a thick plaster-of-Paris cast from my toes to my abdomen. I spent the next two months in Raigmore Hospital at Inverness in a Thomas Splint, a device that held my leg in an elevated splint with weights attached to my leg to keep the bones straight. Unfortunately, bone union was delayed because of too much traction, an error pointed out by the orthopaedic surgeon who came once a month from Aberdeen. I spent my last month in Gray's Hospital in Elgin; that involved a 12-mile round trip for my mother from Lossiemouth, rather than a 60-mile one to Inverness.

As a result, I missed the entire autumn term and did not return to sports till the summer cricket season. It was hard to catch up academically, but I left with sufficient exam passes to get into university. I needed two GCE A-level passes out of the three subjects. I took Chemistry, Physics and Biology. I concentrated on Physics and Biology and passed both. For this, I must thank Ian Balfour-Paul, the biology master; he supplied me with textbooks to read while I was in hospital. I graduated from Merchiston in June 1953.

On balance, I enjoyed school, especially the camaraderie with other boys, playing sports and learning so much. I did not enjoy the cold. In midwinter, we had to walk around in open-necked shirts, blazers and shorts. At night, I shivered in my bed in a Spartan dormitory of twelve beds, with windows open even when it was snowing outside.

National Service

Before I could go to university, I had to fulfill the legal obligation to do National Service, which meant two years in the armed forces. This had been introduced on January 1, 1949, for able-bodied men between 17 and 21, initially for 18 months, and, after the outbreak of the Korean War in 1950, it was extended to two years. I joined the Air Force in the hope of flying one of the splendid fighter planes I had watched at Lossiemouth airfield, such as Buccaneers and Super Sabers. But it was not to be because bad eyesight—astigmatism—ruled me out. Although I was not to know it, National Service was to end two years later. Candidates for aircrew training had to accept a commission of at least three years, preferably twelve years. One of the assessment groups I was in included a university graduate; despite already having a pilot's licence, he was turned down.

At Merchiston, I had been in the Combined Cadet Force, one afternoon a week during term, with

National Service 1953

a two-week field camp after each summer term. So RAF basic training was not too stressful. The Drill Sergeants were loud and aggressive. "You are a nig-nog! What are you?" The billet had to be meticulously clean and equipment meticulously laid out, all designed to weld the motley collection of recruits into an obedient unit. The Windsor knot for a tie was forbidden. It seemed the Duke of Windsor's abdication, deserting his post, was not to be forgiven. At the end of Square Bashing, the Sergeants and recruits came together for a farewell party enjoyed by all.

During basic training, I had two interviews with a view to being commissioned as an officer. The first officer's report to his senior assessor was not flattering. The second officer read out parts to me, which I well remember: "a slight youth" – True. "He appears to think his public school education gives him the right to be an officer." – True. "Lacks aggression." – True. I stayed in the ranks.

The training course to become a radar operator was in Wiltshire during a severe winter with much snow. Our Nissen huts were inadequately heated. The coal for the iron stoves in the teaching and bunk rooms ran out, so we scavenged wood for fuel. When that ran out, we sat wrapped in our greatcoats, fingers frozen, as we listened to lectures. The best way to get warm was to take a bath, at least when there was hot water. The downside was that all the light bulbs had been stolen – so I bathed in the dark; all the bath plugs had been taken, so I brought my own. It was during this period of degraded living that I decided to apply for the Medical School of Edinburgh University.

During my initial training, all recruits were asked to state whether they wanted a home or overseas posting. I opted for overseas, looking forward to seeing some of the Empire at government expense. It was not to be. After training, a lad called McLean from Edinburgh and I were posted to the RAF camp at the well-named Cold Hesledon, on a hill near the coast north of Hartlepool, among the coal mines of Durham. Instead of flying aeroplanes I spent my working time underground in a radar control bunker — ironic because the strain on my eyes was worse than if I were flying.

When another circular came round asking for volunteers for an overseas assignment, I applied, even though I had at that time only a few weeks left to serve. Much to my surprise, I was accepted. A few days later, I was on a plane to Malta to take part in an annual military exercise. The plane was a DC-3, the work horse of the World War II. Parked on the tarmac, the fuselage was at an acute nose-up angle to the ground; it was quite a climb from the entrance near the rear to the front of the cabin. It rattled like anything and was very noisy. It was a relief to get out several hours later.

It was August in Malta, in the middle of a heat wave, with temperatures over 100 degrees Fahrenheit during the day. I was quartered in a Nissen hut with a corrugated iron roof; it was like an oven during the day. It was pleasantly cooler on night watch, a light breeze coming off the sea stirring the dust on the parched ground. During the first ten days, there was intense activity when the 'enemy' sent waves of planes to attack the island, and I helped the valiant defenders to hold them off. Afterwards, there was free time when I and the others who had been rushed to Malta's defence waited for flights to take us back to the UK. During the war, Malta had withstood devastating bombing by the Germans, who sought to capture the island fortress. They failed and the island was awarded a George Cross for its valour.

I was happy to explore the island. Mdina, the ancient capital, was within walking distance. Huge walls, built 3,000 years ago, were surrounded by a deep and wide moat. The area was the perfect place for a football match. Valletta, the current capital, was an exciting mixture of ancient churches and houses with narrow streets leading down to the Grand Harbour. Some of the Mediterranean fleet was in the harbour, with many of the sailors on shore leave. I watched one sailor taking the steps two at a time as he followed a woman upstairs from a bar. I had neither the money nor the inclination to do likewise.

In Malta, I discovered the most thirst-quenching drink for a hot day — a crushed-ice lemon and sugar concoction in a long glass — it was life-saving. I was happy to rejoin forces with the group that had done radar training with me in England and had spent their National Service two years in Malta.

Other outings took me to one of the wide sandy beaches on the north shore for a wonderful swim, and a visit to a blue grotto on the south coast. To reach there, I had to climb down a cliff to a huddle of fisherman's houses; there I hired a boatman to take me round the cliffs to a sea cave. It was not a spectacular cave but a wonderfully gentle and relaxing experience to be on the water, just the boatman and myself, after the days of hectic activity, heat, people and dust.

I flew back to an air station near London, caught a train up north to my base, picked up my leave pass and was back on a train to London that evening to join the rest of the family for a week's sightseeing in London.

One benefit of National Service was to take me out of the social bubble in which I had lived up to that point. My comrades were a mixed bag of men — no women — from streetwise salesmen, apprentice tradesmen, to people right out of school like myself, hoping to go on to tertiary education. I learned that despite being a 'public school boy' with a posh education, I was no smarter than some men from working class backgrounds. We got along well, and cheerfully, knowing that our time as National Servicemen was limited. The camp had a football team and a cricket team.

We played matches against other RAF units.

The experience also took me to places I had never been. During my time in Durham, a group of us was invited down a coal mine by a mining engineer. Fitted out with hard hats, we went down in a wire cage lift, walked along narrow tunnels with rail tracks to the working point where the seam of coal was drilled out. A hard, dirty, dangerous job that had been the occupation of generations of miners, such as our guide.

One mining family was extremely kind, occasionally asking a group of us to tea on Sundays after service at their Methodist Church. Their home, in a terrace built for miners, had a living room and kitchen downstairs and bedrooms upstairs. Coming back from the mine covered in grime, all the miners had to look forward to was a tin tub of hot water, in front of the fire in the living room. Another experience was to go with my friends to a dance hall in Sunderland. A couple of visits made me realise that a single-sex school education had not prepared me for such events. On a different level, a memorable outing was to Newcastle to see *Romeo and Juliet*, starring Richard Burton and Claire Bloom – a stunning performance.

By the end of my National Service, I was earning, as a Senior Aircraftsman, the significant salary of £3 a week. My official discharge assessment reported: Bearing – very smart; Conduct – exemplary; Cooperation – very good; Abilities as a tradesman – Good; and Leadership – good. The last category was benignly inaccurate – at no time did I have any leadership opportunity.

It was during my time in the RAF in Durham in 1955 I learnt that I had been accepted to study Medicine at Edinburgh University. This was on the basis of my 'A-Level' results and a supportive letter from the headmaster of Merchiston, Cecil Evans. Thanks to his letter, I was not required to attend an interview. This was a life-changing moment. I was delighted at the prospect of spending the next six years studying at Edinburgh University. It was going to be a drain on the family finances but my parents celebrated the news with me.

Edinburgh University is one of the most famous institutions of medical learning in the world. Founded in 1726, it is the oldest medical school in Britain. Admission was, and is, very competitive. In my year, only ten per cent of applicants were accepted. I chose to study medicine because the subject I enjoyed best at school was Biology. My parents had suggested I become a lawyer like my grandfathers, but were happy with my choice of medicine.

At school I had just one short meeting with a career adviser who had suggested forestry. Good advice. Since I retired from practicing medicine, I have had time to enjoy trees, and have for years supported the 'Trees for Life' organisation that is intent on rewilding Scotland.

During my first term at Edinburgh University, I wrote back to my former RAF colleagues, inviting them to meet me at Murrayfield Rugby Stadium, and received the following reply: -

> *The Inmates, Cell 27C   29 Nov 1955*
> *Dear Sprog, (a colloquial term for a new recruit)*
>   *I (and the rest of the inmates) were glad to hear that you seem to be enjoying the pleasures of civvy street. The lads caught me in one of my rare sober days and thought it was about time we replied to your scraggy little note. So here it is.*
>   *First of all from all of us Scotsmen and in some cases, i.e. Musk etc. Scots boys, the first international at Murrayfield is a date and the War Memorial is just the place, allowing of course that I am in a fit condition to distinguish the Memorial from the Scoreboard. Ross, Musk and myself sailed through*

our Medical the other day (a turn up for the books) so it is only a matter of hours now. (Before discharge from the RAF). *Arthur Cook and Bill McLean have gone from the billet now and things are a wee bit quieter than they were. Last Thursday was the combined demob party of Arthur, Bill, Jack Oldfield, Bruce Youll etc., even Joe Harvey was pissed that night. Jack Oldfield was his usual self, standing in the middle of B Billet with a pick digging a hole in the centre of the floor.*

Thursday is another big night, Porky, Jack Fisher Moseley and Nott all go on the Friday so it should be quite a night. This means of course that I shall be senior man, the English blokes will be falling over each other in the bogs on Tuesdays (cleaning duty) for a while, with Musk S/M of A Billet and Wattie Wilson S/M of B Billet. X Should that be censored (Musk thinks so) it looks a reign of terror is about to begin down in the twenty sevens.

That's all the news from Stalag 92, John. Ken, Brum, Jack, Jim, Hoppy, Joe, Ross Arthur, Webby, the two Ians, Graham and Geoff all ask for you and hope the 'Uni' is going OK,

All the best
Jim the drunk.
PS After the match the Clochan of course. Just like old times.

None of them turned up at Murrayfield, but I did meet Jim and a friend at a Bay City Rollers concert during the University Charity Week the following summer.

Becoming a Doctor 1955-1961
Between 1955 and 1961, I spent six years at the Medical School of

Edinburgh University. It gave me the skills I used for the next 40 years and the option, like my father and others in our family, of working and living abroad. My parents strongly supported my decision to train as a doctor

My entry into the medical school in 1955 caused a major change for the family. My parents rented out Ardival, the family home in Lossiemouth, to a Doctor McConachie who had joined Dr Simon in the General Practice next door, and bought a large house in Morningside, a pleasant middle-class neighbourhood in the southwest of Edinburgh. It served several purposes — a stable and comfortable place for me to live during my studies; my sister Eleanore could attend St Dennis, a good day school where my mother had been, and my mother could enjoy the rich life of Scotland's capital city. She continued writing, and published a book, *The Minister's Wife*. It was published to coincide with the annual Assembly of the Church of Scotland — good timing. Her pen name was Anne Gardiner.

I think my father may have been a reluctant party to the move. After returning from India, he greatly enjoyed his retirement in Lossiemouth. He worked hard in the garden, clearing land for vegetables and a hen-run and raspberry and gooseberry enclosure. For several years, he was secretary of Moray Golf Club. He enjoyed it, and was, I am sure, highly efficient. It also gave him the opportunity to get to know local people. There was a wide social division between the fishing community and the 'gentry' in the area.

The fishing community had been established at Lossiemouth for over a hundred years, a close-knit community that played football and enjoyed a round of golf. Incomers from the south with their fine houses and speaking BBC English were a breed apart. It was not a matter of religion, there were six different church denominations in the town, each with their own church.

It was not a matter of race, everyone was Caucasian and British, apart from one Italian family I knew who owned a shop, Rizza's, which sold the best ice cream in town.

In Edinburgh, my father started a new career. Beginning as a driver for the Red Cross he became a regional controller of transport. He set an example to us children of correct manners, scrupulous honesty and carefulness in all he did, as well as consideration for others. He was reserved in a very Victorian way, having been born four years before the end of the reign of Queen Victoria. He had lived in the reigns of five British monarchs. He was a conscientious Elder of the Church of Scotland and a Royalist. He was always kind to us, maintaining discipline by setting an example rather than by command. There was much about him that we did not know. He did not want to talk about his army life, World War I or his experience with the Indian Army. Nor do I remember any conversations with him and my mother about the Partition of India, the prospect of which precipitated his departure. My mother kept diaries — but, after her death, my father burnt them all. "Too personal", he said. A real shame.

At university, I found that I was surrounded by excellence, among the students as well as among the faculty. On the first day, I discovered four other Merchistonians starting with me –Alastair Philip, Bobby Burt, David Reed and John Baird. Not having had to do National Service, all had come direct from school. All went on to distinguished careers in medicine. John Baird joined the RAF once he had qualified as a doctor, and ended up as Air Chief Marshall Sir John Baird, Surgeon General of British Forces medical establishment. Alastair Philip built a distinguished career in Neonatology in the US. Bobby Burt became a senior executive for an American pharmaceutical company and John Reed emigrated to Canada and became a successful surgeon in

Penticton, British Columbia.

My prime focus at university was in passing the exams. The first two years were the hardest because of the subjects involved. My least favourite was biochemistry, and relearning how to study again having left school two years before. Once the course became clinically based it was easier and more interesting.

My social life, outside my family circle, involved perhaps one night a week. I had saved £120 during National Service, a nest egg for planned travels in the holidays. For running expenses I received £1 a week from my father. This covered my lunch at the Men's Union, about two shillings daily, and little else. On Sundays we all went to church.

In my year, there were 120 students in the medical faculty; like me, they had signed up for five to six years. It was among them that I made my closest friends. We had limited social contact with students in the Arts; they came to University for only three years, took their classes in different locations from ours and lived in a different world. We male medical students were based at the Men's Union in Bristo Square close to the medical school buildings and the Royal Infirmary. The women students had a separate social centre—the more foolhardy or adventurous coming to Friday night dances at the Men's Union.

My year was the last one to study Botany. In the summer term, I cycled down from Morningside to the Botanical Gardens for the early morning lecture, then cycled back up the hill to the Men's Union for lunch, unhurried because my next lecture was not till the afternoon. On a fine morning, it was a lovely way to spend the time. Cycling around hilly Edinburgh was an excellent way to keep fit. But I hated those streets with cobbles, especially dangerous when wet and where tram lines were running. Once I was nearly killed, when my front wheel was caught in a tram track and I was thrown onto a taxi—happily on the side, not underneath it.

I was fortunate to be taught by many distinguished professors. Here I would like to remember them. In our pre-clinical years, we had Professor Michael Swann in Biology. He used to walk up and down the stage while giving his lectures. Only once did he stop, when a student laid a small device on the stage, which exploded when he stepped on it—he was not amused. He was famous for his research on cell division. Later he became Principal and Vice-Chancellor of Edinburgh University, chaired the BBC, was awarded a knighthood and later a Life Peerage.

My Professor of Physiology was David Whitteridge, a large man with a great sense of self-importance. Later he achieved his ambition of being appointed to the Chair of Physiology at Oxford. In one lecture, he expounded on the result of one of his experiments; it proved that, if you expanded one viscus, like the urinary bladder, it constricted peripheral blood vessels. From then on, when someone wanted to be excused to urinate, he or she would say, "I am going out to warm my feet."

Professor of Anatomy was George John Romanes, a small man, an excellent lecturer and famous neuroanatomist. I have vividly contrasting memories of two anatomy demonstrators; one was an elderly, distinguished and friendly gentleman, a medical missionary in China for many years until driven out by the communist revolution in 1949. The other was a young Australian surgeon in training, brusque and unpleasant.

During our clinical years, the heads of departments were giants, indeed. Sir Stanley Davidson was the co-author, with Sir Derek Dunlop, of *The Textbook of Medicine*, the standard text at our university and worldwide. He was softly spoken and dignified and had a distinguished war record as a doctor and a world reputation in nutrition. He was nearing retirement when I knew him. Sir Derek Dunlop was a great man when I met him as a student; he was the Professor of Materia Medica at Edinburgh University. Tall, thin and elegant, he was an excellent and stylish lecturer. Only once was he booed, good-naturedly, by the class at a lecture when he started talking of minims (drops) of thyroid extract. His lectures had always stressed the scientific rigour of exact doses of medication. I am told that he was a superb after-dinner speaker, because of his meticulous preparation.

Sir John Crofton, Professor of Respiratory Medicine, was based at the City Hospital. Of Anglo-Irish descent, educated in Ireland and England, he had a distinguished career as a doctor in World War II. In his clinical unit at City Hospital, he introduced and developed what came to be known as the 'Edinburgh Method' for tuberculosis treatment. This involved the use of multiple drugs taken simultaneously to reduce the chance for drug-resistant strains of the tubercle bacilli to develop; he combined this with careful monitoring of patients to ensure that they adhered to the prescribed medication regime. His team were able to demonstrate that mortality, and the spread of the disease in the community, could be reduced almost to zero if medication was properly prescribed and properly taken. The incidence of tuberculosis in Edinburgh declined rapidly. Crofton spent much of the rest of his career travelling around the UK and the wider world spreading this method. I came to know him better when I was a postgraduate student at the City Hospital. Small and dynamic, he impressed me with his energy and authority. He was instrumental in supporting my wife Judith during her career both as a student and later during her work on tobacco control. He was good company and always intensely inquisitive about knowledge and world affairs relating to tobacco. Years later, when Judith and I returned to Edinburgh on annual visits from Hong Kong, we always called on him and his wife Aileen at their home in Colinton or took them out for a meal. He had enjoyed a remarkable life and was always forward looking—the mark of a great man.

Sir Norman Dott was a man of immense achievement and small physical stature like Sir John Crofton. He was Professor of Neurosurgery at Edinburgh and had built up a world-renowned unit at the Western General Hospital. I spent several weeks there as an undergraduate and six months as a House Officer. Professor Sir John Bruce, Professor of Surgery, was a distant figure; he had a distinguished career in World War II, academically and professionally. Professor Sir Michael Woodruff of Experimental Surgery was famous for being the first person in Britain to do a kidney transplant.

Professor Geraint James was Professor of Orthopaedic Surgery; his claim to fame among students was that, at a mature age, he married a student in a year below mine. Professor Ian Donald was Professor of Obstetrics and Gynaecology. I do not remember him, but do recall when a group of us students were living in the University Simpson Memorial Maternity Hospital—Professor Donald's domain—and organised a very successful Burns Night Celebration in the hospital residents' dining room. The party spilled over into Sandy Bell's tavern down the road.

Less famous was the head of Dermatology, who told us that he was sure that the waves of venereal disease that washed into Edinburgh each autumn were the fault of the people who came up from London for the Edinburgh Festival. Head of Neurology was a distinguished Dr James Slater. Tall and slim, he was an excellent lecturer. He latterly suffered from a muscular weakness, from which he died. Sadly, the autopsy revealed that he had been killed by pernicious anaemia, B12 deficiency, an eminently treatable neurological condition. His son Tony was a classmate of mine.

The Professor of Psychiatry, Alexander Kennedy, was a large, extroverted man and amusing lecturer. He was the psychiatrist called on to assess all the convicted murderers in Scotland. According to him, they were all mad. Dr Sir James Cameron was the consultant in charge of the first clinical ward at the Royal Infirmary that I attended. A small quiet-spoken man and excellent teacher, he was often away at medical college meetings. His deputy was a Dr Donald Batty, a flamboyant character who had a daunting reputation as an examiner and tutor. At the first meeting between him and the group of ten students including me, he began by stressing the importance of observation in making a diagnosis. He turned to one student, David Thomson, and said, "You look street-smart", which he was. He turned to another student and told him he looked stupid—he did indeed fail his exams. He turned to me and said I looked naïve, probably having seen the look of shock on my face at hearing his last diagnosis.

As part of the medical course, we had to administer twelve anaesthetics and deliver twelve babies. The anaesthetics I completed in two sessions. At one, I gave ether on a cloth mask to children who were having tonsillectomies. At the other at the Royal Infirmary Accident and Emergency, I gave nitrous oxide to patients having minor surgery. I completed the child deliveries in one week at a hospital, Bellshill, halfway to Glasgow. I recall with sadness one beautiful blond, 15-year-old girl who came in at full term for an emergency Caesarean section. "Too pretty for her own good," was the surgeon's remark. I decided I did not want to pursue either specialty.

During my university years, I continued to play sport. The main one was golf; I played once for the University. The University had a student concession with all the municipal and many private golf courses. I rode on my bicycle, with my clubs on my back, to all areas of the city, and paid my two shillings

1960 University John in white jumper and kilt, Castle esplanade, Tiddlywink competition

for a game. I also played Squash for the King's Building Team, playing against other university teams.

My only international sporting experience was with the Tiddlywinks team. The Edinburgh University team was sponsored by Guiness, the Duke of Edinburgh was the patron. Edinburgh won the Scottish Universities championship but represented Scotland, unsuccessfully against Cambridge for the British University's title during their Rag Week — it was a lot of fun. We had one charity Tiddlywinks demonstration, on the esplanade at Edinburgh Castle.

I liked music and sometimes went into the Old Quad the refectory at lunch to hear student jazz bands who played there once a week. During my time at Edinburgh, the British Musicians Union lifted their embargo on foreign bands playing in UK. So I was able to hear some great bands like Louis Armstrong and his All Stars. Traditional Dixieland jazz was all the rage, Ken Colyer, Chris Barber and Humphrey Lyttleton were at the height of their success. Inspired by them, I bought a clarinet and taught myself to play it, with the forbearance of the rest of the family. I gave up when I left University.

During the time the family lived in Edinburgh, we had living with us for three years my cousin John Fleming from Keith studying for a Chemistry degree at Edinburgh University. For one year, we had another cousin, Alastair Mackay, staying with us while he studied Scottish Accountancy. Both were good company. Eleanore finished school and went on to secretarial college in Edinburgh. Donald we saw briefly on his leaves from Africa. It was a rare time to have so many members of the family together.

Early in my final year at Medical School, I had to start thinking about where I would complete my one-year pre-registration hospital training. I had passed the ECFMG (Educational Commission for Foreign Medical Graduates) exam showing English competence that would allow me to go to the US. The Vietnam War was still on, however, and I had no wish to be conscripted. Many hospitals in the Commonwealth were approved by the General Medical Council as training centres. I wanted to go abroad, so I applied and was accepted at two places, St Johns in Newfoundland and Nassau in the Bahamas. I chose Nassau. It was a colony so I had to appear for an interview at the British Commonwealth Office in London. I was accepted on condition that I passed my final exams, which I did.

A DOCTOR'S LIFE IN HONG KONG

Lossiemouth, Dad, Mum, John at Covesea 1959

1961 Graduation Edinburgh University

Chapter Five
1955–1961
Crossing the World: Travels as a Student

Skiing — 1955

In the loft above the garage at the family home, Ardival in Lossiemouth, there was an old pair of wooden cross-country skis with leather bindings that had belonged to one of my uncles. They were about ten feet long and had no metal edges. On these I had my first ski outing, with the Edinburgh University Ski Club, a weekend at Glenshee in 1955. There was nothing to ski on but a few icy patches of snow near the top of the hill. Without steel edges on them, my skis were hopeless. We stayed at the Youth Hostel in the valley. A kilted character rather like Burl Ives with a guitar, led us in singing Scottish folk songs. Despite the poor skiing, it was a great weekend.

Skiing in the Black Forest — 1956

I spent Christmas 1956 with a university group at Feldberg, a ski resort in Germany's Black Forest. It was organised by Hans, a German student, who, as we learnt later, had not organised anything like this before. To keep costs down, he had chosen the cheapest options. Hans, Pierre from Paris, Hugo from Africa, two girls from the US and I set off together from Edinburgh. We travelled overnight by train to Freiberg, where we spent one night at an army camp previously used by French occupation forces. I was entranced with Freiberg, a very attractive city, and visited again years later.

The next day the others hired whatever ski equipment they needed. I had my ancient long wooden skis, without steel edges, designed for cross-country skiing, RAF 'square-bashing' boots, thick RAF trousers, sweaters and my golfing jacket. I was definitely not a ski fashion statement. Later that day, we took a mountain train up to a station in the Feldberg region of the Black Forest and, from there, a bus to a farmhouse/ski-lodge at the foot of the ski run that boasted one ski lift. We stayed in a dormitory with two-tier beds in spartan rooms of a stone-flagged bunk house; in the summer, it was probably a cowshed. During the first two days, there was not enough snow for the ski lift, so Hans gave us lessons — we were all beginners. Sadly, on the second day, Hugo fell, travelling at all of five miles an hour, and ruptured the medial ligament of one knee. He was carried off to a nearby nursing home run by nuns.

During that first week, Hans excused himself to spend Christmas with his family; homesick Pierre left for Paris, and the American girls departed for warmth and sunshine in Italy. For them, the final straw was when the local butcher killed a cow on the premises; he filled two large metal basins — placed in the passage outside our bedrooms — with cow innards and proceeded to make sausages.

A second group from the university arrived for the second week, a day late. The courier at Victoria Station in London was instrumental in their missing their boat-train; they lost their sleeping car reservations and had a terrible trip. On arrival, they were disconcerted to find that I was the sole remaining member of the first week's group. The next day Hans turned up and went with them back to Feldberg to hire equipment. Then it thawed. Altogether, I had about six days' skiing. Despite the chaos, I enjoyed it and looked forward to my next ski trip — but the next time was 24 years later!

Hitchhiking

As a child, I had travelled many thousands of miles in India in great comfort; since then, I have always been keen to travel. I was disappointed that my two years of National Service yielded just two weeks in Malta. I viewed a degree in Medicine as a passport for world travel. All Commonwealth countries accepted a degree approved by the British General Medical Council. In addition, like many in my academic year, I sat and passed the American ECFMG examination, started in 1955, which gave the option of working in the US.

University holidays presented the perfect opportunity for travel. I had saved enough money during National Service to finance my ambition, but only by the most economical means — hitchhiking. The trip to St Andrews was a start, the trip round Europe was a trial run for my ultimate aim, to cross North America. In 1957, the Vietnam War was drawing to a close and Jack Kerouac had published *On the Road*, a book that inspired a wave of travellers.

Keep Your Hands Off — 1957

In July 1957, I started my hitchhiking career, to watch the British Open Golf championship at St Andrews on the east coast of Fife, 50 kilometres, or 30 miles, north of Edinburgh. The Royal and

Ancient Golf Club of St Andrews was established in 1754 and is one of the oldest in the world. The winner was Bobby Locke from South Africa. Somewhat rotund, he had developed a swing to cope with his girth, a swing that started the ball way to the right of target and brought it back to exactly where he wanted it to go.

On this trip, I learned two lessons. Firstly, always carry a good map. On the way north, I should have ended my first lift at Milnathort before getting to Glenfarg; instead, I carried on up the Perth Road as far as Bridge of Earn. Fortunately, all roads led to St Andrews for The Open so there was no trouble getting another lift. I camped in a tent on the hillside to the south of the city, uncomfortably, in cold and wet weather.

The second lesson was not to take chances with suspicious drivers. On the final day, a well-spoken middle-aged gentleman fancied me enough to offer me a lift all the way back to Edinburgh, on the understanding that I would spend the night with him in Perth — it must have been my kilt that turned him on. I made sure I did not meet him again and hitched a lift back in another car to Edinburgh that evening, without compromising my honour.

From Paris to Nice by Cadillac!
My second hitchhiking trip was a summer expedition to Europe in 1957.

In the 1950s, hitchhiking was very popular amongst students. It was cheap — the Government limited the money permitted to be taken out of the country to £25 per year. I could speak a little French and had phrase books in French and German; I had heard that many people spoke some English, so I was not worried about communicating. Youth Hostels were present in many large towns and scenic areas. I carried a tent as a backup. My parents were no doubt concerned about me but never tried to dissuade me.

JOHN MACKAY

I started in the evening on the A1 road at Tranent, on the outskirts of Edinburgh, where I was dropped off by my father. I had learned that the long-distance lorry drivers travelled by night and were the best bet for a lift. Indeed, I made good time as far as mid-Yorkshire; there I stood for a long time in the early hours of the morning, tired and beginning to question the merits of this form of travel. Eventually, a lorry driver picked me up. He said, "I am not meant to pick up passengers, you know." A Good Samaritan.

He dropped me off near London, a journey of 200 miles. I took the subway to Victoria and a bus from there to Canterbury; I arrived at the Youth Hostel just before the closing time, 10 p.m. Next morning, I took the ferry to Calais and checked into a Youth Hostel in the town that evening. I must have looked genuine as a student hitch-hiker. I wore a kilt and carried a rucksack displaying the Youth Hostel Association badge and a Scottish flag. The trip nearly floundered in Calais. I left my wallet containing my passport and nearly all my money on the counter of a family grocery shop near the hostel. To my surprise and embarrassment, it was handed back to me in the hostel, before I had even noticed it missing — what good fortune.

My first lift in France was appropriately enough in the 'deux chevaux' Citroen of a farmer and his wife delivering vegetables. I sat in the back amongst the produce. This was one of the most iconic French cars. A few lifts later, I was in Paris. I stayed at a hostel for several days, while I explored the delights of the city — churches, museums, parks, the Eiffel Tower, the banks of the Seine. They were delightful days leading to footsore early nights.

My next objective was the Mediterranean coast. I had been standing on the main road south from Paris for only a short time when a very long black Cadillac drew up. I could not believe my luck when the driver, a young man, told me that he was going all the way to Nice. He turned out to be the nephew of the distinguished old lady sitting beside him; she was a member of the Russian nobility who had fled to Paris after the 1917 revolution. The limousine glided along in a manner so much smoother than the bumpy ride amongst the vegetables in the Citroen. But, in the end, I look back on my first ride in France as the more comfortable. The first day went well. We stopped in the evening at Vichy; they stayed at the Hotel Ambassadeurs, recommended by the Michelin Guide, and I at a Youth Hostel.

The next morning, I was walking through the market square to their hotel at the appointed time for departure when I saw the Cadillac approaching. I waved it to a halt, apologised for being late and climbed in, somewhat to their embarrassment, I think. Maybe they had decided that the novelty of a hitchhiker on board was interesting for one day only. They continued to be pleasant but not chatty with me, talking to each other in Russian. I was prepared to accept some coolness in return for the pleasure of wafting down to Nice in a Cadillac. We travelled on the direct route south, down the Rhone valley through Clermont-Ferrand. I remember dramatic hill-top villages around Le Puy. That afternoon we stopped at Avignon. I had time to wander around the ancient town, the Pope's Palace and the bridge made famous by the song, *Sur le Pont d'Avignon*.

I spent that night in my tent at a camping site on the west bank of the river Rhone. It was not restful because of the mosquitoes. I was waiting at the gate of their up-market hotel when they emerged the following morning, so there was no chance of missing my ride. By the time we reached Nice, the Countess had relaxed and was chatty. She recommended Cannes as the place for young people to have fun, but I had decided on Nice because it had a Youth Hostel. It was situated on the road leading up the hill at the eastern end of the Promenade des Anglais. As it happened, the Hostel was full, so I spent the first night at a Relais, an even cheaper establishment, of small rooms filled with bunk beds and smelling of cheap alcohol. The next few days I enjoyed more comfortably at the Youth Hostel. It had a wonderful multi-national atmosphere—friendly, relaxed and full of characters. It was run by a North African Frenchman, possibly Algerian, assisted by two English girls, with one of whom he was having an affair.

An American girl stayed for a couple of days, to catch up on sleep. She said that she had hitched a lift on a lorry whose driver had been happy to accept payment in terms of sexual favours. There were two young Frenchmen, whose hitching modus operandi was for one of them to wear a long blonde wig to attract the motorist; his companion sat in the ditch out of sight, only emerging when the ride was secured. The beach at Nice was a disappointment after the wide expanses of sand at Lossiemouth. It was all stones, too hot to walk on barefoot, and crowded with people getting browner and browner in what was the fashion in those days.

I remember a long conversation with a retired musician. He had been a cellist with the Mantovani Orchestra, at that time world famous, but had been forced to give up because of rheumatoid arthritis of the hands. He showed me his hands, distorted with the disease—what a personal tragedy. I hitched to Monte Carlo for a day, wandered round the town, the palace, the harbour with fancy yachts at the quayside, the casino and had a swim at a stony bit of beach in Menton. I decided that Monte Carlo did not cater to hitchhikers.

From Nice, I hitched along the coast to Italy and up to Milan. The Youth Hostel there was in the centre of town within walking distance of the cathedral and La Scala Opera House. The ice-cream vendor there was an artist, sculpting multi-coloured flowers in ice-cream cone vases. They tasted as good as they looked, fabulous.

From Milan, I travelled north along the shores of Lake Maggiore to Locarno, wonderfully scenic, and then by train up into Switzerland because it was grey and raining. I stayed at a Youth Hostel in Lucerne. Next morning after hours without a lift, I took a train from Lucerne to Basel, and from there had a lift to Freiburg on the Rhine; and the following day down the Rhine valley to Heidelberg. The Youth Hostels in Germany, Yugendherberger, were wonderful in comparison with those in France or the UK. They were new, spacious, immaculately clean, and well patronised. I still remember the plate of soup I had at Heidelberg, a great bowl of broth so full of vegetables, barley and meat that it was a meal in itself. The only downside was the fact that there were so many hitchhikers that the entrances to the autobahnen were lined with travellers. No hitching was allowed on the autobahnen themselves.

I travelled in style down the Rhine by boat, from Mainz through the gorges. I drank in the sight of medieval villages clinging to the banks of the river and grapevine terraces climbing up to fairytale castles on top of the hills. I sat on the top deck with a friendly American couple and will always remember his name because he gave me an infallible word association to remember it by: 'Bayer', as in aspirin. I spent one night in Cologne; I could still see the signs of heavy destruction from wartime bombing. The cathedral was very impressive.

Hitching on into Belgium, I stayed for one day in Brussels and one in Bruges, just a short way from Ostend and my return ferry to Dover. Having counted my pennies very carefully throughout the trip, I worked out that I could afford one very good meal, so I treated myself to a plate of steak and chips and a glass of beer. That night in Bruges, there was a son et lumière performance in the main square; it gave an account of the city's history, a wonderfully theatrical event. On the final day, I took a train to Ostend, the port for the ferry to Dover, hitched lifts into London, and finally took a train to the home of my uncle Rowand Mackay at Tadworth in Surrey. I had been through five countries in Europe for a month, at a cost of just £20!

It was a joy to return to the luxury of a family home and a bedroom to myself, and have the satisfaction that I had done what I had set out to do. What happened the next day could not have been a bigger contrast. While I had been away, an invitation had come to my parents to attend the wedding of Victoria Henry, daughter of a friend of my father, a fellow Indian Army officer. It had been sent to my Uncle Rowand who handed it to me the morning after I arrived: the wedding was to be held in London that very day. My parents could not go but would be happy if I would represent the family. My uncle gave me a blank cheque to hire a morning suit and Aunt Gwen gave me five pounds before I took the train into town, still in my kilt and sports shirt. Moss Bros were very smooth and efficient; their staff did not bat an eyelid at the unusual appearance of their client. In no time at all, I was fully kitted out to attend a formal wedding, with my hiking gear stowed in the suitcase provided.

I left the case at the Westbury Hotel where the reception was to be held and crossed Hanover Square to St George's, a fashionable church, for the wedding. At the reception afterwards, I talked with the bride, an absolutely gorgeous redhead. It was a surreal feeling to be sipping champagne in the opulent surroundings of a society wedding, after a month of living on the breadline. The reception over, I made my kilted way out of the hotel and back to Moss Bros where I handed in my smart clothes.

The next day I left Tadworth by bus for Kingston on Thames, and hitched from there, with a couple of hours of sightseeing at

Oxford on the way, to Bourton on the Hill, a lovely village in the Cotswolds, to stay with my uncle Culbard Mackay and aunt Nita. My final day of hitching took me from Worcester to Newcastle, with many lifts and much rain. At 8 p.m., I was standing outside the railway station in the rain; so I did the only sensible thing and took a train for the last 120 miles home to Edinburgh. The train was almost empty so I spent the journey stretched out in a first-class compartment. I had set off alone but enjoyed great companionship from fellow travellers at every stage of the trip. It had been a great experience.

North America 1958: Crossing the Prairies
Emboldened by this successful European trip, I decided on a similar journey the following summer in North America. My plan was to fly by the cheapest route possible across the Atlantic, work briefly in a hospital in Canada to earn money, then hitchhike to the Pacific coast and back, staying with relatives and friends on the way. And that is exactly what I did.

I wore the same outfit as the previous year—kilt and sports shirt—carried the same rucksack, but without the tent. I had only used it once in Europe. Made of canvas, it was bulky, with wooden tent poles and not mosquito- or rain-proof; it was a far cry from the modern lightweight tents with nylon fabric and aluminium struts.

Icelandic Air had the cheapest student flights across the Atlantic. So, in July, I flew one of their propeller planes from Prestwick near Glasgow, via Reykjavik and Gander, to New York. The plane landed in the early hours of the morning, so I spent part of my first night in US in the traditional spot for vagrants, Grand Central Station. The waiting area was a cavernous place with islands of seating. Many bodies with bundles of belongings were lying or sitting around, disturbed from time to time by patrolling policemen who checked for possession of train tickets.

In the morning, I arrived at the William Sloane House YMCA, a large building with a throng of young people milling around the foyer waiting for rooms to become available near midday after check-out time. I had a bad moment when my luggage disappeared. Eventually I tracked it to the luggage store downstairs and retrieved it by describing the exact contents of the rucksack to a highly sceptical member of staff. In the end, I was given a room to share with a Frenchman.

That day I had a new experience—I was cheated by a professional! He was a young Canadian who said he was from Montreal and had been playing ice-hockey for a team in US. He had temporarily run out of funds for some reason or other, would appreciate a loan, and gave me the address of his home in Montreal where I would get the money back. I gave him US$10 that I could ill afford. When I arrived in Montreal, I found the address to be, of course, fictitious—a good learning experience.

I was happy to head north out of New York the next morning. Lifts were not hard to come by. Most people thought I was from a Canadian regiment or a Boy Scout. I was warned off the State Highway by police; in future, I took care to hitch from the side of the access roads. I travelled up the Hudson River Valley, with the Catskills and then Adirondack Mountains to the west and the Green Mountains of Vermont to the east. By nightfall, I was in upstate New York in lovely, wooded country dotted with small lakes on which stood summer weekend cottages; I camped out on the verandah of one of them for the night.

The next day I crossed over into Canada, at the head of Lake Champlain, in a car driven by a North American Indian. I made it to Montreal with him, and found my way out to Dorval, the lakeside suburb where my father's cousin, Charlie Young, lived with Gisele, his French Canadian wife. Wonderful hosts, they took me with them to spend the weekend with a friend, May Lochhead; an elderly widow, she spent the summer in the Laurentian Mountains north of Montreal. She had a marvellous pine-built house on a slope overlooking a lake, with mature pine forest all around. She had a boathouse with a canoe and a motorboat. Around the lake, about a mile in diameter, were several similar summer houses. I learned how to paddle a canoe on a straight course and explored the lake. We took our meals on a balcony overlooking the lake; they were preceded by numerous glasses of sherry drawn from a barrel. The fresh air, the scent of pine, the stillness, the healthful tiredness after a day's activity chopping wood or paddling the canoe or fishing, combined to make it a blissful place.

Hospital Orderly
Before leaving home, I had arranged a job as an assistant ward orderly at the famous Allan Memorial Institute of the McGill University Teaching Hospital in Montreal. I checked in there on the Monday and found myself a cheap student lodging near the hospital. I worked at Allan Memorial for three weeks. I explored Montreal, a delightful city, probably because it was so European and reminded me of Paris, with an extra North American buzz. The most interesting part of the work was connected to a programme run by a Dr Ewen Cameron on the treatment of depression. It was at a time when physical therapy was being researched as an alternative to psychotherapy and psychoanalysis. Some patients were sedated with barbiturates; while they were semiconscious, they were fed a continuous tape recording telling them that they were really fine. If this did not work, they were given a course of electro-convulsive therapy. A strong dose of this therapy would leave them confused and lacking memory of recent events. Many years later, I discovered that Cameron was funded partly by the

Central Intelligence Agency (CIA) of the US.

The hospital had a world-famous surgeon, Dr Wilder Penfold. He was renowned for his research in which he would expose a patient's brain, then bring them out of anaesthesia and have them tell him their sensations when he stimulated the cortex of the brain. I watched from the observation balcony of the operating theatre while this was happening. I left the job before the month was completed because I was given the chance to go back to the summer home of May Lochhead for a week. The week with her was a delight. I did many useful jobs around the estate — clearing fallen trees from the long woodland path to the road, remnants of the winter storms, rebuilding a bridge using pine trees and much else besides. It was fun and was much appreciated.

To the Pacific

When it was time to start my journey to the West Coast, Charlie Young drove me to the western outskirts of town and dropped

1958 Norris Mackay's farmstead, British Columbia

me on the Trans-Canada highway. A train thundered by, drawn by an enormous locomotive; it gave the melodious lonesome wail that only seemed right in the open prairie. There was a long way to go. I had my usual feeling of excitement and nervousness at the prospect.

In no time, I was in Ottawa, the national capital. I stayed at the YMCA for a day admiring the Westminster-style Parliament buildings and the view from there down over the river and the rafts of logs being floated down to the paper mills. The next stop was Toronto, where I stayed with a Canadian whom I had met at the Edinburgh Festival. I had spent an afternoon showing him around the city and taken him to a ceileidh in a church hall just below the castle esplanade where we joined a hilariously chaotic eight-some reel.

My friend was lodging with people in a suburb on the lake shore and had planned for me to stay at a room he had in town. However, his landlady insisted that I stay with them, which was even better. My main memory of that visit was of being invited to play golf at a country club to the west of the city. My host and I played nine holes, had lunch, and then played the second nine, which seemed to be the standard practice. I played well enough to impress my partner and myself.

Now I faced a long haul all the way to the West Coast before I had another address to home in on. It was 4,400 kilometres (2,700 miles) from Toronto to the Pacific Coast. I hitched towards Sudbury, finally picking up a ride in a Volkswagen 'beetle'. The driver, Jim, was a young Englishman who had gone through drama training in London and was now running a community entertainment organisation in Winnipeg. He was driving all the way back, about 750 miles and was happy to have company. We headed due west from Sudbury to Sault Ste Marie. The road through Canada went round the north shore of Lake Superior and was not in good condition; so we crossed into the US and drove through northern Wisconsin towards Duluth, Minnesota.

We stopped for the night at the side of the road, after dark, when Jim had been driving for at least 400 miles. Sleep would have been difficult in the car at the best of times. On this night, it was made impossible by the most dramatic electrical storm I had ever seen. Incessant arcs of lightning, crashes of thunder and torrential rain continued for hours. We were concerned that there might be no road left to drive on the next day, but, by daybreak, the skies began to clear and we could get going.

At Duluth, we crossed back into Canada and motored through beautiful, wooded country around the north of Lake of the Woods. Stopping for petrol at a rare filling station, we noticed that one of the rear tyres was on the point of bursting. It was a retreaded tyre bought only recently, so Jim was rightly furious at having to buy a new one. We reached Winnipeg that evening, and I spent the next two nights at Jim's apartment. Situated on a flat plain, the city had nothing to recommend it; the houses were largely built of wooden board and unattractive.

West of Winnipeg, the road ran over gently undulating prairie. I picked up a ride with a farm machinery salesman in a new Ford Edsel who was grateful for company. That day he took me to Regina, and on to Calgary the day after. On the way, we passed places with evocative names like Portage La Prairie, Indian Head, Moose Jaw, Swift Current, Maple Creek and Medicine Hat. From time to time, he would turn off the main road onto a potholed farm track to see a client farmer. He believed that there were only two ways to drive along potholed roads — either very slowly or very fast. He tended to drive very fast.

After hours and hours of looking at the plains, it was exciting to see the first faint outline of the Rocky Mountains on the skyline. Keen to get into the mountains, I spent only one night at Calgary and hitched on to Banff the next day. It was breathtakingly spectacular. One photograph I took from up one of the mountains won a prize at the Edinburgh University Photographic Club. I hitched on, over the Kicking Horse Pass and down to Golden in the Columbia River valley. The Trans-Canada highway was still under construction round 'the big loop', so, at Golden, I took a train for the spectacular ride through Glacier National Park as far as Revelstoke.

Here I met a group of students from Cambridge University who were working on the highway. Most were in a work gang shovelling dirt and digging ditches; one said he thought they must be the most efficient gang in that section. They pushed themselves very hard. Another member of the group had been smart enough to get a job as a surveyor, so he stood around holding a measuring pole all day. Wages were huge. I applied for a job the next morning, but there was nothing on offer. That night I slept in the park, under a bench. Two teenagers sat at a nearby bench discussing a party they were going to put on. At one point they noticed me and I heard one say to the other, "He's probably a hobo." I certainly felt like one.

From Revelstoke, I had lifts right along the shores of beautiful Okanagan Lake. Charlie Young in Montreal had given me the address of a farmer at Penticton, at the southern end of the lake. The family was most hospitable and happy to have me stay for a night. They laughed when I said I would like to earn money picking fruit. "Only the Doukhobors do the picking," they said, "You should work in the canning factory." The Doukhobors were the poorest sector of the community. They were Russian evangelicals who had fled religious persecution in the early 20th Century and settled in Canada. Anyway, the peach harvest was over on their farm; I was invited to eat as much as I liked off the trees. The peaches were luscious.

The next day I travelled south, nearly to the border with USA, before turning west again, over the Cascade Mountains and down to the Fraser River at Hope. Some miles down the river, where the road ran along the north bank, I reached the homestead of Norris Melville Mackay, my father's cousin, and his wife Norah. They had been expecting me and were happy to take me in. I stayed with them for a week; one day I earned a little money harvesting tomatoes at a neighbouring farm. On another day, I went out on a boat with a fisherman netting for salmon on the Fraser River. Unhappily, the fish were not running; rather than let me return back home empty-handed, he 'borrowed' a fish from his mate in another boat. Evidently, Norris and his wife Norah were well known and liked in the area.

Norris had trained as an electrical engineer in Manchester at the beginning of the century, when electricity was just becoming important as a source of power and lighting. He could have done very well in Britain but was seduced by the idea of going to Canada and opening up the country. Like many others, he ended up on five acres of poor soil, as a homesteader. To make money he used to work for the British Columbian Hydro-electric Board. He married Norah, from a village which we visited just up the river; it had wooden board houses set round a common, as near to an English hamlet as can be. Unhappily, she had rheumatic heart disease and was told she should never have children. No sooner had he built his wooden house, wonderfully well done too, than World War I broke out. He, of course, volunteered to join a Scottish regiment. He used to have a horse that helped him work the fields, but it was worn out and eventually died. At the time I was there, they grew a little corn, but they were essentially retired, living on his war pension. He was a fine man, kind and cheerful.

My next contact address was with a Mrs Phil Black who had

been a neighbour at Lossiemouth. To reach her, I hitched into Vancouver and took a ferry to Pender Island, one of the islands in the channel between the mainland and Vancouver Island. I stepped off the ferry onto a wooden pier at this lovely, wooded island, and the first thing I saw in a field of lush pasture was a herd of highland cattle, long horns, shaggy red coats and all. I stayed just one day in that restful sanctuary. I would have liked to have stayed longer but always with me was the thought that I had to be back to New York on a specific day for a charter flight to the UK that I could not miss, and here I was at the opposite edge of the continent. I have never been the true traveller, one with no deadlines to keep, able to stay wherever he or she is for as long as he or she wishes.

From Pender, I took the ferry to Vancouver Island and hitched down to Victoria. Here I had the address of a niece of Norris Mackay and found another bit of Scotland. After greeting me at the front door, the lady of the house asked, "Now then, would you like an egg to your tea?" The next day was a Sunday. I remember it well because it was the day of a fishing competition in the bay off Victoria. I was invited to go with the daughter of the house and her boyfriend. Very unfortunately in the excitement of departure, we left behind the spare can of petrol. So, instead of restfully trolling for fish, we took turns rowing the dinghy — and caught nothing. There were many dolphins around, frightening the fish, so the others did not catch many fish either. The following day I travelled back to Norris and Norah.

Friends of theirs, with a bigger car, had offered to get me started on my way back to the east coast by driving me across the border to Bellingham in Washington State, where they were to visit friends. My first lift across the border came from a couple of young men, labourers on a road construction project, who told me they drove 100 miles daily from Seattle to their work site. In the back of the car was a crate of beer to keep them going. After only a short while, they said they were tired, and handed the driving over to me — happily for just a short spell.

On the outskirts of Seattle, we were pulled over by the police for speeding. The driver leapt out of the car as soon as he stopped and walked to the police car to show his licence and be booked. He explained later that he had already been fined for drunken driving, and, if the police had seen the crate of beer in the car, he would have lost his licence.

One of them insisted that I stay with him and his family in their shanty-town style wooden shack in Seattle. The car belonged to his brother-in-law who needed it back, so we were off again within minutes of arrival at his home, to check out a car on offer in another suburb. We found the seller's place at the bottom of a valley, bought the car, an old sports two-seater, and set off home with the two cars. After half a mile, the sports car stalled. Successive efforts to jump restart it by coasting downhill were unsuccessful; this left us at the bottom of the hill again, out of touch with the other car. Some time and many phone calls later, long after dark, the other car turned up and towed us home. Next morning at dawn, we were off again, still in the brother-in-law's car, for them to get to work. They obligingly dropped me off at the exit point for the highway leading east. I was sorry to say goodbye to such happy-go-lucky characters.

The Longest Ride Ever
This was the start of an amazing day's travel. The first pick-up was with a young man in a van headed for Chicago — 3,300 kilometres (2,000 miles) from Seattle. In the next 24 hours, we travelled almost nonstop. He himself was driving for all but a couple of hours, and covered 1,900 miles. We drove through the Cascade Mountains to Ellensburg, across the Columbia River

valley to Spokane, and over the Rocky Mountains to Billings, the start of the prairies.

The radio was on most of the time; we had to re-tune from time to time as we moved through different broadcast areas. The favourite song was *Volare* by Domenico Modugno, who had just come third at the Eurovision song contest. I can still remember the melody. We drove through North and South Dakota, and Iowa, avoiding Minneapolis. I asked to be dropped off near the ring route south of Chicago. I had to wait for an hour or so in the early morning before my next lift. I spent the time watching the children of the small village going to school, feeling like a visitor from another planet.

Once I got going, I easily found more lifts and, by afternoon, had crossed Michigan State to Detroit. From there I crossed over the border back into Canada, to stay with a friend of my parents who lived in Windsor, Ontario. After a couple of days for rest and recuperation, I spent a day hitching to Toronto, where I met my friend again. The plan had been that he would drive me to New York, but it turned out that he did not have leave to spare, so he gave me $10 to cover the train fare for the last 500 miles. I spent a couple of days with him, going to a college basketball game and enjoying milkshakes, jukeboxes and McDonald's culture. On my way to New York, I stopped at Niagara Falls for a day, staying at a motel. The falls were magnificent. The shops there had a remarkable amount of tourist gifts. I bought a cardboard poster that proclaimed, "Once a Knight, Always a Knight, but Once a Night is Enough!" I kept this lubricious object hidden away for many years, until the marriage of a former flat-mate of mine named Trevor Knight. The perfect wedding gift, I thought. In the event, the people at the wedding reception were stuffy and a trifle embarrassed when they saw the sign.

Back in New York, I checked in to the YMCA for my last night, counted my pennies and went up to Times Square to take in the bright lights. I have two memories of that evening. One was of sitting in a restaurant on Times Square trying to get through an immense helping of chicken-in-a-basket, when a police officer came in with his gun, club, radio and other equipment and was treated to a free meal and drink. The second was going into a classy cocktail lounge and listening to the piano playing of Ahmad Jamal, a very cool star of the jazz scene in those days. I could not get over the fact that everyone else was chatting to each other rather than listening to the music.

As a present for my father, I bought a very smart grey nylon tie, just right for going to church. He was very pleased with it—but greatly taken aback when he examined the lining to find it decorated with a luscious pin-up. I fancy he did wear it for laughs, but not to church. The flight back to Glasgow on Icelandic Air was uneventful. At Customs, I unwisely declared the camera that I had bought in Montreal and found I did not have the necessary £5 to cover import duty, so I had to come back the next day with money from my father to collect it. On my return to Edinburgh, my father met me at Waverley station with the words, "You are an amazing chap." From him, this was a memorable complement.

Student Attachment and Security Guard 1959–1960

During my last two summers at university, I was unable to do such long-distance travelling. I was limited by the requirements of the medical course and the need to earn money to finance a holiday. I was required to do electives, in medicine and surgery, each lasting two weeks; we were obliged to attend the wards and operating theatres to observe and assist if called upon. I did the surgical elective in the neuro-surgical unit at The Royal Infirmary in Edinburgh, under Professor Sir Norman Dott, a world-famous surgeon. I found this a fascinating experience, although I did not see myself as a surgeon, being more inclined to psychiatry. His unit was known around the world for developing neurotaxic surgery for parkinsonism.

For the medical elective, I chose psychiatry at the Fulbourne Hospital near Cambridge. I was able to explore and enjoy Cambridge, helped by a fellow medical student called Dave Preston, a Canadian from Ottawa, who had a motor scooter on which we drove around town. The Fulbourne was a Victorian establishment set in large grounds with lawns and surrounding trees. I found large open wards, some with dangerous patients strictly guarded, depressing wards full of elderly demented people incarcerated for life and shorter-stay wards with psychotics, depressives and schizophrenics actively receiving treatment.

One episode remains fixed in my mind. Two patients with intractable depression were on the day's operating list for leucotomies, procedures in which, under general anaesthetic, a small burr hole is made at each temple and a fine knife is inserted to divide some frontal cortex fibres from the rest of the brain. An exalted specialist surgeon had come down from London to perform the operations but, to his great annoyance, the anaesthetist did not turn up on time. After an uncomfortable delay, the anaesthetist turned up full of apologies. The surgeon carried out the operations at great speed and shot off back to London. The result was that one patient recovered well and was more relaxed and easier to manage; the other became a vegetable.

Since then, I have been back to Cambridge many times and always enjoyed it. My brother Donald had spent a year there as a post-graduate studying Tropical Agriculture under a Colonial Development Service Scholarship. I can well understand why he enjoyed it so much. In addition, both our sons went to Cambridge

University, and our younger son Richard continues to live there, so Cambridge is still on our itinerary.

During my last summer holiday in 1960, I worked as a night security guard in London for Securicor for a couple of weeks to earn money. For part of the time, I was at a deserted cigarette factory in the Camden Town district; then at a paper-collecting centre on the south bank of the Thames next to the Battersea Power Station. It was interesting because there was a large amount of reading material, printer's rejects. But these jobs were dark, frightening, not something I would like to do permanently. The upside was that it left the days free to enjoy London, go to the theatre and explore the city. I stayed with my cousins Jill and Barbara Thomson at their home in Belsize Park.

Scandinavian Safari – 1960
With my hard-earned money, I was able to take my last trip as a student, to the Summer School in Scandinavia. It was organised by Scandinavian students and designed to give serious medical instruction at four different universities, with a generous amount of sightseeing thrown in. I flew from London to Copenhagen where I joined the others. We were a motley collection – five Brits, French, Germans, Americans and a couple of Yugoslavs who were out of the communist fold for the first time and had a very large bottle of Slivovitch to help them enjoy it.

From Copenhagen, we travelled to Aarhus University for two days. On one of them, we went to the highest point in Denmark, 567 feet. Our academic focus here was orthopaedic surgery, taught by a professor from Aarhus University. From Aarhus, we travelled up the Jutland peninsula to take the ferry across the Skagerrak to Norway and Sandefjord, the centre of the Norwegian whaling fleet. From there we drove to Oslo via Edvard Munch's home, where we saw his painting, *The Scream*.

Oslo was delightful. We were taken round the Parliament building by one of the student hosts; his father was an MP from Bergen. We saw the Olympic ski-jump site, climbed to the top of the jump and wondered at the courage of the competitors. We took a trip down the Oslo fjord to the most southerly lighthouse in Norway; there we swam in freezing water. Most memorable were the Vigeland Gardens, a sculpture park in Oslo with wonderful figures on the hillside, and *The Kiss*, a monumental statue in marble of a man and a woman kissing.

A train took us into Sweden, to Gothenburg (Goteborg) for a couple of days. One day we were taken on a ferry up through the islands to have a magnificent seafood meal, with the usual too many toasts with aquavit. Back in Copenhagen on the last leg of the trip, we visited the Tivoli Gardens, the Tuborg brewery and a castle that could have been the inspiration for *Hamlet*. I had one night away from the group to meet a friend, a classmate from Edinburgh, Bill Newey; he was doing a student elective at one of the city hospitals. We went to a pub with friends at the harbour. It was wall-to-wall with people; we drank and listened to a great jazz band, then on to a party afterwards. The girl I was introduced to during the evening turned out to be from a village way outside Copenhagen. By the time I had escorted her home and returned to the city on a commuter train, it was almost time for breakfast. The following evening, after a full day of activities, I fell asleep on the couch of a bedroom occupied by two girls of our party. I woke up with some embarrassment the next morning to realise where I was.

After the end of the Summer School, I took a train to Stockholm. I spent several days there enjoying the Viking museums and walking around the city. It is always fascinating to explore new places, but I did miss the camaraderie of the group. I took a train back to Copenhagen and from there a ship back to Newcastle. It was fine and calm until we sailed into the North Sea. From then onwards, we were butting into a strong headwind and moderate seas. I found it safer to spend the night on deck, wrapped up in blankets on a deckchair. It was exhilarating to watch the swells surging past, and the clouds scudding past the moon. Those that went below did not join me for breakfast the next morning.

Hospital: Canada or the Bahamas? 1961
During my final year at university, I realised that my investments in Littlewoods Football Pools were never going to support me. I had to get a job. My final selection lay between hospitals in St John's, Newfoundland, and Nassau, capital of the Bahamas. The St John's job was attractive because I had spent one summer in Canada and enjoyed it immensely. The Nassau job was attractive because I had never been to that part of the world, and the climate would be a great deal more pleasant than in Newfoundland. I was also influenced by a fellow student, John Lund, a Bahamian who reassured me of the standard of the hospital, and the pleasures of the islands. In the end, I opted for Nassau. But first, I had to travel to London for an interview with a panel at the Commonwealth Office. All went well, so I signed a contract for a one-year Preregistration job at the Princess Margaret Hospital in Nassau, starting in July 1961.

Chapter Six
1961–1963 and beyond
The Bahamas

Leaving home is never easy. Opting to spend my medical preregistration year in the Bahamas meant that I would not see my parents again for a year. I have no doubt they had hoped I would find a job in Scotland but understood my wish to travel, just as my father and two of his brothers had done. Donald was by now working in Northern Rhodesia; later Eleanore would spend three and a half years in Canada. Our family typified the Scottish diaspora, educated people going abroad to the Commonwealth, to learn, to contribute and hopefully to make a good living.

I flew west from London to New York, and then south to Nassau, the Bahamian capital, arriving on July 27. The Princess Margaret Hospital was set on a low hill; there are no high hills on the island. A wide drive led up to the main block, an H-shaped structure, with two floors, painted white and pink. The junior doctors' residence to the right of the drive was a single-storey wooden building with wide balconies at the front of four bed-sitting rooms with ensuite bathrooms, and fans for cooling and no air-conditioning. There was a communal, central dining area

A DOCTOR'S LIFE IN HONG KONG

1961 Nassau, Bahamas, Princess Margaret Hospital

1961 Nassau, Bahamas, view over hospital

with kitchen. Behind the building was a tennis court.

During the next few days I was introduced to all the other doctors. Stanley Cooper was the chief physician, trained in London, tall, serious about clinical standards and a good teacher. There were two Medical Officers, MOs, one was Welsh, the other, Cecil Bethel, was a Bahamian; they each ran a medical ward of a dozen beds. The paediatric ward of about 20 beds was run by an English woman specialist paediatrician. Two preregistration doctors covered the medical and paediatric wards.

The two surgical wards were on the second floor. The chief surgeon, Bentliff, was an Englishman trained at the Westminster Hospital, an excellent general surgeon, tall, with an imperious manner. The second surgeon, Huggins, was a Trinidadian Chinese, small, quiet, and a diabetic. The two obstetric and gynaecological wards were run buy a consultant. Two Medical Officers worked both in surgery and Ob/Gyn, Jason McCarroll,

1961 Nassau, Bahamas, Juan Perez, Jan Evertz, John

and an Irishman, assisted by another two preregistration doctors.

My fellow preregistration doctor colleagues were a Dutchman, Jan Evarts, from Curaçao, and Graham Somerville, a graduate from Edinburgh University who was married to Jose.

Jan was a genial fellow, musical, with a pile of great Latin American records, but too relaxed about his medical duties and too fond of his drink. His employment ended abruptly, when, in a drunken binge he went up to the nurses' quarters and created a disturbance. He found a job in British Guiana from whence he reported the nurses were friendlier.

His replacement was totally different. Andrew Sherrington had qualified in London, was very bright, an academic. He had been qualified for two years, the first spent as a translator of French, German and Russian for the World Health Organization in Copenhagen; the second year working in the editorial unit of the Lancet. Uninterested in clinical medicine, he had chosen Bahamas as the least bad option to get his registration. He was a naturalist, collecting geckos, which he would feed with insects. Once he caught a beautiful hummingbird that he kept in a cage and fed with honey. He was saddened when it died.

He subsequently made a distinguished career working for the Library of the American Medical Association in Washington, then administrative jobs in Canadian medical journalism. I met him twice after we had left the Bahamas, once at his mother's apartment near the Albert Hall. She was a distinguished-looking old lady of Russian origin living in a grand but gloomy apartment and relying on meals on wheels for her lunch. Years later he came to visit me in Hong Kong on his way to somewhere, just the same person. I took him around the colony, ending up at a bar where we had one drink and declined to have anything to do with the hostesses.

When Graham Somerville, a very competent doctor, finished

his training, he went back to England and worked as a GP, until a sadly premature death from Parkinson's disease. His replacement was a married white Jamaican named Hunt, keen on sailing; he built a dinghy on which I joined him sometimes. He had qualified at the University of the West Indies in Jamaica. With his mates he would drive over from Kingston to Montego Bay for the weekend to pick up American tourist females; he reported with disbelief that sometimes the white Southern Belles would hook up with black Jamaicans rather than himself and his white chums.

There were two other doctors working in Accident and Emergency, Cubans, who had left comfortable and successful lives on the island, to emigrate when Castro took over. The older Cuban was a real gentleman, in his fifties who had been a paediatric consultant in Cuba. The younger was an engaging character in his thirties who had been the Cuban middleweight boxing champion. He was an Obstetrician/Gynaecologist, an inveterate womaniser and he proudly showed us an album of pictures of all his conquests. During his time in Nassau, he seduced a member of the Cuban embassy and later had to take her to Miami for a termination.

There were some specialists with whom I had less contact: an English psychiatrist with a Bahamian girlfriend; a chest surgeon who ran the TB establishment situated away from the hospital. He also performed open heart cardiac surgery, like opening up mitral stenotic valves. There was also an ophthalmic surgeon, Steele-Peterkin, who was the first to describe the effect of chloroquine crystals on the eye.

I started off my medical career with three months of medicine under Cecil Bethel, a very genial and helpful mentor. I met him and his wife a year or so later when he was in London sitting for the MRCP, a post graduate degree to become a Member of the Royal College of Physicians. The next three months were spent with the second Medical Officer. The consultant wards and rounds with the Senior Physician, Stanley Cooper, were the most exacting and instructive part of the week. The only part of my medical six months that I did not enjoy were the emergency calls from the paediatric ward, usually infants with dehydration from gastroenteritis requiring venous 'cut-downs' to provide intravenous fluids.

The Bahamian islanders were generally strong and healthy. The young men were prone to getting sexual diseases; gonococcal urethral strictures causing acute urinary retention were not uncommon. The saddest patients were illegal immigrants from Haiti who were brought in half-starved and anaemic from hookworm, and with tuberculosis. One Haitian came in with gross hydrophobia, rabies, for which we had no cure, just sedation. He died quickly.

On the surgical side, the first three months were under the gentle guidance of Dr Huggins. He was an experienced surgeon but had never taken a surgical fellowship. He was obliged to pause sometimes during operations to read up on the operation protocol in his textbook, and have a sugary drink to ward off diabetic hypoglycaemia.

The second three months were under the uncomfortable rule of Bentliff. He and I quickly realised I was not a potential surgeon. He had no time for lack of skill or aptitude. The senior theatre male nurse, Daniels, was a very large, black Bahamian who was constantly told he should go back to the jungle from whence he came, and swing on trees. Even the genial Daniels was sometimes exasperated by these comments.

Bentliff was a law unto himself. On one occasion while on his regular visits to the paediatric ward, he stopped beside the beds of two infants with severe hydrocephalus who had been

1961 Bahamas, Paradise Isle

there for weeks and who would inevitably die soon: he injected potassium into their cephalic veins to finish their sad lives. The ward sister, a Roman Catholic, was upset but could do nothing about it. Some years later Bentliff moved to Bimini, just across the Gulf Strait from Florida, where he continued in surgical private practice.

It was not all work in Nassau. Grand Bahama Island is a very flat coral island surrounded by crystal clear water and coral reefs. I had a wonderful time swimming, snorkelling and sailing. I used to swim at dawn before going to work, and again sometimes in the afternoons.

From a letter to home dated August 26:

> *My big excitement this week has been my boating trip on Sunday. The two Americans who own a boat, Danny and Charlie, took me out for the day, along with the chef of The Pilot House and his wife and kid, and two young American couples complete with two-gallon jars of Planters Punch,*

a crate of beer and two guitars. The chef provided the food. We sailed to a neighbouring island and spent an hour or so trolling for fish, without success. We then moored off a beautiful white coral beach and swam, sunbathed and sang songs till 3 p.m. The water was incredibly clear, and no sharks within a hundred miles. We docked back at Nassau just before sunset then went up to the chef's place for a steak supper. Next time we go out I am going to be allowed to sail the boat. I can't wait. I have joined a club just over the wall from the hospital which has a swimming pool, kidney-shaped, with coconut-laden palms leaning over it and little tables set in shady corners — just like a Hollywood film set. Several of the hospital staff are members. The beauty of it is that I can spend my time swimming and sunbathing while I am on call for the hospital.

There are a few disadvantages to the place about which I will tell you when I have space but at the moment everything in the garden is looking very nice indeed.

There was a tennis court in the hospital grounds where I used to play with other doctors and friends.

'The shops close at 5 p.m. every day, half day Friday, so if I want to do any shopping, I have to ask for the afternoon off. I get about one day off a week. I have spent practically nothing so far, saving up my pennies for a scooter or a car, and for part share of a speed boat a group of us have our eyes on. If we get it, we will be able to go water-skiing, fishing, and go on expeditions to one or other of the local islands.'

I played one round of golf on an uninteresting course in town, the Nassau Country Club; and two games of cricket for the hospital team, in one of which I was our team's top scorer, our best player was Bunty Rolle, a large West-Indian bowler and batsman from Jamaica.

> 'My big adventure of the week took place on Friday. I was detailed to go on a plane to one of the outer islands about 140 miles away to pick up a boy of 15 who was severely ill. We took off at 11am in an orange and green twin-engine sea plane, a Grumman Goose. I was the only passenger on the way out. The first half of the trip was over a deep ocean channel running between island groups – about 60 miles wide. Through the crystal clear water I could see to the bottom of the sea for the last half of the trip over shallow water between an archipelago of little coral islands.
>
> We reached the little settlement shortly after noon and picked up the boy who was not so seriously ill after all – pneumonia. Half the population was on the jetty to greet us – all the men, the women all seemed to be gathered round the unfortunate boy.
>
> Coming back, we made good time (I amused myself by trying to spot sharks – saw only one) until we had gone nearly half way, then suddenly bits started dropping off the starboard engine and oil streamed out. Our shadow on the water showed a long plume of smoke coming from the engine. I expected the pilot to try and limp home on one engine, but he made for the nearest spot of habitation and landed. He found that the engine was completely finished and would take a week to repair so we beached the plane. I went off and found the local D.C. and district nurse and arranged to stay overnight, after we had called on the wireless to Nassau to be told that there were no planes available to relieve us.
>
> It was a beautiful little community, clean, well ordered

and with delightfully friendly Bahamians. Palm-thatched cottages, palm trees, fishing boats up on the beach and nets hanging up to dry – I was all set to spend the next month there; the clinic had everything to treat my patient; in fact, I was having a much-needed swim when a relief plane arrived produced at short notice from somewhere and we were all whisked back to Nassau much to my regret."

For my first three months in Nassau, I explored the town on foot and on bicycle. The hospital drive led down to Bay Street, one lane each way, which ran along the north shore of New Providence Island, lined by small shops and bars. The Pilot House Club was at the east end. The waterfront was one block north. A good harbour, protected to the north by Hog Island, about a square mile of a long, thin, undeveloped spit of sand and coral covered with scrub and bordered by nice beaches. Now it is Paradise Island, the site of a luxurious resort with its own airstrip and two bridges connecting it to Nassau. The harbour was the base for fishing boats, small inter-island ferries and trading vessels. Private boats, yachts and power boats were anchored on the eastward side by the shore, beyond the harbour quays.

The total population of New Providence Island was 110,000, 90 per cent of them Africans whose forebears had arrived as slaves to plantation owners or as freed slaves following the American War of Independence in the 1780s. They lived 'Over the Hill' to the south of Nassau; the whites and wealthy lived along the northern strip of coast.

The island had a colourful history. During the war with Spain, Nassau became a base for privateers who raided the Spanish and French treasure ships. When the war ended in 1696, the privateers started raiding British ships also, becoming true pirates. They became powerful enough to set up a self-governing

Pirate Republic, which ended only when George I sent out a new Governor, Woodes Rogers, who arrived in 1718, pardoning those who wished to remain. The others had to base their piracy elsewhere.

When I arrived in Nassau the only 'pirates' were 'The Bay Street Boys', successful businessmen with offices on Bay Street. Twenty years after I left, and ten years after it became independent, the Bahamas was still a tourist haven, but had also become a staging post for criminals running drugs from South America to the US.

After three months in the colony I had saved enough of my £50 a month salary to buy a car. I bought a very much 'pre-owned' 1950 Austin Popular two-door saloon for £100, recently resprayed and looking smart. I had great fun with this car touring the island. The maximum speed on the island was 30mph and there were no hills, so the car was able to cope despite occasional problems with bad wiring, failed windscreen wipers, and a window that would not shut. The most amusing moment, in retrospect, came when I once accelerated too fast and the man in the front passenger seat fell over backwards, seat and all, as the plywood flooring gave way.

I wrote home about the car in November:

> My car is now going very well after a 'grease job' and a new part in the steering so that now I do not have to travel a wavy line down the centre of the road. Mind you, like my late lamented bicycle, the brakes are never likely to bring me to a skid stop, or any stop at all on a wet day – just as well there are no hills to speak of on the island. Things keep dropping off in the most disconcerting fashion. On Saturday, the inside door handle on the front passenger seat came off with a happy tinkle of scattered nuts and bolts.

When we arrive at any place now, I have to leap out and let my passenger out by opening the door from the outside – in what I take to be an impressively well-bred manner.

When I left, I abandoned the car as unsaleable.

Without the distraction of television, the evenings were spent reading, playing bridge, visiting friends, going out to one of the four cinemas, or calling at clubs or calypso bars.

I became good friends with an artist, Brian Arthur, who ran Chelsea Potteries from a studio dominated by a huge Banyan Tree on East Hill Street. Chelsea Pottery had been established by David Rawnsley in 1952. I met David when I visited the original Pottery in Radnor Walk, London, after I returned to the UK.

The main celebrations in Nassau were at 'Junkanoo' on Boxing Day and at New Year. The New Year celebrations were particularly exuberant. The whole population joined in marching down Bay Street behind bands and colourful floats, everyone blowing whistles, beating drums or ringing bells, shouting and dancing, fuelled by rum.

There was one private hospital in Nassau, the Rassin Clinic, started in the 1950s by Latvian-born, Meyer Rassin, an ex-army surgeon. It is now 'The Doctors Hospital'.

I was entitled to one holiday during my year in the Bahamas. I went with an English lawyer, his name I forget, to Jamaica for five days. The plan was to land at Kingston, hire a car and drive round the western end of the island to Montego Bay from where we could fly back to Nassau.

We stayed in Kingston overnight only, put off by its reputation for violence. We had two nights at Ocho Rios. On the second day my friend was ill, so I drove on my own up the Rio Grande valley, famous for the rafting trips down the river. The scenery was very lush and green, banana plantations, stands of immense bamboo

1962 Jamaica Ocho Rios, John

and rain forest on the mountains. Coming around a right-hand corner I was met head-on by a bus going downhill at speed. I swerved to the side of the muddy road my wheels almost over the edge of the cliff. Momentarily the bus and I were stationary. Before it inched past a Jamaican man leaned out of the bus and shouted, "You lucky raas", raising a laugh from the other passengers.

We had one day at Dunn's River Falls, another beautiful beach area with the falls coming down over rocks in a cascade straight onto the beach. Montego Bay was less attractive, many tourist hotels, even so, being off-season the beautiful beach was not crowded. Jamaica possessed an excellent contrast to the Nassau — mountains.

Once I had finished my year's training in Nassau, I stayed on for one more month to fill in a gap at Accident and Emergency. I could have stayed longer to make a career there and continue to enjoy the Elysian Bahamian lifestyle, but I was determined to get specialist training, which meant returning to UK. To that end

I had applied for a job as a House Officer in Neurosurgery at the Western General Hospital in Edinburgh. To my surprise I was accepted, possibly because of my student attachment there three years before.

My return trip could have been the same way as I had come out, by air via New York. Instead, at the end of August 1962 I flew to Miami for a look at the playground of the rich, took a Greyhound bus to Washington to explore that city, on to Montreal to visit my relatives, Charlie and Gisele Young, and from there flew to the UK.

Edinburgh

I had only a few days at home in Lossiemouth before starting work in Edinburgh. I was fascinated by neurosurgery and learned enough to make occasional but critical use of my training in later years.

Sir Norman Dott, who was world-famous, had just retired and had been replaced by Professor Gillingham. My immediate boss was Philip Harris who had just come back from further training

1962 Ardival, Lossiemouth

JOHN MACKAY

1962 Ardival, Lossiemouth, Mum, Dad, Donald

in US, learning how to do the anterior approach for relief of cervical spondylosis, a dramatic technique and very successful. In Ray Gilchrist's unit they were doing the first X-ray positioned thalamo–paladotomies for parkinsonism. One of the Registrars was Peter Wu from Hong Kong on a government scholarship, during which he passed the Surgical Fellowship, FRCSE and Medical Membership, MRCPE.

The other House Officers and I lived in a flat at the top of the hospital, very convenient for getting to work, and there was plenty of that. We clerked in the patients, managed day-to-day needs, talked to relatives, but had relatively little time in theatre — the Registrars assisting the surgeons doing the intricate operations required to seal bleeding aneurisms and remove tumours. It was interesting to watch the surgeons operating on patients with Parkinson's disease, 'the shaking palsy'. With the patients sedated but conscious, they opened windows to the brain by drilling through the skull under local anaesthetic, passed probes into the brain and by talking to the patient and watching the trembling limb identified the right place to destroy that minute area of brain causing the movement.

All was not work. I bought a car and with it could travel, play the rare game of golf, and get up to Lossiemouth for a break around Christmas. We had one party at home, at Ardival, at which my Bahamian calypso records went down well.

Assessing career prospects at this time, I realised that to become a hospital specialist I would have many years of work and study, and I would have to compete against serious competition, and with pay that would hardly support getting married and having a family. The alternative of General Practice did not appeal, being regarded as an occupation that was taken up only by failed hospital would-be specialists; this was at a time before the GP Charter was negotiated, after which General Practice became better paid for more reasonable working conditions; and it became a specialty discipline in its own right.

At this point a routine visit to my dentist provided an answer. Dr Livingston-Blair had been my dentist since my student days, so he knew me well. He showed me a letter he had received from a fellow Edinburgh graduate, Dr Gren Wedderburn, enquiring if he knew of any suitable doctor to join Drs Anderson & Partners in Hong Kong as a general physician. I showed this letter to all the people in my circle in Edinburgh. The reaction was always, "Hong Kong is a long way away," and "once you step off the academic ladder, you will never get back on again." On the contrary, I was attracted by the offer of a three-year tour in the exotic East followed by six months leave and a prospect of study leave. Peter Wu was a catalyst, extolling the virtues of Hong Kong and showing pictures of the colony. I was particularly taken by a picture taken at night of the floating restaurant in Aberdeen Harbour, ablaze with lights and activity.

I wrote in my application and was interviewed in Edinburgh,

at his flat in Garscube Terrace, by then Senior Partner George Watson. He offered me the job, to start in six months after I had done further training in hospital medicine. To meet this requirement, I chose to go to the General Hospital in St. Helier, Jersey, where I expected to get general medical training rather than a narrow training in a medical specialty in Edinburgh.

JERSEY CHANNEL ISLANDS

The time in Jersey was valuable in that it gave me more training in medicine. I got on well with my seniors, and was pleased to find that I knew more about some subjects than they did. The medical consultant came in daily but spent most of his time at his busy private clinic.

My neurosurgical training came into play on one occasion. A young girl was brought in having fallen into a swimming pool and nearly drowned. On careful questioning it was clear that she had suddenly fainted and then fallen in. A lumbar

1963 St Helier, Jersey

puncture showed blood in the cerebrospinal fluid: she had had an intracerebral bleed. (This was before the days of brain scans and MRI). Hasty transfer to London and surgery for an arteriovenous malformation saved her life.

On another occasion a young woman, on holiday with her parents from a small village in Wales, was brought in having had an epileptic fit. On examination she was at full term pregnancy. She was having eclampsia. The parents were shocked. They remarked that up till then, they had not known that their daughter even knew how to have sex. Immediate transfer to the maternity ward and the baby and mother were saved.

Jersey in the summer was a delight with two golf courses, many beaches, cosy country pubs in one of which I first heard the Beatles' latest hits.

One misty afternoon, I was sitting in a pub close to the airfield when the crew of a Jersey Airlines plane came in: the captain immediately going up to the bar and downing a pint of beer. A fellow crew member told me that the airport had been fogged in with only the church spire acting as landmark. Faced with the alternative of spending the night with his passengers at an airport in France, a considerable expense to a small airline, or having a shot at landing, the captain had opted to give it a try — successfully.

Barn dances were held at weekends, in real barns on farmsteads, this was the swinging sixties.

My sailing career nearly ended prematurely somewhere in the English Channel in the summer of 1963. One of the doctors at the General Hospital in St Helier had a small boat, a Silhouette, about 24 feet long, a sloop-rigged craft with twin keels and an outboard engine.

He agreed to lend it for the weekend to fellow anaesthetist, Bill, and a theatre orderly called Tom. They invited me to join them on a trip to France. I accepted like a shot. On the Friday afternoon, Bill drove me to the bay where the boat was perched on the sand, standing on its twin keels. We climbed on board and settled in while the tide came in to float the boat.

Quite some time later Tom turned up, apparently delayed by difficulty in choosing which tie to wear that evening when we went out on the town at St Malo, only about 30 miles away.

Tom was the only one who had been on the boat before, so he was elected captain. He had an additional qualification, having once been a used-car salesman he was elected Chief Engineer as well. He went to work on the engine that had been submerged in rain water as it lay in the well of the deck during the preceding week.

By the time the tide had come in sufficiently to float the boat, Tom had managed to start the engine, which coughed and spluttered with rain water in the system somewhere. I had been elected 'Navigator' because I had been in the RAF and therefore could read maps. There was a map on board, with all sorts of notations on it with which I was entirely unfamiliar. However, France was very close to Jersey and could not be missed if we travelled in a southeasterly direction.

What we did not have was a Tide Table, without which no one ever goes to sea in the English Channel. It was an unexpected disappointment when we found ourselves bobbing slowly along, past the entrance to St Helier Harbour as dusk was falling, at a time when we had hoped to be strutting on the pier at St Malo.

The breeze was failing, our engine was malfunctioning, and the lights of St Helier beckoned through the gathering darkness, but we decided to press on. The other two went down into the cabin to sleep while I took first watch. It was very dark, the clouds covering the stars; a gentle breeze wafted us along a calm sea in a south-easterly direction, according to the compass.

Suddenly a large, jagged rock slid past to starboard. A shout from me brought the others on deck. Our captain calmly sized up the situation, decided to drop the sails, put down the anchor, and went back to his bunk.

Lying in the well of the cockpit I was alarmed to see more rocks sliding by. We were dragging our anchor in a strong tide race. Tom was unfazed. The anchor will catch on a rock underwater before the boat hits one on the surface, was his opinion.

At daybreak we found we were at the northern edge of a great shoal of rocks that I identified as the 'Minkies', more correctly, Les Minquiers.

We hoisted sail and gingerly snaked our way between the rocks until we came to the main channel running NE to SW through the middle of the shoal. There were a few houses on one island, part of France. We had made it to France!

We anchored in the channel and had some food. Tom went to work on the engine again to get the water out of the system. At this point we decided that we had better head for home.

The wind had dropped completely so we had to motor. We pulled up the anchor and set course due north for Jersey, the outboard chugged away smoothly putting out a cloud of black smoke. The captain and chief engineer slept down below. Only when he surfaced a couple of hours later did Bill and I learn from him that the black smoke indicated that we had been running with the choke fully open, wasting fuel.

This was to prove a serious error. As evening fell and we were again chugging past the entrance to St. Helier harbour, the fuel ran out. A scant zephyr of a breeze gave just enough power to our tiny sails to get us into the anchorage of the Royal St Helier Yacht Club.

Happy to be back on dry land again we headed home for a good night's sleep.

The following day the owner of the boat reported that the outraged Commodore of the yacht club had berated him for docking without permission and commanded him to take his scruffy boat away. For good measure, the owner also pointed out that it was just as well that we had not made it to France proper because we had failed to clear our departure with the immigration authorities in Jersey.

In retrospect this was absolutely the foolhardiest of expeditions. That it was completed without serious mishap was a matter of undeserved good fortune.

A fellow doctor and I rented a small house in the countryside for a month. His mother came to stay there for a while, followed by my sister Eleanore and a female friend. It was a delightful retreat from the hospital residence.

Eleanore remembers, "He invited me to stay for a week in Jersey, all expenses paid, when he was working at the hospital in St Helier. It was a delightful contrast to my existence as a

1963, Jersey, Cliveden Cottage

poorly paid secretary at the Department of Physical Chemistry in Cambridge when I was saving for my air fare to Montreal and a new life in Canada."

Eleanore did go to Canada. She worked in Montreal for 3.5 years, then returned to Scotland to get the qualifications to go to university. She earned a degree in Biology at Stirling University, completed teacher-training and worked for the Open University." Since then she has married, has two children and five grandchildren. I am proud to have such a talented sister.

Hong Kong
Getting There: Rocky Mountains and Arctic Circle

Having completed my six-month medical job in Jersey, I returned home to Lossiemouth to enjoy a last stay with the family before going to Hong Kong. I left Britain in October 1963. I was not due to start in Hong Kong until December. My original plan had been to spend six weeks on a Blue Funnel cargo-passenger ship. When I found out it was no more expensive to fly the long way around the world via North America, I decided to use the intervening two months to see as much of the United States as I could. My budget was limited so I bought in the UK a special holiday offer, a $99 air ticket that allowed me to travel all over the USA on feeder airlines, on as many flights as I wanted within two weeks. I flew to New York, spent a couple of days there and then took a train to Boston.

I stayed for three days in Boston with a friend of a friend in his flat; I explored the city and found the Harvard area very attractive. One afternoon my friend took me for a drive through the New England countryside, the trees were brilliant with autumn colour and pumpkins for sale lay in huge piles by the side of the road. My last evening was a disaster. Instead of going out for dinner, I spent it in bed violently ill with food poisoning – I believe from a clam I had eaten at lunch.

In Boston, I activated my air ticket. I flew to Atlanta, Georgia, changed planes and on to New Orleans, Louisiana, for two days. The French Quarter — what a wonderful place that was! I wandered round the old streets soaking up the music and atmosphere of warm southern casual living. The best place was an open bar where four old African American men were playing wonderful Dixieland Jazz. Down the street was another typical establishment, a piano bar, whose pianist specialised in playing the college songs of all the customers. They only had to shout out where they were from and he was off with some thumping tune. The place was, naturally, packed with college students.

By way of contrast, I went on a conducted tour of an original New Orleans home of a hundred years ago. Our guide was an elderly lady elegantly dressed in a long black dress with white lace ruffles on her neck and wrists; she gave a polished discourse on the furniture and the way the white gentry lived in those days. At the end of the tour, in the front parlour, one of the other visitors offered her some money. With the most delicate of gestures, she indicated that the money was of no interest to her but could be left on a tray resting on the table by the door.

From New Orleans, I flew to Oklahoma City for a change of planes. I was reminded of the signature tune of the stage musical *Oklahoma*, about the wind sweeping across the plains. This really was prairie country, with wide horizons and wheat fields. Next stop was Denver, Colorado, where I changed to an even smaller plane for a spectacular ride, between rather than over, the Rocky Mountains, stopping once at Bluff before reaching Grand Canyon, Arizona. It was after dark when the taxi driver left me at a motel, with an instruction to enjoy the view in the morning. How right he was. At daylight, I found myself perched on the western edge of the canyon, 3,000 feet above the valley floor.

After breakfast, I walked down from the cool heights covered with fir trees at the rim, on a dusty trail winding down the precipice to the valley floor at around 2,000-feet altitude; it was a hot desert environment with cacti and thorn bushes lining the Colorado River. The climb up to the rim of the canyon at 5,000 feet took a deal longer: nearing midday, the sun was hot, and the altitude made a difference. Most people were riding on mules.

That afternoon I flew on to Phoenix, Arizona, a small town of wooden-board-fronted houses lining wide, empty streets, like something out of a Western cowboy movie. Next morning, I took a plane to Los Angeles. On the flight, I discovered I had left my passport at the hotel in Phoenix. The elderly lady sitting next to me on the flight was very sympathetic; she invited me to stay with her in Los Angeles while the passport was couriered to her home. I accepted gladly, and everything turned out well because of her generosity. I spent one day sightseeing with her, going to the magnificent Marine World, and took delivery of the passport the next day.

I was keen to go into Mexico, if only to say that I had done so. I took a bus down the coast to San Diego and across the border to Tijuana. I quickly realised that this was not really Mexico, more a recreation area for sailors from San Diego. I went into a seedy-looking cinema and found it showed blue movies; I resisted the advances of a hooker, and swiftly returned across the border. Next stop was San Francisco. I spent several days there enjoying its unique character, relaxed, and friendly—the first city since New Orleans to appeal to me.

Alaskan Airways was a designated domestic, feeder airline because it had no international routes—hence the incongruous opportunity to fly 1,500 miles to Alaska and back again at no extra charge. We landed at Anchorage, a real frontier town with only two kinds of shops—fur and liquor. The next morning I flew on a tiny plane to Nome and Kotzebue above the Arctic Circle. Nome was an Eskimo fur-trading station on the western seaboard; it consisted of a few wooden huts raised above the ice on piles. Caribou furs hung up on lines, above the reach of the dogs. Fortunately for me, it was sunny, without a breath of wind, because I was wearing the same clothes I had on a few days earlier in the heat of New Orleans. Even so I felt the skin of my face tighten in a most extraordinary way when I stepped out into the cold, dry air. On the plane, I had been talking with a young dentist returning to the base hospital. He invited me to look around the hospital, and keep warm in the hour we had on the ground before the plane took off back to Anchorage.

That same day I flew back to Seattle, arriving in the evening and checking in to a motel for one night before a flight the next day to Hawaii. That afternoon, November 22, 1963, President John Kennedy was assassinated in Dallas, Texas. On television, I watched a shocked newsreader make the announcement. The next morning everyone I met was in mourning. What a tragic end to the dream of Camelot. In Seattle, even the skies were grey, with a persistent rain. I was glad to move on. Such assassinations became part of US political life during the 1960s — Black Muslim activist Malcolm X in February 1965, civil rights campaigner Martin Luther King Jnr in April 1968 and, two months later, John's younger brother Robert Kennedy, a US Senator and Presidential hopeful.

Hawaii & Japan: Waikiki Beach and Skillful Drivers
The next stop was Hawaii, to stay with my second cousin Alistair Philip, his wife Elin and their two small daughters. He was working as a neonatologist at the Straub clinic, the most prestigious medical group in town, which had its own hospital. I greatly enjoyed magnificent Waikiki Beach, where I swam

and attempted to surf. I also explored the rest of the island. It was a paradise of warm winds, sunshine, beaches, palm trees, brightly coloured shirts, and South Seas music. The final stop on my journey was Japan. In Tokyo, I stayed at the YMCA for three days. I took one tour to a famous shrine on top of a hill north of the city. The road up was narrow and had a succession of hairpin turns. I marvelled at how the drivers of the large tour buses managed to negotiate the corners; it was, I decided, by virtue of very short wheel bases of the buses relative to their length.

My second tour was to the south, to Kamakura, and the Great Buddha at the Kotoku Temple. When we returned to Tokyo, the guide, a young university student, insisted on taking three of us tourists to a coffee house; he wanted more conversation so that he could improve his English. Certainly, very few of his countrymen could speak it.

Before reaching Hong Kong, I needed an inoculation. I called the British Embassy and was directed to the Tower Practice, so named because it was situated near the main radio transmission tower. Interestingly, it had been the place where Gren Wedderburn, a Partner and my future colleague in Drs Anderson & Partners in Hong Kong, had worked before moving to the colony.

I almost missed my plane to Hong Kong. The airport bus that I had arranged to pick me up at the hotel did not appear, so I took a taxi. What the head doorman said to the driver I can only guess, but the effect was dramatic. He drove like a man possessed through heavy traffic on wet roads, swerving from lane to lane, and got me to the airport in time. I was happy to give him a large tip. In the last six weeks I had caught fifteen flights on time so I was determined to make this last one successfully.

On December 3, 1963, I landed in Hong Kong.

CHAPTER SEVEN
A New Life in Hong Kong

Like many people who came to work in Hong Kong, I had a short-term contract of three years, and knew that after three years, if I did not like it I could move elsewhere. I did not imagine that, six decades later, I would still be living here. Apart from

1964, Kowloon neon lights

summer visits to my family in Britain and holiday travel around the world, I have lived much of my life here. So it is for many expatriates in Hong Kong: they come for three years — and stay for a lifetime. The next three chapters will explain how this came about.

It was on December 3, 1963, that I flew into Hong Kong. I was met in Hong Kong at Kai Tak Airport by George Watson, Senior Partner of Drs Anderson & Partners, and his wife Elizabeth. I had met both at my interview in Edinburgh six months before. He drove to West Kowloon where we boarded the vehicular ferry to cross the harbour; there was no cross-harbour tunnel in those days. Then he drove up the winding Peak Road to Mount Kellett, and the Matilda and War Memorial Hospital; it was an exciting introduction to the dramatic scenery of Hong Kong.

The hospital was named after Matilda, wife of Granville Sharp. After marriage in India, the couple arrived in Hong Kong on Christmas Day 1858, just 17 years after the colony had been established. Granville set up a successful company in business, commerce and property; he became a wealthy man. His wife devoted herself to charity work; she died of pneumonia on August 22, 1893, aged sixty-four. Six years later, Granville died during a visit to England. In his will, he left money among his relatives and a portion to be used to build a hospital, named after his wife, that would provide free treatment and accommodation to poor and destitute Europeans — but not Chinese, such was the culture of the time. The 24-bed hospital opened on January 27, 1907, and treated 84 patients in its first year. All the staff were British. The site was at the top of Mount Kellett on Victoria Peak, the highest point on Hong Kong Island. Before World War II, only Europeans could live in the Peak area. After 1945, the facility was renamed the Matilda and War Memorial Hospital; in 1951, it reopened with a new wing and new equipment and began to accept paying patients. By the time of my arrival, it had become one of Hong Kong's leading private hospitals, serving both Chinese and non-Chinese, with the name Matilda International Hospital.

At the hospital, I shared a flat with two other young doctors working for the same practice. Stewart Rance was a gregarious, lively Englishman who worked as a GP with an interest in Obstetrics and Gynaecology. Niall Cullen was Irish, a specialist Obstetrician and Gynaecologist who had qualified in Ireland and done his specialist training in the US. He was serious about his job but enjoyed the good life when not working. The three of us shared a spacious penthouse flat above the new Grayburn wing of the hospital. Two well-trained Chinese domestic helpers, a Shanghai couple Sun and Ah Wong, looked after us; he did the cooking and served at table, while she cleaned the flat.

1964 Matilda Hospital, Sun and Ah Wong

The view from the flat was magnificent. To the east, we looked over the wooded hills of Hong Kong Island running down to the southern coast, Repulse Bay, Deep Water Bay and Aberdeen Harbour with its immense fishing fleet. To the south was Lamma Island sitting like a large amoeba, the coastline very irregular and bays and headlands with a high hill at the centre. To the west, clothing the hillside below the hospital were the fields of

1963 Grand Canyon, USA

grass for the cows of The Dairy Farm at Pok Fu Lam. The cows themselves were mostly in byres; they were let out for meagre exercise in the adjoining paddocks. Out to sea was the dumbbell-shaped island of Cheung Chau and behind that the bulk of Lantau, the biggest island in the colony.

A serious drought since November 1962 had left Hong Kong with virtually no water. Reservoirs in Hong Kong and Shenzhen were depleted. Water was rationed to four hours every fourth day for households. People made use of standpipes at the road side. Rice paddy fields were abandoned. Hospitals were exempt from water rationing. Our flat at the Matilda Hospital became a popular venue for our friends to come in for a shower. Shipping tankers brought in water from up the Pearl River. The emergency ended in the summer when a typhoon filled the depleted reservoirs. Spurred by this drought and conscious of the ever-increasing population, the government constructed off-shore reservoirs, Plover Cover and High Island. They were created by joining together islands to enclose an area of salt water which was then pumped out and replaced by fresh water, a unique engineering concept at the time. A treaty was signed with China to supply water by pipeline from the East River, now Dongjiang River, in Guangdong.

Over the next days, I met the other doctors. Three worked

in Edinburgh House in Central Hong Kong—George Watson, a surgeon and the Senior Partner; Freddy Watson, an Obstetrician and Gynaecologist, and Tony Dawson Grove, a general practitioner who had been Senior Partner. He had worked in the Practice before the Japanese Occupation of 1941-44 and helped to restart it after the war; he was the only one of us who could speak good Cantonese.

I also met the three who worked in the Kowloon office in the Peninsula Hotel. One was Gren Wedderburn, a surgeon who had trained in Edinburgh and came from a missionary family. During the war, he had been in the RAF as a doctor in India and Burma. After the war, he joined a practice in Shanghai until it was forced to close by the communists. He moved to The Tower practice in Tokyo. He was recruited with Drs Anderson & Partners in unusual circumstances. At a rugby match in Hong Kong, he was captaining a team from Shanghai playing a local team. Allan Eberle, a member of the Practice, refereed the game. After the match, he approached Wedderburn and invited him to join; he accepted. The other two were Peter Drummond Smith, a GP Paediatrician, and Ron Wylie a skilled do-anything GP, including anaesthetics, Obstetrics and Gynaecology. Later, when he returned from home leave, I met Dr Eberle, a large and very English gentleman and a physician. All the doctors had qualified in the UK.

The partners who lived on the Island owned beautifully situated houses, high up on The Peak, looking north over the harbour, except Tony Dawson Grove who had a beautiful house on Headland Road overlooking Repulse Bay. Those partners resident in Kowloon lived in smart rented apartments on Kadoorie Avenue, except Ron Wylie who lived in Havelock—also known as 'Hard Luck'—Terrace, in a small flat that had been built for workers of the Whampoa Dockyard at Hung Hom.

Later he rented an upmarket house on Kadoorie Avenue.

I had a busy schedule. I visited my patients in the Matilda Hospital before driving down the Peak to visit others at the Canossa hospital on Old Peak Road. From there, I drove to Causeway Bay where I held a clinic for the workers at the nearby British American Tobacco factory. I once had a fascinating tour of the factory, with its modern automatic machinery and rich aroma of tobacco; every month the staff presented me with a carton of 200 cigarettes. I did not smoke, so I passed the carton to my colleagues. It is inconceivable today that I or any other doctor would accept such a gift.

From 10 a.m. to 1 p.m. and 3 p.m. to 5 p.m., I saw patients at the Anderson & Partners consulting rooms in Edinburgh House. Lunch was usually a sandwich in the men's reading room of the Hong Kong Club, which I had joined. On the way back to the Matilda Hospital, I might have home visits and look in on my patients at the hospitals. I had a half day on Friday. On Saturdays, the office closed at 1 p.m. On the weekends, we took turns to be on call. During the week, all the doctors were expected to be on call for all their personal patients.

My patients came from all parts of society, from Taipans and their families to lowly employees of their companies with whom the Practice had contracts. For example, I treated everyone at the Peninsula Hotel, from the manager down to the housemaid. Even more interesting were the hotel guests coming from all parts of the world.

The Hong Kong population when I arrived was three million, it had increased by one million over ten years, and was to double in the next sixty. Life was more leisurely, quieter and less crowded than it is now. What has not changed is the ability to enjoy the country parks that cover 40 per cent of the area of Hong Kong.

To get around the island in a hurry, I bought a second-hand

sports car, an Austin-Healey Sprite. It was a nippy little car and fun to drive, especially in fine weather with the hood down. On cold days, I wore a duffle coat and a deer-stalker hat.

Sailing to Manila

For leisure activity on my own, I delighted in exploring Hong Kong Island, the New Territories and the Outer Islands. When my colleague Stewart Rance went on leave, I took his boxer dog with me on these expeditions. With Rance, Wylie and Cullen, I went sailing in their Flying Dutchman from a mooring at the Hong Kong Marina at Hebe Haven in Sai Kung. At that time, there were no other Marinas in Hebe Haven; the bay was clear of boats, great for water skiing. Their boat was a very sporting, plywood-hulled dinghy, with ballast provided by a crate of beer. Inevitably, we did not think of returning to the marina until dusk; by then, the wind had failed, and we had to paddle back. Then we raced back in our sports cars to Tsim Sha Tsui — there were no speed limits outside city boundaries — and had a Chinese meal at a favourite restaurant on Kimberley Road. Then we returned to Hong Kong Island before the last car ferry left at midnight.

Often, we were invited out on the yacht belonging to Alec Pearce, a well-known stockbroker. It was a wooden sloop-rigged cruising boat about 35 feet long. His boat man Ah Mok had been with the vessel for years and kept it in immaculate condition; when we were allowed to take the boat out without Alec, he made sure we did not do anything foolish. Two episodes on that yacht remain in my mind. The first was when I out-tacked *Reverie*, Chris Von Sydow's yacht, while beating into Rocky Harbour through the narrows between High Island and Fu Tau Pun Chow. At that time, *Reverie* and Chris were the fastest racers in the yacht club. The second was when we were out in Mirs Bay and the weather had turned bad with rain, strong winds and a heavy swell. I took

1964 China Sea Race Griffin

over the tiller while everyone else disappeared below deck, apart from Ah Mok and me; I steered it round to a sheltered anchorage at Junk Bay to await the passing of the storm, finally sailing into the harbour to its mooring at the Royal Hong Kong Yacht Club at Kellett Island.

Between these two boats, I learned the rudiments of coarse sailing. It was not until I joined the Royal Hong Kong Yacht Club that I learned the finer points of yacht racing. I was proposed for the Yacht Club by Dr John Park who worked with a rival medical partnership, Drs Vio and Partners. As luck would have it, he was also a Merchistonian. He was one of the club's leading sailors, having represented it in Dragons at international regattas. He took me out twice in his boat. He had his own regular racing crew, so introduced me to a happy bunch of more casual racers who had an L Class yacht, a heavy wooden boat and not as exciting as the newer classes; so, after a number of races, I changed over to crew in the Flying 15s and cruisers.

The culmination of my sailing career came in 1966. I competed in The South China Sea Race from Hong Kong to Manila. This 600-mile race was started in 1962 and had been won then and in 1964 by von Sydow's *Reverie*. So I fancied our chances in *Griffin*, which was a sister ship, a wooden-hulled, 40-foot yawl designed by Sparkman and Stevens. Our boat was skippered and owned by an American from Manila. The second watch was led by a similarly mature American friend of his. The rest of the crew from Manila were Jess Villiereal, a businessman, a former US Air Force pilot, and a Filipino boatman, who did most of the hard work.

The race began off the Royal HK Yacht Club at Kellett Island on a grey windy day. Our skipper judged it perfectly and we were the first boat to sail out of the harbour. That first night was rough. I was sick as a dog once it was too dark to fix on the horizon. Thereafter, we had light winds for two days, and one day of almost complete calm. On the afternoon of the third day while we were sitting sweltering in the sun, we were surprised to see another yacht ahead of us near the horizon, move off at good speed. Later we learned that it was a Japanese boat that had sailed down to Hong Kong, arriving the day before the race. They had forgotten to take on board any water, and the crewmen were dying of thirst. They had to abandon the race and turn on their engines.

The last day at sea was a race in strong winds down the Luzon coast. Further out to sea, our skipper had shortened sail in even a moderate breeze. But now, in home territory, he kept up his huge main Genoa, even though we were carrying too much canvas and the lee rail was permanently under water. We were in sight of *Reverie* for the first two days. When I was at the helm, we overtook her on the morning of the third day. At that point I went off watch. By the time I came on deck again, she was out of sight and we never caught her again. The second watch leader pleased me by saying that I was the best helmsman on board.

The first across the line was *Stormvogel*, a famous plywood maxi-yacht owned by a South African timber merchant, Cornelis Bruynzeel. The winner on Handicap was *West Wind II* owned by David Westerhout. We on *Griffin* were the second of the Manila yachts to finish.

Hong Kong Squash Champion
My other main sport was squash. I played at the Hong Kong Squash Club on Garden Road, only walking distance from the Drs Anderson & Partners office in Edinburgh House. I played about five times a week, at lunchtime or after work. A group of us used to meet regularly to play — an army man, two business executives, a Thai rice trader and me. Finally, we formed a team

called Fiddlesticks, which in 1962 won the Hong Kong league title. Our team broke up because some of the members had been posted overseas. So the next season I played for the Royal Hong Kong Yacht club first team. One of the members of the team was Bill Lane, a friend since then for 40 years.

In the summer, I swam frequently, the only pleasant way to exercise in the heat, either off boats at weekends or at Repulse Bay after work. I remember one very still evening when I swam out to one of the rafts moored well off the beach at Repulse Bay, and went to sleep. When I awoke, it was dark and the sea was alight with fluorescence and a few sampans of Hakka fishermen, their boats islands of lights to attract fish. I lay watching as the boats glided past, before eventually swimming back to the darkened shore.

My other pastime was butterfly collecting, something I had enjoyed as a boy in the Himalayas. From a supplier in England, I bought a complete set of mounting equipment; a carpenter in Wanchai made a display cabinet and, with government permission, I acquired a bottle of cyanide to kill the butterflies. Very quickly I had an interesting collection, particularly of the colourful swallow-tails, Pappillonidae. Even more spectacular were the moths, especially the Luna and Atlas moths. On one occasion, the nurses on the floor below the doctor's residence at the Matilda Hospital rang up to report that a bird was trying to break through the window into their duty room. Going down to rescue them, I found that it was an Atlas moth — wingspan thirty centimetres — flattened against the window, attracted by the light. After we turned down the lights and with gentle encouragement, the moth flew away. Many years later my children, then at primary school, asked me why I killed butterflies. It was a good question. I pleased everyone by donating the collection to their school.

For entertainment, there were numerous cinemas, some showing English-language films, amateur dramatic groups and an amateur orchestra under its founder Dr Solomon Bard. City Hall opened in 1962, with the first modern theatre, exhibition gallery and library in the city. Occasionally, a troupe of theatrical players or a band came on tour. I remember one evening when I had just got back from work to the Matilda Hospital and heard on the radio a live broadcast from City Hall of the unmistakable and exciting sound of Chris Barber and his Dixieland Jazz Band. I waited till the interval, drove down from the Peak, parked in Statue Square and joined the audience for the second half of the show — a great way to end the day.

I had spent a lot of time exploring Hong Kong in my car and on foot. My photographs from that time show a Hong Kong vastly different from today.

On the island I had observed the streets crowded with trams, cars, and the occasional rickshaw. I was once offered a ride in a palanquin, a covered litter for one passenger, consisting of a seat carried on two horizontal poles by two liveried retainers. It was stationed on King's Road at the bottom of the hill leading up to the senior officers' quarters of the Swire's Tai Koo dockyard at Quarry Bay. Embarrassed, I chose to walk up, carrying my medical box, to see my patient.

Many of the streets were lined by shop houses, ground floor shops facing onto covered pavements, with living area in the two floors above. At night, the buildings blazed with neon signs in extravagant colours.

The hillsides were occupied by ramshackle communities of 'squatter huts', wood and corrugated iron structures packed close together. Irregular pathways leading to water stand-pipes. I had cause to dive into a labyrinth like this near Diamond Hill in Kowloon on a medical visit, guided by a young woman whose parents still lived there, having given her an education that had allowed her to emigrate to Canada.

The Kowloon Walled City was an anachronism left over from the British lease of the New Territories from the Chinese in 1898. The walls of the original Chinese city were removed by the Japanese to extend the landing strip for planes in 1942. Over the years, residents and many new immigrants from China had built another wall as high as 14 storeys, consisting of apartments packed closely together. Outside the Hong Kong or Chinese government regulations, the community prospered as a manufacturing base, and haunt for drug addicts. I went in once to see for myself the narrow passageways with open drains, tangles of power cables, shops, hairdressers, offices: a complete community. Jackie Pullinger worked in the Walled City for many years as a teacher in a Christian mission and at a drug rehabilitation centre. She wrote about it in *Chasing the Dragon*. It was demolished in 1993 to 1994 and converted into a beautifully landscaped public park that my wife Judith and I visited on one of our friend Jason Wordie's walkabout tours.

Further north, beyond the Lion Rock, there were small villages scattered among the fields, some of them still with their original walls. Water buffalo, large black beasts with wide horns, pulled the ploughs in the paddy fields. Two rice harvests were possible each year. I watched the crops being gathered and winnowed by hand. Ten years later, the rice cultivation had ceased because of diversion of streams to fill fresh water reservoirs, and because cheaper rice was being imported.

Some ancient villages have been conserved. I like to visit the Sheung Yiu Hakka village on the Pak Tam Chung Nature Trail. It is complete with living rooms, a kitchen, agricultural implements, a pig pen, a terrace for drying rice, and an adjacent lime kiln where coral was heated to create lime for building.

The northern slopes of Tai Mo Shan were still herring-boned with the former tea cultivation terraces. The Kadoorie Farm and Botanical Garden still grow some tea on the mountain.

For my first two years, I stayed at the Matilda Hospital. During that time, Niall Cullen left to return to the US, Stewart Rance left for a long home leave, so I took in a friend, Frank Knight. Frank moved out when he married one of the nurses. At the wedding reception, I presented to him the card that I had purchased at Niagara Falls with the caption, "Once a Knight Always a Knight, but Once a Night is Enough!" I thought it very apt, but the other guests were less enthusiastic. My next flatmate was a very pleasant young Englishman, who was engaged to a local girl. He was asked to leave when it was reported to the hospital authorities that the Chinese girl, his fiancée, had been visiting the apartment. His departure left me living in splendid isolation attended by the two servants—the king of the castle, but not for long.

Moving to Kowloon
When Ron Wylie left for long home leave, I was transferred to the Kowloon practice to replace him; the practice was based in the Peninsula Hotel. A new doctor, Cam Gribben, from New Zealand, joined the practice. With his wife and two children, he moved into the Matilda flat. I knew no one who lived in Kowloon. I moved into Ron's small, ground floor flat in Havelock Terrace, a row of dwellings built for workers at the Hong Kong and Whampoa Dockyard in Hung Hom. The discomfort of living in these insalubrious surroundings was offset by the presence of Ron's efficient Chinese cook/housekeeper, and of Ron's pride and joy, a Mini Cooper S that he raced in the Motor Sports Club, often with aviation fuel bought from a friendly supplier. With his advice to keep it functional, I sometimes took it out for a drive.

Across the road was a resettlement estate for refugees from China—H-shaped concrete blocks six floors high. Each consisted of a row of rooms, one per family, with an open passageway at the front connecting the rooms to the communal washrooms. There were toilets and kitchens in the link between blocks. Over Chinese New Year in 1966, I was confined to the house as I was suffering from mumps. Any chance of rest was destroyed by firecrackers exploding every day from morning till 11 p.m. Long strings of firecrackers hanging from the balconies were lit at the bottom and blasted their way to the top, showering the pavement with shreds of red paper. At the other end of the road was the dockyard and, next to it, the China Light and Power coal-fired power station. From its high chimney, smoke poured out and travelled with the prevailing wind over the Kowloon Peninsula.

I found, very soon, that living in Kowloon had its good points. I was now working out of consulting rooms on the mezzanine floor of the Peninsula Hotel, the best hotel in the city and admitting patients into St Theresa's Hospital and the Baptist Hospital. The other Anderson & Partners doctors working in Kowloon were Gren Wedderburn, the surgeon, and Peter Drummond-Smith, the GP who did paediatrics and deliveries. Wedderburn was married to Jean and had three daughters of marriageable age.

Peter Drummond-Smith was born in Hong Kong; his father had been a director of Jardines, the 'Noble House' of China traders. Peter was educated in Edinburgh, and unmarried. Ron Wylie was the odd man out, having been born and educated in Glasgow, whereas Gren, Peter and I had been educated in Edinburgh. Ron had worked as the doctor for a jute factory in India for two years before coming to Hong Kong; he happily recalled that in India, he had lived alone in a company house with seven servants.

Wylie returned from his leave, liberating me from the six months living in the docks. At the same time Gren went on holiday for two months, leaving me to look after his luxurious apartment in St George's Court on Kadoorie Avenue. Kadoorie Avenue was, and still is, the prestige location to live in Kowloon. Peter Drummond-Smith was already in residence in St George's Court, also in Kadoorie Avenue. Two weeks before the end of my contract and return to Scotland, I was joined by my brother Donald and his wife, Jo. He was on holiday from work for the Colonial Office as an agricultural specialist in Northern Rhodesia. I greatly enjoyed showing them around the colony that I now knew so well.

In December 1966, I finished my three-year contract in Hong Kong and agreed to renew it for a further three years. I was very happy to do this, because I was enjoying my work, the people I was working with, and the lifestyle in Hong Kong. The Senior Partner had agreed to give me three months of paid Study Leave on top of my six months regular leave so that I could earn a postgraduate specialist degree. I could look forward to a Partnership during my next contract and an increase in earnings.

I looked forward to the next six months of leave. It would be a delight to stay with my family again. We had stayed connected with weekly airmail letters, but it would be good to be back in Lossiemouth with them. My only sadness was that I would only be with them at intervals; I had committed to study for a higher degree in medicine, which would mean living much of the time in Edinburgh. I had signed on for a course at Edinburgh University on Advances in Medicine. This involved a three-month course of lectures and clinics, followed by a clinical attachment to a specialist unit for another three months. With this in mind, I had during my three years in Hong Kong been studying regularly, keeping up to date with the latest journals and absorbing lessons from my daily practice. Passing this exam was important to me.

Twilight of an Empire

These three years for a colonial expatriate like me were a time of privilege.

Of the private clubs that I joined, The Hong Kong Club was very exclusively for leaders of business and professionals.

The first Chinese member of the Royal Hong Kong Yacht Club was appointed in 1963. A Hong Kong Yachting Association was inaugurated with European and Chinese members so that a sailing team could be sent to the 1964 Tokyo Olympics.

The Hong Kong Golf Club Captaincy was first given to a non-Caucasian, Dr G. Choa in 1972.

In the days before the Labour Legislation of 1968 brought in a six-day working week, the countryside and seas were largely empty at weekends.

The senior members of government and the Civil Service were British. Governor Sir Donald Black was followed in 1964 by Sir David Trench. British army regiments occupied a large area of land scattered between Stanley peninsula, Central Victoria, Kowloon Peninsula, Stonecutters Island Clearwater Bay Peninsula, Sek Kong, and at the border. The Royal Navy were based at Tamar, the Royal Air Force at Kai Tak.

The coming 1997 change of sovereignty would bring with it an acceleration in change to society. The wealthy elite by then would more likely be Chinese. My circle of expatriate friends shrank because of people returning to their homelands or settling in places that were more economical to live in, like Malaysia or Thailand. I have found new friends among those like us who are staying on, and friends in the local community. Colonial privilege is fading to be replaced by economic privilege.

Chapter Eight
A Partner in Practice

I begin this chapter with the six-month study break in Edinburgh from December 1966 before my return to Hong Kong.

Cupid Strikes and Lions in Africa
The first thing I had to organise before returning to Edinburgh was a place to stay. I wrote for advice to Dr John Cruikshank, a fellow graduate of the university. He put me in touch with a friend of his, David Burns, who had a top-floor flat at the Queen Street end of North Castle Street; everyone called it Haggis Heights because it was situated above McSweens, a butcher famous for its Haggis. Staying with David was the start of a long and happy friendship. I had a small bedroom with a dormer window and shared all other facilities with David. He was a small, jolly and rotund man, a lawyer trained in Edinburgh, of independent means from a rich Fife farming family. His main interests were music and art; his flat was home to a grand piano and an impressive array of modern Scottish artwork. I was quickly introduced to his wide selection of friends, lively young professionals.

The medical course was hugely interesting and rewarding in terms of knowledge. I regularly drove up to Lossiemouth to see my parents, but not often enough; it must have been hard for them to know that I was back in Scotland after being away for three years, and yet not close to them. In Edinburgh, I again met Anwar Ahktar, a fellow medical student and now a doctor at the City Hospital. He was an interesting man. He had been brought up in India, his father an Indian professor of Economics and his mother an Englishwoman who always wore a sari. During his student days, Anwar lived with his mother in a small flat in a dingy tenement in the Fountainbridge district of Edinburgh; its only claim to fame was the fact that Sean Connery, the James Bond of that time, had lived there.

The Membership Examination at Edinburgh required that a specialist subject be offered. I was thinking of making Geriatrics my specialty — but one visit to the City Hospital made me change my mind. With my postgraduate group, I was in a lecture theatre attending a clinical pathological conference on respiratory disease chaired by Professor John Crofton. A junior doctor from his ward was presenting a case. She was so attractive and made such an excellent presentation that I was determined to meet her again. It really was love at first sight. I was too shy to approach her directly and asked Anwar to introduce me. Her name was Judith Mary Longstaff. To be close to her, I chose the City Hospital, where she was working, for my Medical Attachment. We met soon after, and happily Judith liked me too.

The romance blossomed despite my dedication to completing my studies and passing the Membership examination, and her heavy duties as a Pre-Registration doctor. Immediately after passing the Membership exam, I proposed, and was delighted she accepted. There were only two weeks before I had to return to Hong Kong, so we had to rush to organise the wedding. Judith

1967 With our parents at the wedding reception

did an amazing job to arrange a Registry Office wedding, only possible because of a last-minute cancellation, and a reception at the North British, one of the most famous hotels in Edinburgh at the east end of Princes Street. For my stag night, I took David Burns, my best man, to the Victoria Grill, one of David's favourite watering holes. We held the marriage ceremony on July 8, 1967.

1967 Wedding Reception, Edinburgh

Despite the short notice, guests at the reception included both Judith's and my parents and people from around the world — my sister Eleanore who came from Canada; my Senior Partner, George Watson and his wife from Hong Kong who were on leave in Edinburgh; Judith's sister Margaret and family from California, and her cousins from London and Northumberland.

Our honeymoon was at the Trossachs Hotel on the north shore of Loch Achray in the Trossachs National Park near Stirling. It lasted only a weekend, which was much too short. On the Monday, Judith had to return to work at the City Hospital to finish her last three months before full Registration, and I had to return to Hong Kong.

I travelled as far as Gatwick Airport—only to find to my horror that my passport had expired. I had to wait in London for two days while the passport office in Petty France renewed it. I had arranged to return to Hong Kong via Northern Rhodesia where I would meet Donald, his wife Jo and newly adopted son Innes. I had to fly first to Nairobi in Kenya. In Nairobi, I took the chance of a one-day safari in an adjacent game reserve, before catching the connecting flight to Lusaka.

I had a wonderful time there, including a flying visit to the Victoria Falls on the Zambezi River, an awe-inspiring sight, a wide river suddenly disappearing into a narrow chasm, twice the height and breadth of Niagara Falls that I had seen four years before. David Livingston named it 'Victoria' to honour his Queen.

From Lusaka we drove east to spend a few days at the Luangwa Valley Game Park. On our first outing, Donald surprised me by announcing that the lion we saw was the first one he had seen in Africa despite having lived there several years. We saw herds of elephants wading across the Luangwa River, a tributary of the Zambezi River, coming from Nyasaland, which had become the independent Republic of Malawi in July 1964. The safari camp was a collection of round houses and a central area where we ate and socialised; it overlooked a pool frequented by hippos. There, we met some South African marksmen who had been brought in to cull family groups of elephants to keep the numbers down and prevent degradation of the forest. The local gamekeepers were loath to do the job themselves. I still have the impala-skin pouffe that Donald and Jo bought for me.

Hong Kong: Riots and Protests
I returned to Hong Kong in July 1967. I went back to the doctor's flat at the Matilda Hospital; in their turn, Cam Gribben and family were now on leave. Three months later, Judith joined me at the flat. When the Gribbens came back from leave, we moved over to Kowloon, to a series of 'leave flats', all in the Kadoorie Avenue area. One belonged to Peter Drummond-Smith at St George's Court; another was the house of the manager of American President Lines on Braga Circuit; a third was owned by a Cathay Pacific pilot and finally an apartment of our own in St George's Court.

In 1967, Hong Kong was being wracked by riots and demonstrations by Chinese pro-communist supporters against the colonial government. They were following the example of Red Guards in the mainland. It was the start of ten years of chaos and disruption in China during the Cultural Revolution that lasted from 1966 to 1976 and pushed the country close to bankruptcy. In Hong Kong, the protesters used roadside and petrol bombs. In 1967 alone, 51 people were killed, including police officers. Of the demonstrators, 800 were injured and more than 1,800 arrested. Nobody knew whether the protesters were acting for a particular faction in Hong Kong or Guangdong Province or on behalf of the central government. While the police could, with difficulty, contain the protests, they would not be able to resist an invasion by the Chinese army. The fear of such an invasion hung over the city, causing many people, especially the wealthy, to leave.

I admired Judith for coming to join me in Hong Kong despite this dangerous situation. The Bank of China building in Central was like a fortress; red flags hung out of the windows and patriotic Chinese songs and speeches were blasted by loudspeakers. On one occasion, we were looking at flats in the Garden Suburb of Yau Yat Chuen; on trying to leave the area, we found the only exit route had been blocked because of an unexploded bomb. We had to leave our car there, and come back later after the bomb had been defused. One of the casualties of the riots was a bomb disposal officer who lost both of his arms.

When she first arrived in Hong Kong, Judith said that all she wanted to do was lie on a beach in the sun; this was not surprising since she had just spent a gruelling year of hospital work in the cold of Edinburgh. But that sentiment did not last long, within two weeks she started going to Cantonese classes, worked in a charity medical clinic, and then as a civilian employee of the British Military garrison. Colonel Walsh, the Chief Medical Officer who employed her, was a distant cousin of mine. She was scandalised when he told her that, because she was a woman, he could only pay her 75 per cent of a man's salary. Until this changed, the British Forces and South Africa shared the dubious distinction of having their job advertisements ringed in black in the British Medical Journal.

Three honeymoons in Asia
The first honeymoon was when Judith and I made a weekend trip to Macau. It was in the midst of the Cultural Revolution in China. In Macau there were red flags flying from every building. The British consulate had closed, its walls were covered in graffiti. Loudspeakers blared 'patriotic' messages. We visited all the touristy sites, the fort, the lighthouse, the A Ma temple, the St Paul's cathedral façade, walked the Praia, went into Stanley

JOHN MACKAY

1967 View from Tai Mo Shan looking over Deep Bay, John taken by Judith

Ho's casino where we played baccarat, watched Jai Alai with an enthusiastic betting crowd. This game was played in an elongated court with the right side open, the ball being flung at the end wall at high speed using a hand-held wicker basket 'cesta'.

A Different World from Hong Kong: Pedicabs not Motor Taxis
Judith and I had our second honeymoon on an Easter long weekend in Manila, timed to coincide with the arrival of the fleet at the conclusion of the South China Sea Race from Hong Kong.

The most memorable part of that trip was an adventure with friends, the Houstouns, up the river to the Pagsanjan Falls. The water was low so in a few places our two boatmen carried Judith and me up over the boulders as we sat in the heavy wooden canoe. They were barefoot. Their strength and sure-footedness were impressive. At the falls there was a deep pool where we all swam. Getting under the fall itself was no joke; the force of the water was powerful.

The third honeymoon was in Taiwan in April 1968, We flew from Hong Kong to Taipei, and found it not to our liking. Streets were crowded and noisy, flanked by poles festooned with telephone and power lines as in America.

We quickly arranged for tours outside the city. The first one was a bus trip down the east coast highway to Hualien. It was well named a 'highway'; the road was etched into beetling, friable cliffs along the coastline. We were in the last row of seats and were bounced around unremittingly on the pot-holed roads, but took comfort that in the case of disaster we would have the best chance of survival.

The experience was not helped by the story we heard that a few years before, the Taiwanese driver of a similar bus had realised that his passengers were all mainland Chinese, so drove the bus over the cliff, killing everyone on the rocks far below.

The horrors of the journey were forgotten the next day when we travelled by bus up the Taroko Gorge. This was a spectacular drive up a single-lane road that followed a river up towards the centre of the island, through mountains seamed with marble. The narrowness of the gorge meant that much of the road had been tunnelled through the mountains. We stayed that night at a small Chinese-style inn set at the confluence of two rivers. Lawns and ornamental statues enhanced the feelings of being at a spiritual retreat, surrounded by towering cliffs and lulled by the sound of the rivers.

We flew back to Taipei from Hualien—one way by bus was enough.

Our second trip took us by train down the plains on the west side of the island to Taichung, and thence by taxi up into the mountains to the resort area at Sun Moon Lake. Here we spent two days, happily rowing on the lake that was over a mile in diameter and had a heavily indented and wooded coastline. We

1968 Sun Moon Lake Taiwan, Judith

found our own secluded corners of the lake in which to moor and lie in the sun.

Back in Taipei we visited the Palace Museum, an impressive building in a valley just out of town. It was constructed on the orders of Chiang Kai-shek to house the treasures of China that the Kuomintang forces had carried with them when they had been driven out of the Mainland by the communists led by Mao Tse-tung.

The exhibits dated from the 'oracle bones', shoulder blades of animals on which were cracks that were interpreted by soothsayers thousands of years ago. There were many beautiful things to see, but to really appreciate them one would have to have a deep knowledge of Chinese culture.

Back in Hong Kong

For the next three years, we stayed at St George's Court, in Kadoorie Avenue. During this time, our two sons arrived, Andrew was born in March 1969 and Richard was born in

1970 Proud father, Andrew and Richard

July 1970. Andrew had a difficult face-to-pubis delivery at St Theresa's Hospital on Prince Edward Road. On the way home from hospital with Judith and Andrew, I said that I was not feeling well. Judith was disbelieving, expecting me to be of help after her difficult delivery, but it turned out that I had typhoid, and was off work for two days and off baby duties for longer. Richard was born at the British Military Hospital, Judith had access there because she had been working as a Civilian Medical Officer for the Army.

While our children were young, we took our home leaves in Britain. We divided the time between Saltburn and Lossiemouth, the home towns of our parents. After my parents died, the venues became Saltburn and our house in Edinburgh. One leave was during the winter months, cold and grey, so we stopped off at Hawaii on the way back to Hong Kong, to visit my second cousin

1977 In Hawaii

and former school and university classmate Alistair Philip, his wife Elin and their two girls. We stayed at a large hotel on Waikiki Beach. The warmth and sunshine greatly boosted our spirits.

When the boys were older, we took them on skiing holidays, to Thredbo in the Snowy Mountains in New South Wales in Australia, and to Kashmir. Judith injured the medial ligament of one knee in Kashmir and did not ski again on that holiday. Andrew and Richard came first and second in the Under Fifteen Indian Ski Championships.

Our last skiing holiday together was in New Zealand. We had hoped to do cross-country skiing at The Hermitage at Mt Cook National Park, but there was no snow at that level. Instead, we walked to the snout of the glacier and its lake. We flew to Queenstown and skied there. Other excitements at Queenstown were a ride in a jet boat on the river, and a dramatic flight over the mountains to see Milford Sound, a narrow strip of water

1980 Gulmarg, Kashmir

surrounded by high mountains—very dramatic. Since then, I have not skied, but the boys have remained keen on the sport.

Judith's parents came out twice to stay with us. Unfortunately, my parents never did; my mother died in 1971 and my father a year later. They did have the pleasure of seeing their grandchildren when Judith and I and the boys returned to the Britain for a holiday in 1971.

That year, we received a notice from our landlord, the Kadoorie Estate, raising the rent by HK$100 per month for the next three years, to more than HK$2,000 for the first time. Shocked by this calamitous news, we set off that very afternoon, a Friday, my half day, to look for some place to buy. That was the only way to protect ourselves from future rent increases. Judith had seen an advertisement for a house on Clearwater Bay Road. What we found was ideal—a bungalow set in a wide garden, and surrounded by the landscaped Bluet Garden. The owners were a New Zealand couple; he was a Cathay Pacific engineer, who had decided to return home for the education of his boys. They were the healthiest children I had seen in Hong Kong, running barefoot through the garden, swinging on trees –things our two could not do in the car park below our St George's Court flat. On the spot, we put in a bid at the asking price, to be told that someone else had already made another bid. Happily for us, the other bidder could not raise the finance, so the house was ours.

When we moved in, we brought with us the Chinese helper who had looked after us in Kowloon, but she did not like living in the countryside. So Judith went to Manila to interview Filipina maids and hire one, Flor Abenoja. Ever since, we have had Filipino helpers, all Flor's relatives. We have lived in the same house for the last 50 years. It is the family home for Andrew and Richard. Happily for Judith and me, they are always pleased to come out from the UK to visit us, in turns, every second year.

In 1973, we returned to Edinburgh for a four-month leave, renting a house in Coltbridge Terrace in the Murrayfield district, close to the national rugby stadium. It suited us perfectly, so we put in a bid for it but were told it was not for sale. We spent the next three months looking around Edinburgh for a house. We came to know the city better than we had ever done before. Eventually we bought a house just up the road, 10 Garscube Terrace, also in the Murrayfield district. It was a handsome Victorian three-storey building, owned by Professor Tamas Wilson who had been Professor of Surgery at Edinburgh University. His wife had just died and he wanted to retire to the country. We spent the next weeks going to the sales and buying furniture, which we stored in our rented house until Professor Wilson vacated his home. We rented the house out and did not start living in it, for two to three months each summer, until after I retired. We sold it in 2019, reluctantly. We loved the space and elegance of the house, and the beautiful garden into which I had put so much thought and happy hours of nurturing. We sold it because it was too big for just two of us.

In 1988, we seriously considered the purchase of one other place, Old Mills House, in Elgin. This was a large mansion with acres of garden bought by my great-great grandfather, William Culbard, in 1889. His descendent, my uncle Rowand Mackay, bought it. After he died, his wife Gwen lived in it until she was no longer able to manage. She went to stay near her son Alastair in the south of England, at Buckfast in Devon. One idea was for us to buy the place and my brother Donald and his wife Jo would move up from their home in Cornwall to manage it and run a cattery or kennel, and we would holiday there together. We had all loved staying there, a place that had been in the family for a hundred years.

It was very unfortunate that we only found the notice of sale

1973 10 Garscube Terrace, Edinburgh

after our return to Hong Kong at the end of a long leave. It was a month after the Sale Notice had been sent, and two days before the sale offer expired. We had to decide very quickly. In the end we decided NO. Alastair was asking a much higher price than we had expected. He said that there was room to build three more houses on the estate. Second, the stock market had plummeted, so we had less capital to throw around. Third, we would need to spend a huge amount to bring the house into a livable state. And, fourth and most importantly, as Judith pointed out, it would be a constant drain on our capital and was nowhere near where most of our friends lived, around Edinburgh. At the time, Donald was disappointed. But, finally, he realised that he and Jo were much better off staying in Cornwall. We were very happy with our second home in Edinburgh.

Schooling in Hong Kong and Britain
Andrew and Richard were educated in both Hong Kong and Britain. They began at the YMCA playgroup next to the Queen Elizabeth Hospital, with the United Services Recreation Club to which we belonged just on the other side of Gascoyne Road in Kowloon. The playgroup had the use of a full-size grassy field and a clubhouse, which made it unusually well equipped. Transporting them there and back from Clearwater Bay Road was a challenge. We solved this by employing a series of nannies who could drive the Volkswagen we bought specifically for the purpose. Sometimes I drove them in, with two children from the Pearce family, our nearest neighbour, in my Triumph Spitfire; it was a real squash. The best of the nannies was Kiki Rasmussen Fleming, an exuberant Danish woman who had been a fashion model, and who is a friend to this day.

We liked the quality of schooling in Hong Kong in the English Schools Foundation system. So we had no qualms about sending the boys to Beacon Hill School for their primary education and to King George V for their secondary education. A bus picked them up and brought them back, each bus being required by regulation to have an adult to keep the children under control while the driver drove, and to take charge in the event of an accident. I was regularly a 'bus mother' going in to school. This was a tougher job than the end of school-day run when the children were tired and less likely to hurt each other and damage the bus. At primary school, they did well socially and academically. Andrew played the lead role of Jesus in the Christmas nativity play — always a sign of future success and Richard surprised us all by being an accomplished Master of Ceremonies at a school 'Music Hall'.

The most difficult decision came when they were 13 and 12. Should we send them to a boarding school in Britain? This was the choice of many British parents in Hong Kong and foreign countries around the world. Some even sent their children to preparatory schools in Britain at the age of eight, so parents and children spent at least eight months of the year thousands of miles apart from each other. Telecommunications then were far less advanced than today. Regularly, headmasters of these prep schools came to Hong Kong to encourage parents to send children to their establishments. They argued their schools could more easily manage and institutionalise them to prepare them for the rigors of Public School. But what was the emotional cost of this separation to both children and parents? We constantly debated this question. Kia Bell, a child psychologist and friend, advised us wisely that we should keep the boys at home until they were at least twelve. By then, they would be imprinted with our values, and emotionally mature enough to cope with being away from us during term times.

So what finally made us decide to send them to the Britain? We had a strong wish that they should grow up regarding Britain, rather than Hong Kong, as their home. We also believed that, for their future professional careers, Britain would offer more opportunities than Hong Kong; sports facilities here were limited because of the lack of space. What made the decision difficult was that both boys were doing well academically and had many friends at King George V, however the number of these friends was dwindling as they were sent back to Britain for schooling, or their parents were posted out of Hong Kong.

We chose for them Trinity College, Glenalmond, an all-male boarding school eight miles west of Perth, in the centre of Scotland. It was founded in 1847 and is affiliated to the Scottish Episcopalian Church (Anglican). On 300 acres, it had space unimaginable for a school in Hong Kong. My old school, Merchiston, had just changed headmasters and was performing badly academically, whereas Glenalmond was regularly getting boys into Oxbridge. A teacher friend of ours in Edinburgh recommended Glenalmond, and when we met headmaster Dr Musson, we were impressed.

In September 1982, we left the two boys at the school, for the start of the autumn term. It was heart-breaking for us. We had not been apart from them for any time since their birth. We wrote a letter every week—there was no internet for instant communication.

Andrew settled in well, being the more gregarious and sportier, but it was more difficult for Richard, who was 18 months younger. Richard took up the bagpipes and still plays them. They both played in the school orchestra, Andrew on classical guitar and Richard on trumpet, then trombone. They were both in Skrines House under Housemaster Bill Crowe; he had been at Merchiston, junior to me. In his final year, Andrew was Head of House and nearly Head of School, a natural leader. Richard was more individualistic and less competitive. He developed good friendships with like-minded pupils.

Judith and I missed having them around and looked forward to the school holidays which we spent with them either in Hong Kong or in Britain, or on ski-trips. Judith travelled back often to join them for half term breaks and took them to Saltburn. Sometimes our good friend David Burns hosted them. Happily, we all kept very close as a family. We were also able to spend more time on our own interests. We took up golf again and Judith began to travel extensively as her career took off as an international anti-tobacco activist.

Both boys were academically successful and went on to Cambridge University. Andrew had wanted to go to Edinburgh University to read medicine but there were no vacancies that year for overseas students. He went to Pembroke College in Cambridge and enjoyed a wonderful time there, being cox of the Pembroke College rowing eight, and playing badminton for the College. His clinical years he spent at Glasgow University; his first choice, Edinburgh was not available. Richard attended Fitzwilliam College and read Natural Sciences; he specialised in Environmental Science. Showing commendable enterprise, he persuaded his parents to finance his purchase of a small house. He earned a second degree at Brunel University on Environmental Law and Management.

Judith's Career Advances
Since Judith's arrival in Hong Kong in 1972, her career had advanced rapidly. After her work with the British Forces, she became a part-time researcher in the Paediatric Department of Hong Kong University under Professor Eileen Field and Dr Flora Baber; they did the first longitudinal survey of the growth of infants in Hong Kong. They discovered that Chinese infants grew as fast as European ones until they were weaned off milk.

Then their parents gave them a rice-based diet which lacked sufficient protein, so they fell behind the European children in terms of growth and milestone development. The government immediately set up a campaign to introduce an alternative source of protein at weaning: today's youth tower over us now.

Judith was keen to earn a postgraduate degree in Medicine. She persuaded Professor Alec McFadzean, head of the Medical Department at Hong Kong University, to let her become an unpaid medical officer with responsibility for some patients in his wards; but she was excused from night duty. The professor was an autocratic man who had rebuilt the university medical school after the Japanese occupation. He had turned it into a world-recognised institution. His juniors were in awe of him and saw him as an exceptional teacher and researcher. Each day Judith had to travel from home to the Queen Mary Hospital at Pokfulam; it was a long journey by Hong Kong standards, at least an hour. It was made easier for her by the opening of the first road tunnel under the harbour. Professor David Todd succeeded Professor McFadzean, and allowed her to continue. Her hard work paid off; in Hong Kong she passed her first, written part, of the Membership examination for the Royal College of Physicians in Edinburgh; after three months of further study in the UK, she passed the second written and clinical parts, first time. She spent the next seven years as head of a medical ward, and Deputy Head of the Medical Department at the United Christian Hospital in Kwun Tong. From there, she developed an interest in Public Health and a commitment to combat the tobacco industry — a most successful career, which is best described by herself in her own books...

Treating Rich and Poor
During my thirty years with Drs Anderson & Partners, the medical scene in Hong Kong developed rapidly. When I arrived,

the nine doctors in the Practice were all expected to do primary care in addition to their own specialty. We had our own X-ray equipment, laboratory and dispensary. Gradually this changed. When I left the partnership in 1993, it had developed referral centres in Central District in Hong Kong and in Tsim Sha Tsui in Kowloon, staffed largely by specialists who saw referrals from a dozen Primary Care clinics scattered round the territory. We had a sophisticated examination centre with X-ray and ultrasound, a laboratory with automatic analysis that could cover most tests and an extensive pharmacy. By the 1990s, specialists in private practice could cover all eventualities. Previously, for tertiary care, we had to send patients to the Queen Mary University Hospital.

The administration in the Partnership changed as the practice grew. In my early days the senior partner took home at the end of each month a significantly larger share of the profits than the other partners, their proportions grew as they became more senior. Assistants were on a fixed salary. There was an office manager who helped the senior partner regarding business decisions. Monthly Partners Meetings were held where major decisions were made, assisted by a bottle of Black Label Johnny Walker, and numerous cigarettes.

By the time I left the Practice, the meetings were held in a smoke-free room and the Johnny Walker was a distant memory. The administrative staff had grown. All the partners had an equal share of profits, apart from the senior partner whose share was only marginally greater.

Hong Kong Practice. Drs Anderson & Partners – the first hundred years, by Katherine Mattock, tells the story of the Practice until 1978.

My own academic career advanced steadily. I became the first doctor in the Practice to have a postgraduate degree in Medicine. Seven years later in 1971, I was one of the first three doctors in

Hong Kong to have the degree from the Royal College of General Practitioners in the UK. My last visiting card read: MB ChB (ED), FRCP(G), FRCGP(UK), FHKCGP, FHKAM (Fellow of the Hong Kong Academy of Medicine). I also had a Fellowship of the American College of Chest Physicians FACCP and a Diploma in Aviation Medicine.

I was a clinical tutor for students from Hong Kong University Medical School and an editor of the Journal of the Hong Kong College of General Practitioners, in which I published a number of research articles. I joined the Hong Kong College of Physicians when it was founded in 1985 and continued to publish articles on the history of medicine in Hong Kong in 'Synapse', the journal of the College of Physicians (HKCP). In 2001, I was Assistant Editor of 'Synapse' when Professor Philip Li, a world famous nephrologist, later the President of the College, became Editor. Philip Li was succeeded by Dr Carolyn Kng, a Singaporean educated in Britain and Australia, a geriatrician, a marathon runner and mountain trekker. My main role was to interview and write profiles of distinguished members of the medical profession who had contributed to Hong Kong.

One of my first articles was on Dr Sun Yat-sen who had qualified from the Hong Kong College of Medicine for Chinese in 1892. He became the first President of the Republic of China in 1911.

I had a patient list that covered all strata of Hong Kong society. At one end were the workers employed by large companies like China Light & Power; hotels, including the Peninsula, Repulse Bay, Shangri La and Hyatt; seamen from shipping lines like American President Lines and Ben Line. I visited the ships to attend sick people, to check medical supplies and administer inoculations for typhoid and smallpox. This was the work carried out by Dr William Adams, appointed in 1868 as the first

Port Health Officer, to whom Drs Andersons & Partners traces its origins.

In May 1975 a ship, the *Clara Maersk*, arrived in Hong Kong with 3,745 refugees from South Vietnam who had escaped from the communist Viet Cong. The merchant ship had rescued them from overloaded, sinking boats. The government called on Drs Anderson & Partners to examine and X-ray all of them, before they were placed in refugee camps to await repatriation or ongoing emigration elsewhere. I was the one who had to deal with this mass of sad, undernourished and desperate families. At the peak, there were more than 80,000 refugees in the Hong Kong camps. As the 1997 change of sovereignty approached, the Chinese Government made it clear it wanted the camps emptied before the change of sovereignty. By that time, most of the Vietnamese remaining were classed as economic migrants and not eligible for political refugee status. There were heart-rending scenes as reluctant Vietnamese were bundled onto planes to be flown back to Hanoi. John Murphy, a fellow Rotarian, managed the air charter company that organised the repatriation.

At the other end of the social scale on my client list were titans of industry and commerce and the arts, expatriate and local, and clients of luxury cruise liners. Since Hong Kong was a 'World City', I treated patients of many nationalities. Most of my patients could speak English, but there was always a nurse at hand to translate Chinese

Our home, Riftswood, was on the Clearwater Bay Road, not far from the Shaw Brothers Film Studios, the largest film production company in Hong Kong; it made about 1,000 films. It had a squadron of horses that exercised over the hillside behind the house. From time to time, the cavalry charged with swords and spears at the ready and bugles sounding, at the large gate of a 'walled city'while defenders fought them off — exciting stuff.

My part in the film story came when I was called to see a gorgeous, young, tall, blonde Scandinavian actress playing the female equivalent to James Bond. The stage gun she had been firing had exploded and showered her face with wooden splinters. I had the delicate task of very carefully removing the embedded splinters. To our mutual delight, all went well and she was not left with any scars. My other brush with stardom came when Shaw Brothers called me to a pre-employment health insurance examination on the then very famous Italian actress Gina Lollobrigida. She was accompanied by a very tough-looking female escort. I had to read out the terms of the health insurance contract. On finishing, I was flattered when Miss Gina complimented me on my beautiful spoken English. She passed the examination with flying colours.

All was not work. I, Judith, Andrew and Richard had wonderful adventurous holidays as shown in the pictures below.

Working at the Jockey Club
One of the clients of our practice was the Hong Kong Jockey Club (HKJC). We had to provide a doctor at each race meeting to care for the jockeys and staff, not the spectators. When I first arrived in Hong Kong, the Jockey Club only raced at Happy Valley, the horses were smallish China ponies, the jockeys European or Chinese amateurs. The trainers were a mixed bunch — several Russians from Shanghai who had trained horses there before the communist government banned the sport. An Australian, John Moore was a very successful trainer, with his son Gary riding for him.

The administrative staff were largely ex-military. Being a member of the club, and even more being the owner of a horse, was a matter of great esteem. George Watson was both. Once a month I took my turn, sitting in the Steward's room between

1999 Juneau, Kicking Horse Rapids B.C.

1992 Rapids below Victoria Falls

1984 Ascot Races

races and in the stand opposite the winning post with the other officials during the races. They were a lively bunch. At that time, the leading jockey was Kenny Kwok. Many of the races were rigged by the jockeys, rather than by the trainers. I remember a very keen race-going doctor friend who whispered before one race, "Number 8 is really trying this time." In translation, this meant that the other horses were not.

Over time, the racing became more sophisticated, the jockeys were all professionals and the administration stricter. Race officials scrutinised television replays of the horses and penalised any jockey not riding to the best advantage of the horse. The veterinary side was headed for many years by Allan Auckney and his assistants. In later years, the veterinary hospital was a state-of-the-art establishment with full-time vets and toxicologists.

JOHN MACKAY

The General Manager or Chief Executive of the HKJC was Major General Bernard Penfold, who held the post from 1972 to 1979. In 1973, he introduced night racing at Happy Valley and, in 1974, off-course and telephone betting. In October 1978, he opened Sha Tin racecourse, with a grandstand that could accommodate 80,000 people. Built on reclaimed land, it is one of the largest racecourses in the world. Hong Kong generates the biggest horse race gambling turnover in the world. The HKJC has a monopoly on gambling in Hong Kong. In return for this exclusive right, it pays enormous sums of tax to Government and money towards sports and charitable projects, like the football stadium where the world-famous Hong Kong Seven-a-Side rugby tournament is played.

The Jockey Club financed three public golf courses on Kau Sai Chau Island, the first two designed by Gary Player. All are magnificent courses. The engineer managing these projects on behalf of the HKJC was a good friend, John Halliday. His son Cameron first worked as a navvy at the first Kau Sai Chau golf course; eventually, he rose to become manager of the whole complex, including a golf training academy for professional golfers, administrators and greenkeepers.

In addition to managing the race tracks, the Jockey Club owns Bee's River stables near Fanling in the New Territories where people ride retired racehorses at a riding school. The Bee's River stables were first used as the meeting place for the Hong Kong fox-hunting fraternity. The high point of the Jockey Club's history was when it was used as the venue for equestrian events at the 2008 Beijing Olympics—China did not itself have comparable facilities. The cross-country course took in part of the Fanling golf courses of the Hong Kong Golf Club; some of the jumps still remain to decorate the courses.

A DOCTOR'S LIFE IN HONG KONG

Indians: Late but Charming

Another important group of patients were Indians. A large number of them live in Hong Kong, mostly working as traders and living in Kowloon. I built up a good following amongst them; their only weakness was often to be late for their appointments. Apart from that, they were delightful patients, appreciative and polite. Among them, I treated members of the Harilela family, famous for having started life as very poor merchants in Guangzhou and gradually building up great wealth in Hong Kong from trading, tailoring and hotels. More than 80 members of the family, from different generations, live amicably in a 'palace' on Waterloo Road in Kowloon Tong. Judith and I were invited to their weddings, golden wedding anniversaries and funerals. They held the smaller functions in their great mansion on Waterloo Road and the larger ones in their hotel, the Golden Mile Holiday Inn.

I also met many Indians in the Rotary Club of Kowloon, which I joined in March 1984. I became a member because I felt the need to meet people from different walks of life, after living in Hong Kong for 20 years. I wanted to hear about aspects of Hong Kong outside the medical and expatriate worlds. Among the members I found many wealthy, and some not so wealthy, members of this all-male club who were very generous of their time and money to help the community. The club had members from all over the world. It is the second oldest in Hong Kong, chartered in 1948. When I retired in 1993 from clinical practice, my Indian patients were particularly upset. They could not understand why I stopped work while I was still healthy.

I was also connected to the Nepali community, especially the Gurkhas. While Hong Kong was a colony, there was a Brigade of Gurkhas among the battalions of British soldiers stationed here. One close friend was Jimmy Keir, a jeweller and philanthropist.

He was born in Nepal to a Scottish engineer father and Nepali mother. He was close to the Royal Family in Nepal. Through him, I became the doctor for a princess of the household. She had been desperately ill in Kathmandu and was evacuated to Hong Kong for essential treatment. It was successful, I am happy to say.

One of my second cousins, Hugh Young, was a Major in one of the Scottish regiments stationed in Hong Kong. He invited us to attend a Highland Games at Stanley Fort—it was a thrilling day of pipe music, tossing the caber and a soccer match in which Hugh was a participant. In 1997, the British army left, but a number of retired Gurkhas remained here, working as civilians, watchmen, taxi drivers, traders and restaurant owners.

Russians: Old Believers
The Russians in Hong Kong were an interesting and varied group. Some were horse trainers, whom I already mentioned, and others were merchants. One group was known as the 'Old Believers'; they were religious dissenters who refused to accept the liturgical reforms imposed on the Russian Orthodox Church by Nikon, the Patriarch of Moscow from 1652 to 1658. In the 17th Century, they numbered millions. Some left Russia after the 17th Century and established farming communities in Inner Mongolia in the north of China. They lived a harsh and spartan life. Even in the 20th Century they had to travel for a week to get to the nearest railhead. They wore traditional garb, with many layers of clothing to protect them from the freezing winters. They seldom washed, a fact that made them unpopular with their Chinese neighbours, who were keenly sensitive to the strong smell. After the communist revolution, the United Nations refugee agency brought them to Hong Kong on transit visas, for resettlement elsewhere.

My responsibility was to care for them while they were

billeted in cheap hotels in the city and do health checks on behalf of the countries accepting them as immigrants; the majority went to the US, Canada and Australia. At one time, I was attending two dozen of them in the Canossa Hospital. Several elderly Old Believers were in a medical ward being treated for TB. In those days, in-patient treatment with daily triple therapy was the norm — injections of Streptomycin, and tablets of Isoniazid and Pyrazinamide.

At that time, Hong Kong was a global centre for TB drug treatment trials run by WHO; they were administered in a government TB hospital, the Ruttonjee, by two Irish Columban Sisters, Mary Aquinas and Mary Gabriel. They built on the research started by Professor John Crofton in Edinburgh; he was the first person in the world to claim he could cure TB. The results of his treatments in Edinburgh proved him right. Today treatments for uncomplicated cases can be given as out-patients and last only four months. In the Paediatric department, my Russian patients once occupied the whole ward when they had an outbreak of measles.

I came to know very well a Mr Valentin Sedoff, the translator working for the United Nations High Commission for Refugees (UNHCR). He was a caring man and very helpful to me; but, eventually because of his alcohol problem, he became an invalid. He was found a place in a retirement community in Australia. He had a great friend called George Kriskow, a large man with a bad temper. He became trapped in Hong Kong because, during an interview with an Australian Immigration official, he became angry and punched him. Another friend was an elderly, slight, man called Ivan. The three made a drinking trio. Ivan was quiet and well behaved; before long, he was granted a visa to go to the US. But, at the time of the plane's departure, he was nowhere to be found, and missed the flight. I was called in to make sure he made the next flight. I admitted him to St Theresa's Hospital, close to the airport on the night before the flight, with strict instructions to the nurses not to let him have any alcohol. When I checked with him in the morning, he was resigned to going and leaving his friends behind. Sedoff and Kriskow were there to keep him company, and showed me the bottles of water, all that there was to drink. Later in the day I had an urgent call. Ivan had disappeared again. The 'water' in the bottle had, in fact, been vodka. I sent out Sedoff and Kriskow to find Ivan; they eventually did—he was wandering distractedly near Kai Tak airport—and put him on the flight. Kriskow was the last 'Old Believer' to leave Hong Kong; he had spent two years working as a gardener at a religious mission in Kowloon.

The other group with whom I had much contact were the White Russians who had escaped from Russia after the Bolshevik revolution in 1917. They also moved to China; they were better educated and held jobs in the cities. In Shanghai, a large number of young female Russian 'princesses' worked in the night clubs. After the 1949 revolution, most of them left the Mainland and came to Hong Kong. One family was called Smirnoff; a member was a talented artist, he had spent the Japanese war years in Macao. His wife was the housekeeping manager of The Peninsula Hotel at the time I first started working there. Her daughter, Nina, married the then manager Felix Bieger; they have been friends of my family for many years.

Pre-1945 Shanghai was also home to a large Jewish community, about 25,000 people. Most had escaped from Nazi-occupied Europe to one of the few cities in the world that did not require an entry visa. They joined a well-established Jewish community in the city; some were very wealthy. During the Japanese occupation, life was very difficult. After World War II and the communist revolution, the vast majority chose to leave

China. The Ezra brothers, Cecil and Denzel were sons of a very successful father and had been rich in Shanghai. But they arrived in Hong Kong penniless after the 1949 revolution. They and many other Jews were housed in the Peninsula Hotel, which was owned by the Jewish Kadoorie family. The Kadoories had been wise enough to diversify their investments in both Shanghai and Hong Kong, where they had assets like the Peninsula Hotel and the China Light and Power Company.

Hong Kong: More on Health
Hong Kong is just south of the Tropic of Cancer. Before my arrival, I imagined that I would be treating all sorts of tropical disease. In fact, the climate is tropical for only the four months from June to September and temperate for the rest of the year. Very occasionally, there is frost on the grass at our house, and icicles hang on the top of Tai Mo Shan, the highest hill in Hong Kong, just short of 1,000 metres, 3,140 feet. Whenever the weather forecasters predicted freezing weather, hundreds of people went up Tai Mo Shan to photograph this phenomenon; with global warming, this has happened less often.

The timing of my arrival in Hong Kong was fortuitous. In the 18 years since Hong Kong had been liberated from the Japanese occupation, public health had dramatically improved.

In 1945 the population of about 600,000 was malnourished, and subject to many infectious diseases such as malaria, cholera, dysentery and TB. British and Allied army and civilian Prisoners of War were repatriated to recover their health in their home countries. At the same time, a flood of people returned from China where they had fled from the Japanese, carrying with them more disease.

By the time I arrived in 1963, Tuberculosis of the lungs was still a problem. Many people had TB scars on their lungs and

1987 Hatchet Lake Lodge, Saskatchewan, Canada John, Judith, Lena and George Fleming

many had active disease proven by culture of sputum samples.

Paragonamiasis caused lung lesions similar to TB. This was a disease caused by a parasite that was acquired from eating infected fresh water shrimps that had been infected by snails living in rice paddy fields.

Cholera El Tor was a milder disease than the devastating original cholera, but small episodes still occurred.

Malaria had been eradicated in Hong Kong. The cases I saw were imported. There was only one locally infected person I treated, a boy who had camped out with a school party on the island of Yung Ping Chau in Mir's Bay near the Chinese mainland.

Leprosy had been endemic in Hong Kong. The Island of Hei Ling Chau was a leprosarium created in 1950 and closed in 1975 with a maximum of more than 540 patients. I went there once and found most sufferers had burned out disease but required orthopaedic operations and physiotherapy to correct limb deformities. I saw only two people in my clinical practice, both early cases and curable.

Typhoid, bacillary dysentery and amoebic dysentery still occurred.

Hepatitis A from contaminated food and water was common. The more insidious viral B and C hepatitis passed on by body fluid contact, or at birth were persistent and could lead to liver cancer. Tests to distinguish the different viruses had just been developed and gave a useful tool for identification.

Childhood infectious diseases had come under control when efficient inoculations were restarted after the war.

The result of better feeding, housing and public health actions in Hong Kong is reflected in the fact that life expectancy rose from 64 years in males and 70 years in females in 1961, to 81 for men and 88 for women in 2021, the highest in the world.

The diseases I most commonly treated were the same minor respiratory infections and digestive upsets that occur in the UK, but not always.

I treated one of the first patients in Hong Kong to be diagnosed with AIDS. His was a tragic story. He had recently retired from his lifetime work as a postman in Sydney, Australia. Before retirement, he had undergone an operation, during which he had received a blood transfusion. When he arrived in Hong Kong with his wife on their first post-retirement holiday, he found he had a chest infection. When this did not respond to regular medication, I tested for AIDS; I knew that it was common in Sydney, but there were no cases in Hong Kong. When the test came back positive, the hospital wanted him out. He and I wanted him back in Australia, to die at home. At that time, there was no effective treatment. He had contracted the disease through infected blood during his transfusion — what a horrible misfortune.

Thunder from China
Events in China always had an impact on Hong Kong. On April 15, 1989, Hu Yaobang, a former General Secretary of the Communist Party, died in Beijing. Seeing him as a liberal reformer, students occupied Tiananmen Square in the centre of Beijing to show their admiration and demand that the party change its negative judgement of him—he had been forced to resign in January 1987. Over the next weeks, this turned into protests calling for more freedom of speech and other reforms. Over the next week, the protests escalated, sparking similar demonstrations in other cities. The students erected a 'Statue of Democracy' and built a tent city in the square. The protests became a global news story. The government was divided as to how best to deal with this embarrassing development. The embarrassment was made worse when Russian President Mikhail Gorbachev, on his first state visit to China, was obliged to enter the Great Hall of The People by a side entrance.

The student leaders became more and more overconfident and ignored the advice of many, including then Party chief Zhao Ziyang, to disband the demonstration peacefully. The government declared martial law. On the night of June 3-4, soldiers from outside Beijing were brought in and cleared the square with a tragic loss of life. Some student leaders managed to escape from China, via Hong Kong. Every year thereafter, thousands of people in Hong Kong held a candle-lit march on June 4 to commemorate the victims, until it was banned in 2021. Students in Hong Kong built their own Statue of Liberty.

Hard Decision to Retire

It was not an easy decision to retire from the Partnership in 1993, at the age of 58. I was still on top of my work, but suffering from a degree of burnout. More important was the belief that, now that our two boys had finished their education and were earning good salaries, my savings could comfortably cover my future expenses. There was also much that I wanted to do in terms of travel and sports while I was fit enough to enjoy them. Judith was, and is, deeply engaged in the tobacco control movement and was based in Hong Kong, a very convenient location for her work across Asia. So we decided to stay in the colony; in 1997, its sovereignty would revert to China and it would become a Special Administrative Region.

My departure coincided with the amalgamation of Anderson & Partners with other practices to form Quality Health Care, a health maintenance organisation. During the next two years, I stepped back in as a locum to help out as needed because of staff shortages.

2013 Firing the Noonday Gun to celebrate 50 years in Hong Kong

My last days in the Partnership were full of farewells. The Partnership paid for a superb meal at The Peninsula Hotel, and, as a golden handshake, gave me a set of glassware worth HK$20,000. In his speech, then Senior Partner Cam Gribben, was most complimentary about my contribution to the Practice, and said that I was the only partner about whom there had not ever been an official complaint from a patient.

Felix Beiger of Hong Kong and Shanghai Hotels and the manager of The Peninsula hosted a dinner in Gaddis, its French Michelin-starred restaurant; it featured a special cake depicting me as a doctor. Later at the Practice's annual Christmas party, I was presented with a gold-coloured sailing ship by the Chinese staff of the Tsim Sha Tsui office where I had worked in harmony with them for so long.

Chapter Nine
1976–2016
Exploring China

I have lived in Hong Kong since 1963 so I have had many opportunities to visit mainland China and have witnessed the country's astonishing transformation during that time. This chapter describes my major visits there, from Harbin in the far north to Urumqi in the far west and the capital Beijing to Hainan in the south — and many golf courses.

Hermit Country
When I arrived in Hong Kong in 1963, China was off limits to travellers. The country was heavily involved in supporting North Vietnam against a South Vietnam supported by the Americans and their allies. The only foreigners in China were diplomats and a handful of journalists in Beijing. The nearest I could get to China was the police look-out point at Lok Ma Chau. From the ridge there, I could look across the Sham Chun River and watch People's Liberation Army soldiers patrolling the far shore. Behind them were rice paddy fields. On the Hong Kong side of the river was a high fence to discourage illegal immigrants. By

1976, the Vietnam War was over, and the Cultural Revolution in China was coming to an end. In 1978, Deng Xiaoping encouraged the return of tourism as part of the opening-up of China. In 2020, the China border was again closed in an attempt to stop the spread of the Covid epidemic. Between these two dates, 1976 and 2020, I made many trips into the country.

The most memorable was in September 1976, the year of the Tangshan earthquake in which more than 240,000 people were alleged to have died. All foreigners had been evacuated from Beijing, which had also suffered some damage. Our friends, First Secretary Murray McLean and his wife Kate and daughter, little Kate, had been evacuated to Hong Kong along with other members of the Australian embassy. We had come to know them well when they lived in Hong Kong, where Murray learned Mandarin prior to his appointment to Beijing. At their invitation, Judith and I and our sons, Andrew aged seven and Richard aged six, accompanied the McLeans on the first return flight of foreigners. The Australian Embassy sent a car to meet us at Beijing airport. The road into the city was dimly lit by lampposts, under which students sat to study because they had no electricity at home. There were few cars, most people were on bicycles, without lights or reflectors, difficult to see in the dark.

We stayed with the McLeans in their smart apartment in the embassy area. Across the road were traditional hutongs, streets of brick buildings with clay roof tiles. Many were damaged. New bricks were piled at the roadside so that repairs could be made.

We spent the next five days visiting the Forbidden City, the Summer Palace, the Great Wall at Badaling, where we were the only visitors.

We joined a Sunday party of embassy personnel and journalists for a bucolic luncheon at one of the ancient and crumbling Ming tombs. Murray took us to the tomb of Emperor

Wan Li (1573–1620), which was open to the public. My overall impression was of spacious public places like Tiananmen Square, where crowds of Chinese tourists from the provinces gathered round to see our two little blond boys, one with freckles, possibly never having seen Caucasians before. All men were dressed in the same Mao suits; the suits of cadres were of finer material. The Zhongshan suit was designed by Sun Yat-sen and depicted virtues of the communist system. Women were dressed plainly, with no cosmetics and no high heels. There were no billboards advertising smart clothing or make-up. To me, the appearance was of a simpler, egalitarian society.

The diplomats were confined to the Beijing area. Special permits had to be obtained to visit other parts of the country. Political speculation was excited by spotting fleets of the black, curtained limousines of officials. It was claimed that the listeners in Hong Kong's Little Sai Wan and Tai Mo Shan radio listening stations could learn more than the diplomats in Beijing. Our last two days during that visit were spent in Guangzhou. We were impressed by the Sun Yat-sen Memorial building and a lavish variety show we watched inside it. Other visits took us to a collective farm, clearly a showpiece, where we were entertained by a troupe of students all wearing red scarves, and to a zoo to see a panda, the first one we had seen.

Back in Hong Kong, we heard that Mao Zedong had died while we were in Beijing. It was the end of an era.

'The Roof of the World' 1990

In 1990, we were fortunate to visit Lhasa, the capital of Tibet. Few foreigners had been able to visit the 'Roof of the World'. In October 1990, I flew to Beijing to join Judith who had just finished speaking at a conference there. That evening was memorable because we were invited to dinner at the home of Professor Chen

Junshi, a leading academic and researcher in Social Engineering (Community Health). This was the only time we have ever been invited to someone's home in China, so it was a great honour. It was a modest courtyard house in the traditional style. The living room had a number of framed sheets of calligraphy. Chen's father had been a noted scholar and exchanged poems with Chairman Mao.

The next morning, we flew from Beijing to Chengdu, capital of Sichuan province, with two other delegates who had attended the Beijing conference; we were accompanied by a Han Chinese guide. Chengdu is a large city set in the centre of a fertile basin ringed by mountains. One of two delegates, a Welsh professor, noted in amazement that he could not believe that there was a city in the world of more than 10 million people of which he had never even heard. During an afternoon in Chengdu, we were taken to see a well-known cultural centre, the thatched cottage of Du Fu. He was a famous poet and philosopher. His 'cottage' was a small bungalow set in a pleasant garden of bamboo groves. The second port of call was the grave of King Wang Jian, the ruler of the Shu kingdom, from 807–818 AD.

That evening, after dinner, our guide took us to a karaoke bar. This was the first time we ourselves had been in one; it was the latest fad to come out of Japan. The songs were all in Chinese; the guide had a good time singing while we sat and watched the loud but, as everywhere in the world, often tuneless rendering of songs. One of Judith's colleagues asked her if she could do 'the fox' — the foxtrot, which he had been practicing ahead of her visit. He was overcome with delight to swirl around the dance hall with Judith on his arm, showing off his 'fox' to all his friends.

It was uncertain, until we were at the airport on the day of departure, whether or not we would be allowed to fly to Tibet. In general, foreigners were banned, with occasional flights allowed in for reasons that were not explained. We were fortunate. Chengdu airport was a joint military-civil airport; the civil part was two grubby Nissen huts. We climbed into one of two Boeing 707s which took off to make the flight to Tibet in tandem. It was an old plane, fitted out in spartan fashion, with no in-flight entertainment. The middle-aged stewardess handed out lunchboxes with an assortment of sandwiches, Chinese-style snacks and a carton of juice.

When we had climbed out of the haze of the Sichuan basin, it became clear why we were flying in tandem. The ranges of jagged mountains, separated by deep gorges, would have made it immensely difficult to find a downed plane. We flew over this frightening country until we came to the Tibetan plateau; this was more open, dry, with wide valleys and sand dunes. There was a long drive from the airport to Lhasa city; we almost froze in the unheated mini-bus. We stopped once, to view a large Buddha image cut into the rock face. Lhasa lay on the flat plain between the Lhasa River and the mountains. The Potala Palace dominated the city from the crest of an isolated hill rearing suddenly into view from the plain. We stayed at a recently opened Holiday Inn, the first western-style hotel. The manager was from Singapore and clearly regarded it as a hardship posting. Every room was equipped with an oxygen cylinder.

The first day we took it easy; we had been warned of the ill effects of the altitude. We all had headaches and slept poorly; the guide was the worst affected and suffered from vomiting. Our first outing to the city was to the Barkhor Market, at whose centre is the Jokhang Temple. Every Tibetan wore layers of woolen clothes and thick leggings. The differences lay in the coloured headdresses and the amount of gold jewellery, indicating where the wearer came from and their wealth.

All the Tibetans asked us to give them pictures of the Dalai

Lama. These are forbidden items. Had we carried or distributed such items, Judith would never have been allowed to work in China again. Everyone went round the outside of the temple complex in an anti-clockwise direction, through narrow cobbled streets lined by old three-storey stone buildings; shops and stalls sold religious and other trinkets. In front of the temple, many pilgrims were prostrating themselves on the ground, drawing themselves forward onto their knees, and then prostrating themselves again, moving forward slowly. Inside the Jokhang, the air was heavy with the scent of lamps burning yak butter. A never-ending line of people shuffled slowly round inside, skirting the main hall; it was richly decorated with pictures on the walls, carpets for monks to sit on, and low tables covered by red and gold cloth. Lockers round the sides of the room were painted red and gold, as were the wooden pillars partially covered in colourful drapes.

To the side and behind the main Buddha statue were further alcoves with Buddha images. A door led off the main hall to a workshop where monks were hard at work preparing more little images from yak butter. Preceding us in the throng was a sight that brought home the reverence of this devout society — an old man was leading round a sheep. People explained to us that the man hoped that this action would lead to his sheep being reincarnated in human form in his next life.

Initially, our Han guide was scornful of the Tibetans. He said, "If they earn any extra money, they don't save it, or spend it on housing or education. They just give it all to the monastery or buy gold leaf to stick on the statues. They never improve themselves." The people certainly looked very poor. There was one national wash day each year in May. Girls remained uneducated.

We were reminded that Tibet was a troubled part of China by the sight of PLA soldiers with rifles patrolling the roofs of the buildings flanking Barkhor Square. Between September 1987 and March 1989, there had been demonstrations by Tibetans against Chinese rule. The most serious occurred between March 5 and 7, 1989 in Lhasa. On March 8, China declared martial law and sent in tens of thousands of troops and police. This resulted in the closure of Tibet to tourists for months. We were one of the first groups allowed back in. Even then, no individuals were allowed, only tour groups with escorts.

Our next stop was the Sera monastery on the outskirts of the city at the base of the mountains. This was a teaching centre, where we watched groups of monks debating; they were seated on the ground in circles in the shade of the trees. The senior monk posed a question and the student leapt up, giving a loud clap of his hands as he answered. The monastery itself was built of stone, with tree-trunk beams to hold up the roof. The inside was less ornate than the Jokhang Temple but still impressive with a huge hanging Mandala depicting the wheel of life, red and gold wooden pillars and Buddha images. Monks were studying mantras, surrounded by piles of others. On the porch outside, novices were studying, pausing only to hopefully enquire if we had any biros.

Next came the Norbulingka, the summer palace of the Dalai Lama. It was in one of the rare areas with trees, not far from our hotel. It was a pleasant two-storey building with comfortable rooms furnished in a Victorian style; it had items that seemed incongruous in this exotic country, such as a gramophone and a wireless. No one has lived in it since the current Dalai Lama had fled to India in March 1959, after the failure of a large-scale revolt against Chinese rule. That evening, we went into town again for a dinner and cultural show of Tibetan music and dancing.

The next morning, we were taken to the Potala Palace. We drove up a narrow road that led round to the North Gate at the back of the building. We were shown the outside of the Yellow Palace and into the White Palace dating from the 11th Century where the Dalai Lama used to live on the top floor. We were not allowed to take pictures of the interior; this was a pity, because the rooms were richly ornate, especially the room with shrines to previous Dalai Lamas.

Since we were a medical group, we were taken to the Tibetan Medical Clinic, which had an exhibition of medical writings and drawings — fascinating. There was also a gold statue in a shrine in honour of Yudo Gambo, founder of Tibetan medicine in the 7th Century. I bought a large book *Tibetan Medical Thangka of the Four Medical Tantras*. This was the English translation, published in 1984, of ancient Tibetan medical writings. In the afternoon, we were free to wander. We walked from the hotel to the river, very swiftly flowing, and glacially opaque water about 200 yards wide between high banks of stones. A cowskin boat was ferrying people across. I climbed in for a round trip, hoping it would not capsize.

Our guide from Beijing had been unwell throughout with altitude sickness and recovered fully only when we descended to a lower altitude.

Guilin, 1993

In 1993, our son Andrew and a close school friend, Hugo Allen, came to Hong Kong to stay with Judith and me. They were celebrating the ends of their successful university careers.

Together we flew from Hong Kong to Guilin, a small city in the Guangxi region set on the Li River and surrounded by spectacular limestone mountains. We stayed at a comfortable Sheraton Hotel. Our first outing was a bus ride into the hills of the Guangxi-Zhuang Autonomous Region, where we visited the villages of indigenous tribes. The Miao women wore pink headdresses, the Yao women with very long hair worn like a turban.

The next day we went on a cruise down the Li River. It was a delightful four hour trip down a gentle river surrounded by spectacular hills, each one the subject of a folk legend. The other craft were long rafts on which fishermen sat with cormorants they used to catch the fish. At Yangshuo, we came ashore and boarded a bus back to Guilin. On the way, we stopped at the Fubo Shan cave, its walls covered with ancient Chinese characters and carvings of Gods, and at the Reed Flute cave, where subtle-coloured lighting illuminated the limestone stalactites and stalagmites.

Back in Guilin, we climbed some lesser limestone hills to take in the spectacular views. At one, we were overtaken by a swarm of schoolgirls who had probably never been close to Europeans before. They were very insistent at having their pictures taken with Andrew and Hugo, both very handsome young men. Judith taught the boys how to say in Chinese, "We are not film stars." It did not make any difference.

I enjoyed this trip, unhurried, with family and friends, a new place for all of us to explore.

Three Gorges, 1996
At the annual Chinese conference on Tobacco and Health in 1995, Judith had proposed holding the next conference on a boat on the Yangtze River—and, unexpectedly, this came to pass. She invited me to join her on the boat in 1996.

The conference started in Wuhan. The boat trip of several days was up the Yangtze to Fengjie, just short of Chongqing and back again to Yichang. The Three Gorges dam project was well under way, with the main dam at Sandouping scheduled to start filling in autumn 1997, so time was running out for a chance to see the original river.

I only just made the trip. A week before, I had undergone back surgery in Hong Kong for a slipped disk and was still in pain. It was a hard decision to make; we and the surgeon had severe misgivings about my making the trip, but I knew that this was my only chance to go before the dam started filling. Judith and I flew direct from Hong Kong to Wuhan, a flight of one and a half hours, and were met at the airport by other delegates who had just arrived from Beijing.

We arrived at the Hankow Hotel in Wuhan and were greeted by the news that there was a power failure. With no lifts, I had to walk up to our room on the ninth floor, carrying our luggage, a real struggle. The room lacked heating and water. Somehow, I then managed to descend in candlelight to the second-floor restaurant for dinner, next to a wall of fish-tanks containing nothing but dead fish — victims of the power failure and consequent lack of oxygen. Rejecting what was from then on called the 'Dead Fish Restaurant', we walked down another floor, to a Chiu Chow restaurant; it was smart and clean, much more prepossessing. Professor T.H. Lam from Hong Kong, the only one of us fluent in Putonghua, ordered the dishes. His first choice, reputed to be a local delicacy, was not a popular success. Partially fermented bean curd, it smelt hideous but tasted not too bad.

The last event, or non-event, of the evening was a phone call in Putonghua to our room from a charming-sounding young lady who appeared to be offering some sort of service. She reacted with surprise that 'Dr Mackay', in whose name the room was booked, was female. This was not the only time Judith received such calls in China. A poor sleep on a hard bed (I cannot yet lie on my side), and traffic noise, resulted in a less than restful night.

7:30 a.m. 'English Breakfast' in the room was a mistake. It

consisted of a fried egg, cooling rapidly in a saucer of congealing fat, chopsticks were provided but fingers proved to be more practical. The accompanying portion of sponge cake went well with a pot of coffee sweetened with condensed milk.

Other members of the party had fared better with the dining room buffet of Chinese food.

8:00 a.m. The party gathered in the lobby to check out and proceed on a bus tour. It was heavily overcast and raining, and Wuhan had the reputation of being an industrial city avoided by all sane tourists. But the group was not returning to the hotel and it became apparent that it would be impossibly complicated for me to remain there and rest as I was inclined to do.

So off we went, myself firmly corseted and hoping for the best.

It took an hour for the bus to work its way out of the Hankou city centre to the East Lake, a wide expanse of water interlaced with causeways and offering in the summer, one could imagine pleasant vistas of tree-lined lakes and marble bridges and activities for thousands of cyclists, sailors, rowers, fishers; and there were floating restaurants sufficient to feed the multitude.

In mid-winter it presented a dully monochrome appearance, the only people to be seen were a concerned group of onlookers gazing at the roof of a car which had run off the causeway into the lake.

Our route back took us over the Yangtze River on a one year old suspension bridge, through miles of Wuchang suburbia to the city's most famous tourist landmark, the Yellow Crane Pagoda. A pagoda was first erected on this site, on a hill overlooking the river, many centuries ago. Wars and earthquakes have destroyed various structures since. The present reincarnation dates from 1958, the traditional seven-storeys high. To reach it we walked up a steep stone-paved road past huge masks depicting the classical stage masks of Chinese Opera. Wide terraces, bordered by temples and curio stalls, climbed up the crest of the ridge to the pagoda.

Exposed to the wind and rain I was chilled despite a thick suit, a 'fleecy' jacket and a Gortex waterproof jacket and hood.

It was a relief to get inside the pagoda, out of the wind, and to warm up by climbing to the top floor. The view was worth the climb. In the foreground was the Yangtze, here narrowed between two bluffs and providing a convenient location for the first bridge to be built over the river below Nanking in 1957 by the Russians with separate decks to carry road and rail traffic.

On the opposite bank was the radio and TV tower, the tallest structure in the city, that had until recently carried a large advertisement for Kent cigarettes. The current mayor had ordered it to be taken down in response to a central government directive, thereby losing thousands of dollars in annual revenue.

The cities of the west bank, Hanyang and Hankou, stretched into the mist-shrouded distance.

Returning to the bus again I lay down on the back seat to rest my aching back and to ease the numbness that had spread over the front of my left foot. We drove over the Yangtze bridge and then over a lesser bridge spanning the Han river that separates Hanyang from Hankou.

Our destination was the Hankou Medical University. Here we, the Hong Kong quartet, were ushered into a bedroom suite, unheated, where I dived under the quilt to try to get warm.

After a short rest we joined the other delegates to the conference and members of the faculty in an elaborate banquet of about 20 courses. The afternoon I spent sleeping or reading in bed while the others attended the official welcoming ceremony to the conference, several long boring speeches that I was happy to miss.

5:00 p.m. The ceremonial dinner, attended by the Mayor of Wuhan, the government Vice-Minister of Health, two Presidents of the university and selected delegates, was an extraordinary banquet.

The centre piece of each round table seating eight was a large platter with a colourful picture made out of vegetables, one depicting a trio of golden carp swimming round an island, another one, an eagle with each feather exquisitely detailed.

The toasts with Maotai came first, then half a dozen plates of different starters, then a profusion of dishes so there was not enough room on the table to set them all down.

Vegetables in quantity: snow peas, bean sprouts, cabbage, lotus root. Fish displayed like porcupines, and another fish dish presented in a boat of bamboo, rice-flour swans swimming on a pea-green lake, shredded chicken flour peacocks, soups at intervals and for desert — toffee apples.

This feast and the one at lunch were not, as I had first thought, an example of bounty from our hosts, but were taken off the funding for the conference provided by the UICC.

7:00 p.m. We boarded buses to take us to the river and our ship, a short drive through misty streets, tree-lined, lamp-lit, the old foreign concession part of the city.

At last the excitement of boarding, stepping carefully down a slippery ramp carrying hand baggage, relieved to find the ship an imposing, sleek, white, four deck craft, blissfully heated, and with all our heavy luggage already on board.

Our cabin, on the main deck was small but adequate with two beds, writing desk, en-suite bathroom, and wide picture window.

8 p.m. We set sail, up river to Yichang and the Gorges.

It had been a difficult two days, tiring, cold and sunless.

Everyone had been most solicitous, amazed that I should have attempted the trip only eight days post-operative.

So was I.

As soon as we boarded, we set sail. Our route would be up-river to Yi Chang and thence through the Three Gorges — Xi Ling, Wu (just before Wushan) then Qutang, as far up-river as Fenjie city (just before Chongqing) and then back downstream for a return view through the same Gorges to Yi Chang. There were three decks of passenger cabins, all with outside views. The interior cabin space was occupied by a hairdresser, medical clinic and by the crew who slept on bed rolls side by side on the floor in dormitories. On the main deck, forward of the dining room, was a large lounge; above it was a bar, disco, tables for cards and Mahjong and a large screen video. There were two lifeboats on davits, but no other flotation aids to be seen. Judith asked the conference organisers,"Where are the life jackets and when was the lifeboat drill?" It was telling that not one person could even understand her question, either among the conference organisers or the ship's crew.

River craft passed by regularly, coal barges running downstream, empty ones coming back up and other sightseeing river cruisers like our own, mostly smaller. The river ran surprisingly fast, the main current always on the outside curve, marked by little boat-like buoys with reflector grills on top. The conference started the following morning. After the welcoming speeches, Judith gave the opening address on Sun Tzu and his philosophy of warfare as applied to the tobacco control campaign.

Our boat had to queue at Yi Chang and the Gezhouba barrage

for the lock gates to open and for the craft coming downriver to exit first. The lock was huge, thirty-four metres wide and 280 metres long, lifting shipping an elevation of 70 metres. By the time all the boats were packed into the lock, there were three 76-metre and two 60-metre ferries, one tugboat lashed to a barge, a motorised sand barge, one 30-metre ferry, and four smaller boats. We anchored at the entrance to Xi Ling Gorge to visit the Three Poets and Three Philosophers Cave, dramatically sited in a limestone buttress sticking out at the confluence of the Yangtze and a tributary of opaque green water. This spot was held by Kuomintang troops and marked the limit of Japanese advance during the war. We were told that 20,000 of the inhabitants in this area were killed by a plague released by the Japanese. The cave itself had statues of poets and philosophers and many inscriptions on stone in various styles of calligraphy. The afternoon concluded with a spectacular cable-car ride across the gorge at the Nanjinguan pass; it marked the eastern end of the Xi Ling Gorge, with views down to Yichang and up the river.

That night we were on deck again to see how the ship could possibly sail up the gorge at night. The gorge was indeed pitch black, apart from our ship's two massive searchlights probing their way along the shoreline, rather like a cockroach's antenna helping it to feel along a wall. At intervals, there were navigation beacons on the cliff face, green lights to the right and red lights to the left. Occasionally there was the flash of a bat or a large insect caught momentarily in the spotlight. Above, the black rim of the towering cliffs was outlined by the clear starlit sky. It was a magical moment for Judith and me to share, other passengers having gone below. During the night, the ship travelled up through the Xiling and Wu Gorges and anchored just above the latter, at Wushan. From the deck, we watched the early dawn lighten the sky, silhouetting Wu Mountain in a gentle misty pink.

Pulling Boats Upstream

For one day, the conference paused for a break. So, we embarked on a full day trip in a small river craft about twelve metres long, up the "Lesser Three Gorges" of the Daning River, a 250-kilometre tributary of the Yangtze. Wushan was the commercial centre for the region; its waterfront was busy with small craft, while the large cruise ships were moored on pontoons out in the stream. Long flights of stone steps climbed up from the low water level to the town, perched on the hillside. An ancient walled city, it had become an unattractive huddle of concrete blocks. Spilling down from the town on the right was the garbage dump, presumably washed away each year in the spring floods. Alongside, not wasting an inch of ground, were plots of vegetables. The rich alluvial soil of the riverbank was intensively cultivated. It was a chancy business for the vegetables nearer the water edge; mudslides and sudden rises in water level could sweep away the crops. We were told that, once the Yangtze dam had filled, the water level here would be thirty metres higher and many of the things we saw that day would be under water. We suggested that China could in the future open diving centres to explore the submerged villages.

At some points, a path could be seen chiselled out of the cliff face. Elsewhere a series of square holes in the cliff face indicated where a wooden gangway had been constructed and attached to the outside of the sheer cliff. Before the days of motorised boats, these walkways would have been the only means of access to the valleys between the gorges. They were also the path for humans to rope and pull the boats upstream — an unimaginably difficult job. Even with modern engines, our boat struggled to make way upstream against the fierce currents; the crew also used steel-tipped bamboo poles to inch us forward. Then it was back to the mother boat and the main Yangtze River.

Vertical Cliffs
Next, we passed through the shortest but most spectacular of the Three Gorges — Qutang Gorge. In the fading light, we made our way up between immense vertical cliffs. On the right, a cliff pathway high above the present water level tunnelled or terraced its way upstream, an extraordinary feat of engineering so many centuries ago. At Fenjie, we turned downstream; in daylight, we saw the 45-kilometre middle gorge, the Wu Gorge. It was astonishing because of the spectacular cliffs of the Wu Mountain range plunging into the river. The towering peaks of the mountains were clearly visible; usually, they are swathed in cloud.

The trip upstream had taken us several days, but we were swept downstream in only six hours. Our Captain was aged 68 and the senior captain of the fleet. He recounted he had received as passengers Mao Tse-tung, Chou Enlai, Deng Xiaoping and other leaders of China. Apart from his skills as a navigator, he was a classical scholar and calligrapher. He presented each person at the table with a river stone on which he had written a verse of Chinese poetry.

We left our boat the next morning. Our printed programme asked us to disembark onto buses, leaving our heavy baggage outside our cabins for collection. However, at 6:30 that morning, there were no buses, no porters, and no sign of any Chinese passengers. Not for the first time, arrangements had been changed and announced on the tannoy in Chinese but not in English. It transpired that, because of road repairs, the buses could not get down the steep and narrow road leading from the main road to the quayside. In the end we opted to walk up the 200-foot cliff road lugging our own luggage. We were pleasantly surprised to find that the main Yichang to Wuhan route was a splendid highway through attractive countryside.

To take a voyage up the Yangtze was an unforgettable experience. I am very glad that, despite the recent back operation, I took the decision to go. The overwhelming satisfaction was the knowledge that what I saw on this trip would be lost forever once the dam was closed and the water level had risen, diminishing the grandeur of the huge cliffs bordering the river.

Admiration for the scale of the project was tempered by the knowledge of the millions of people displaced, villages, temples and fields submerged forever.

Golf in China
In 1963 there were no golf courses in China. When the communists took over in 1949, they denounced golf as a decadent sport and closed the courses, mostly around Shanghai and Beijing.

It was not until 1984 that the first new golf course was built in China, at the Chung (Zhong) Shan Hot Springs resort in the foothills just west of Macao on the west side of the Pearl River Delta. It was financed by a former Royal Hong Kong Golf Club member, Henry Fok, and friends from Macao; it was designed by Arnold Palmer, the world's leading golfer at the time. To get there entailed a ferry trip to Macao and a bus ride for half an hour.

I first played there, with Judith, Andrew and Richard in December 1986, at a time when water buffalo were pulling wooden ploughs through paddy fields in the floor of the valley, just over the fence from the course. After an enjoyable round, we returned to the Hot Springs Resort Hotel where we rode go-carts, and Andrew and Richard had a great time setting off firecrackers from pipes embedded in the tarmac play area.

I have played there many times since, with various groups

of golfers. The two courses are dissimilar. The Palmer course uses the natural topography of the land on either side of a canal, whereas the Nicklaus course, which opened in 1993, has been sculpted out of the foothills with much more engineering. Both courses are a delight to play.

Since Deng Xiaoping opened the country to the outside world, many courses have been built, some close to Hong Kong. Japanese entrepreneurs have built many of them for their countrymen, because golf is so very expensive in Japan.

Just across the border from Hong Kong, I played on several courses. The usual format was to join fellow golfers in a bus in Central, ride to the border, get out of the bus to have passports and visas checked, back into the bus for a trip of about an hour to the course. Play a round of golf, have dinner, stay at an hotel overnight, play a second round next morning, have a large lunch and prize-giving and return to Hong Kong that afternoon.

The courses I enjoyed in this manner were Xili, opened in 1995, Zhuhai International 1985, Shenzhen 1985, Pine Valley, Agile, and Palm Island Resort, with three nine-hole courses designed by Jack Nicklaus. By May 1999, there were 86 courses in China; by November 2007 there were 281. At this point, the Chinese government became concerned at the loss of good arable land to golf, and restricted new applications.

In December 2000, I joined a group of golfers from the Hong Kong Club for a two-day visit to Mission Hills Golf Club in Shenzhen. We met at 7 a.m. at Queen's Pier, next to the Star Ferry terminus on the island, and boarded a bus that took us to Lok Ma Chau boundary crossing. Here we had to pass through immigration and customs controls, Hong Kong's and then China's, before boarding the bus again for a further hour to Mission Hills. We checked in to the five-star hotel, had a quick breakfast and then set off to play the Jack Nicklaus-designed course—a beautiful layout, wide fairways, tricky holes, undulating ground. After a late lunch, most of us rested, some went for massages.

At dusk, we set off again, this time to play the last nine holes of the Jumbo Ozaki-designed course. In dramatic floodlighting, this was a most theatrical experience. The course ran through low hills, heavily wooded, with rivers and lakes in the valleys. I scored 43. A Chinese banquet that night started at 9 p.m. and continued until 11 p.m.

Early next morning, we were on a third course, this one designed by British Open winner Nick Faldo. It had remarkable, distinctive, holes. The final hole I shall remember for some time. The match was all square, largely thanks to Jim Petrie, my partner. The hole is a par five with a lake down the right side of a narrow fairway bordered on the left by a string of bunkers and rising ground. We all hit reasonable drives. As usual, mine was some yards shorter than the rest. I duffed my second shot into a bunker and was still 150 yards short of the green after my third—out of contention. My partner made a bold attempt to get on the peninsula green in two but plunged into the water, took a drop, on the green in four, putted twice, for a six. One of our opponents came up short with his approach, found water, on in five; the other opponent hit two good shots down the fairway, pitched carefully onto the green—and was dismayed to see his ball running through it and into the water, on in five. My fourth shot landed on the green but ran about 20 feet past the pin leaving me a difficult putt with a three-foot borrow. And I holed it, to win the hole and the match.

December 2003, Mission Hills
On Wednesday, Judith and I were up early to be at the Hong Kong Golf club at 8 a.m. when we joined a group of Rotarians

headed across the border to Mission Hills for the annual Hong Kong Rotarians golf competition. I won with a gross 92 and with a net 77. In defence of my modest score, may I say that it was the first time I had been on the very demanding David Duval course. It is laid out in a wide valley with very uneven terrain crossed by rocky creeks draining into a large river and surrounded by forested hills. In addition, the greens were rock hard and very fast.

Two other courses were also in the valley and open for play for the first time in 2003, designed by Annika Sorensen and Jose Olazabal. And two others were in the process of construction, designed by Henry Leadbetter and Greg Norman. Along with the original five courses, Mission Hills is now the biggest golf centre in the world, a fact that their publicity people are very happy to tell you. In 2004, the Mission Hills complex was fully opened. This huge enterprise has 10 golf courses, each one designed by a different famous golfer. The courses are set in the low hills just north of Shenzhen, staffed by hundreds of personnel, greenkeepers, caddies, two hotels, a fleet of golf carts. It is all run with military precision.

The most famous golfer in post-1949 China was Zhao Ziyang, Prime Minister from 1980 to 1987 and Communist Party chief from 1987 until June 1989, when he was put under house arrest after the student-led Tiananmen protests in Beijing. Despite his detention, he was allowed to play golf at a course in Beijing; it was his principal recreation away from the confines of his home.

Kunming, 2004

In October 2004, Judith and I went with a group of Rotarians to Kunming to visit a training centre the club was financing, and to play golf. We played on two courses at Spring City, the Jack Nicklaus, and the Robert Trent Jones. Both were spectacular courses overlooking Yan Zonghai Lake. Guarding the clubhouse were Terra Cotta warriors from 200 BC with golf clubs, to back up the claim that golf was invented in China. In fact, there is documentary evidence of courtiers holding long sticks with curved heads hitting balls towards holes in the ground. We also played the Kunming Country Club course and one other, both spectacular.

Hainan, 2012
Mission Hills opened another three courses on Hainan Island. Judith and I went there once with a group from Fanling. It was a unique experience because the courses are constructed on volcanic countryside. Off the fairway and you were picking your way over unplayable ground strewn with rocks of lava. At the time we visited, we met Iain Roberts, former Head Professional at the Hong Kong Golf Club and now Manager at Mission Hills.

Macao
The Macau Golf and Country Club opened in 1993. Judith and I have played there several times. It is set on high ground on Coloane Island overlooking the Pearl River estuary, spectacular and difficult. For many years, the Golf Manager was Lee Parker, once the popular Head Professional at Clearwater Bay Golf and Country Club in Hong Kong. The Golden Gulf Course west of the Pearl River was designed by Colin Montgomery. Built on flat, flood plain land, there was water between most holes, not the easiest course to play.

Hong Kong
Two other golfing locations opened in Hong Kong itself, Discovery Bay in 1983 with three nine-hole courses, set on high ground on Lantau Island. I played there a couple of times. On

the first occasion, a very large water buffalo lay down on my ball at the 18th hole. I chose to take a drop rather than move the obstruction. On my second visit, there was low cloud, so the game was abandoned.

The second location was at Kau Sai Chau Island in Sai Kung. Public courses, the first two designed by Gary Player, opened in 1995. The third and most difficult East Course was designed by Nelson & Howarth. The land was donated by Government free of charge to the Hong Kong Jockey Club which put up HK$500 millon to develop it for the people of Hong Kong. The courses are all challenging, with spectacular views over the sea and mountains of Sai Kung. Kau Sai Chau had been used for many years as a British army training ground; there was spent ammunition all over it and notices on the shore warned people not to venture onto the island. I have played there many times, most memorably my round on the East course recorded elsewhere under 'rough golf'. The development was for our friends, the Hallidays, almost a family business. John Halliday was the Jockey Club chief engineer while his son Cameron, as mentioned, ended up as General Manager.

Xi'an and Urumqi, 2001
August 31, 2001
The purpose of this trip was to attend the 10th Annual meeting of the Chinese anti-smoking organisations in Urumqi, capital of Xinjiang Autonomous Region in the far west of China; secondarily, to visit Xi'an on the way there, a place to which I had never been. Judith had visited it some years before as part of an anti-smoking tour.

We were up at 4 a.m. to catch our Dragonaire flight to Xi'an. The reward was a wonderful sunrise, building to a climax just as we reached Chek Lap Kok Airport. At 10:15 p.m., our plane descended smoothly through a haze of dust to touch down at Xi'an Airport. The surrounding countryside of Shaanxi Province was flat, heavily cultivated. We were met by a representative of the Sheraton Hotel who showed us to a hotel limousine. The road into town was elevated for much of the way above the flood plain. Along one low ridge, we passed several large earthen mounds, the burial sites of Chinese emperors. After half an hour, we reached the outskirts of the city, riding on fine carriageways past clumps of modern buildings. I wondered where the ancient city was going to be amongst all this development.

Shaanxi Province is bordered on the north by the deserts of Inner Mongolia, the border marked by segments of the Great Wall; to the west by the mountains and highland pastures of Gansu; to the south by the lush subtropical forests of Sichuan; and to the east, over the Yellow River, by Shanxi and Henan, further south by Hubei

Xi'an, or Chang'an as it was called then, was the capital of China for centuries, reaching its height of grandeur in the Tang dynasty (618–907 AD), when it was the largest city in Asia, possibly the world, with more than one million inhabitants. It was founded in 240 BC by Emperor Qin Shi Huang, the first to unify all of China.

The Sheraton Hotel was a typical modern building in western style. It must have been one of the first major hotels in Xi'an because, judging by the picture gallery, many heads of state had stayed in the Presidential Suite. It was situated on Fenghua Road, two blocks outside the west gate of the old city wall. We could just make out the wall through the haze.

After lunch, we took a regular taxi for the 20-minute ride (12 yuan) to the centre of Xi'an. The main road was being widened by the simple expedient of knocking down the old buildings bordering the road. The centre was marked by the Bell Tower, standing at the crossing of the main North and South, and East and West roads. In the past, the bell was rung at dawn to rouse the citizens. This early Ming Dynasty building was rebuilt in 1739. was several storeys high and would at one time have towered over the surrounding houses. Now it had to compete with taller, modern glass and steel edifices.

We walked north for one block and then west, where we followed a tour group down narrow alleyways lined with stalls selling tourist trinkets, until we came to the Great Mosque, built by the Moslem traders who had travelled the Silk Route to Xi'an. The mosque was built during the Tang dynasty, in 742 AD. Entering through an ornate wooden gateway, we moved slowly through four courtyards, separated by ornately carved wooden or stone doorways, before coming to the great prayer hall, closed to non-believers. A doorman drowsed at the entrance to one of the huge wooden doorways, a quiet place in the midst of the noisy city.

Leaving the mosque, we walked south through more narrow streets of the Muslim quarter, under the arched gateway of the massive stone Drum Tower, (in the past the drum was sounded in the evenings), to reach the main West Road again. Crossing the main road, we continued in the direction of the South Gate and found ourselves in a street dedicated to western-style coffee shops and a few bars. Hot and tired of walking we were happy to sit in the air-conditioned Cappuccino Cafe drinking iced coffee.

At the South Gate, we paid a small fee then climbed up to the top of the wall, a massive structure, about 15 metres high and twelve metres wide at the top, wide enough for a whole regiment of men to march along ten-a-breast, protected by two-metre-high battlements. The baked clay flagstones of the walkway were imprinted with, presumably, the 14th Century, Ming dynasty makers' insignia. The deep moat running outside the wall was dry. We declined to have our picture taken riding in a crimson-draped palanquin.

The wall appeared to be in an excellent state of repair. Judith recalled a statement in a book detailing the history of tobacco in China which recounted how the walls of Xi'an were at one time festooned with British American Tobacco advertisements.

Coming down from the wall, we turned east into an attractive street of three-storey shop-houses fortunately preserved from development. The shops were selling traditional handicrafts, calligraphy paintings, porcelain and teas. Aiming to go back to the hotel, we hailed one of the tuk-tuks, small three-wheeled open vehicles with room for two passengers propelled by a small, noisy, engine. The driver asked for 30 yuan, dropping his price to 20 yuan, which we still refused, taking instead a small taxi whose driver quoted 10 yuan to the Sheraton. Poor chap — he was stopped by a policeman on duty at the Bell Tower roundabout for ignoring a red light, and fined 50 yuan. Then the direct route up West Street was blocked so he had to make a wide detour.

When we ultimately arrived at the Sheraton, Judith took pity on him and gave him a tip of 40 yuan. He was quite overcome. It seemed the right thing to do and it helped East-West relations.

Monday August 14
We had chosen to go on an all-day bus tour run by C.I.T.S., the China International Travel Service. The bus started at the Sheraton and spent the next hour picking up other clients from three other hotels. In the end, we had with us four Germans, two Japanese and two Brits. Just as we were leaving the last hotel, we saw a huge advertisement, Marlboro Lifestyle, showing a cowboy in a typical western setting. Interesting, because all overt cigarette advertising had been banned in Xi'an, and we had

certainly not seen one. Our guide said there was no time to stop to take a picture, so we resolved to take one on our return.

The traffic in the city was heavy, so it was a tedious drive through grubby suburbs before we crossed over a major river and stopped at Banpo Museum and Neolithic Settlement. The settlement had been perched on a hillside overlooking the Chan River, a tributary of the Yellow River.

Careful excavation since its discovery in 1953 had revealed many houses, round or rectangular, older ones half buried and more recent ones at surface level, walls and roofs of wattle covered in mud. For tourists, a wide area had been roofed over and exhibits of instruments and pottery were on display. Noticeboards were informative, recording habitation from about 5,000 to 4,000 BC. Close by were pottery kilns, and a burial area.

Our guide was knowledgeable, and spoke good English learnt at a Xi'an university, one of 44 universities in the city, she claimed.

A separate building housed a manufacturing plant for making terracotta figures of men and horses and carriages; carpets and porcelain, jades, scrolls and fabrics, all the usual tourist-beguiling items for sale; the same items would have been on sale two thousand years ago when Xi'an was the start of the Silk Road to Asia. Some items were beautiful, but we were not in a buying mood. We already had two terracotta warriors at home in Hong Kong.

Next stop was Huaqing Hot Springs. This used to be the winter residence of the Emperor and his court, a complex of lakes and pavilions at the foot of Li Shan. Dozens of other tour groups thronged the gardens, taking photographs. The buildings were elegant, with their sweeping tiled roofs decorated with mythical figures. One of the main statues was a striking nude of Lady Yang, the Emperor's favourite concubine. Lunch was at a nearby restaurant, with many excellent vegetarian courses, culminating in a delicious dish of honeyed sweet potatoes.

At last, we were heading for the terracotta warriors, passing on the way the mausoleum of the Yellow Emperor, Qin Shi Huang, a great mound of earth a mile from the site of the terracotta army. At the site, there was a mass of tourist buses, thousands of people, stalls selling hats, camera film, postcards and soft drinks. Once through the turnstiles, we left the hawkers behind, crossed a vast square to a long building which on entering we found to be a giant canopy, 230 by 60 metres, over the excavation of the first funeral pit. Our guide and noticeboards told us only a small proportion of the whole site had been excavated since its discovery in 1970. The figures had originally been placed in orderly ranks and columns in deep trenches divided from each other by walls of earth and roofed over with timbers covered with earth.

On excavation, the archaeologists found that the wooden beams had given way crushing the figures below leaving few of them in one piece. General Xiang Yu had set fire to the complex at the overthrow of the Qin dynasty in 206 BC. It was proving to be a gargantuan task to restore the figures, so they were only opening up the site section by section. Distinctive hair styles and uniforms separated the generals from the officers and from the soldiers. Every face was different, modelled on a real person. Originally all the figures had been coloured. It must have been an extraordinary sight; now only a hint of colour remained on a few figures. From the initial pit, we were shown two others, more recently excavated. More than 7,000 figures have been discovered—who knows how many more await discovery. The Emperor's mausoleum has not been excavated.

Photography was supposed to be forbidden but enforcement was ineffective. In the second major building, a museum, there were life-sized figures of court officials. I observed how a young security guard did his best to stop photography, but was insolently ignored by a tall young man, one of a party of Chinese tourists. The heat and blazing sunshine were getting to us all. Judith became quite faint from dehydration and had to be helped to a shady place and plied with water.

Our last stop was on our way back into Xi'an, to the big Wild Goose Pagoda situated just south of the city. This is a Buddhist temple and got its name from a fable that a group of Buddhist monks were desperately short of food. Their prayers for help were answered when a wild goose fell out of the sky at their feet. The pagoda was a seven-storied structure of stone and wood dominating a low hill, the original having been built in 562 AD to house the translations into Chinese of Buddhist scriptures brought back by monk Xuanzhang from India. It was surrounded by formal gardens, ancient trees, stone seats and stone stelae.

Getting back into town in rush hour through streets clogged with traffic was a nightmare. When we got to the Royal Hotel where we wanted to photograph the Marlboro advertisement, the minibus was trapped on the wrong side of the road, so we left the tour at that point, took our photos, and then took a taxi back to the Sheraton. By then we were weary of the noise and dust and heat and were happy to spend the evening in the hotel.

Tuesday, August 15
We had the morning to continue our exploration of Xi'an before taking our flight to Urumqi that evening. After a leisurely start, we took a taxi back to the Royal Hotel to take more pictures of the Marlboro advert with the sun in the right quarter. We then walked down back streets to the Forest of Stelae Museum, also referred to as the Shaanxi Provincial Museum. This turned out to be more interesting than it might have been for a non-Chinese

speaker. Through an ornate gateway, we found a long, rather gloomy garden laid out in formal style with paths running between many trees, leading to pagodas, and halls built in traditional style. Stelae, upright stone slabs or columns typically bearing a commemorative inscription or relief design, often serving as gravestones, were everywhere, small ones flanking the paths, and immense ones on the backs of turtles amongst the trees. There were buildings housing a library of 2,300 stelae, and a museum with interesting exhibits of pottery, temple decorations, and Buddha images. There was a set of six life-size stone horses, the Six Steeds of Zhauling that had been buried in the tomb of Tang Emperor Tai Zhong in 649 AD, his favourite war horses. They were magnificently carved, with a plaque informing us that two of them were replicas — the originals now residing at Pennsylvania University.

We returned to the Sheraton to shower, change, pack, and eat lunch, ready for our taxi to the airport at 4 p.m. Across the road from the airport carpark, I took photographs of a large cigarette advert on top of an office building, with a Chinese flag flying conveniently next to it, to establish locale.

Xinjiang Airways surprised us; there were no aged Russian planes. We happily climbed aboard a new Boeing 737. During the flight, the scenery was dramatic, with ranges of mountains with glaciers on their northern slopes; barren desert apart from the first half hour, the Tibetan plateau on our left. Our meal was a box containing a tasty selection of chicken and rice, a peach cake, with tea or coffee, beer and soft drinks.

We landed after dark and were met by a Chinese Public Health worker with a minivan and driver. We seemed to drive for miles along dimly lit avenues until we came to the city centre and found the streets brightly lit and thronged with people enjoying the cool of the evening. It was a frightening drive, at speed, the driver determined not to give way to anyone—really the Wild West. We were glad to get to our destination, to the modern wing of a large government hotel built in the massive Russian style of a previous age. Many old friends from previous meetings greeted us, including Dr He Yao from the People's Liberation Army and Prof Richard Peto and Dr Chen Zhengming from the University of Oxford.

Wednesday, August 16
The conference hall was full for the opening ceremony. Judith was on stage and gave her formal welcoming speech in Putonghua. Papers were presented from 11 a.m. to 1 p.m. and from 4 p.m. to 7 p.m. Headphones were available to listen to simultaneous translation, but the standard of translation was so poor that it was hardly worth listening. Feeding was a communal affair for breakfast and lunch. The horde of delegates, about 400, descended like vultures on the 30 varieties of foods ranged in rows of hotplates stationed at the centre of the room; they sat down at round tables for ten persons, before returning for more. Waitresses threaded their way through the tables dispensing milk, tea or beer. The feeding frenzy over, the crowd departed as quickly as it had come.

That first evening there was a reception in a smaller room for the VIPs. Even here there were 22 dishes, served by waitresses in traditional Uighur dress. There were speeches and many toasts of *ganbei* (dry cup), with locally made red wine in liqueur glasses. Afterwards there were songs. The Hong Kong contingent sang an anti-smoking song in halting Putonghua and *Jingle Bells*, to which everyone knew the words. The Mayor of Urumqi brought the evening to a close by singing two songs, one of them in Russian.

Thursday, August 17
I attended the presentations in the morning and took the afternoon off.

Friday, August 18
Again I attended the morning session. In the afternoon, I joined a group of 'Foreign Friends' to discuss tobacco topics with a group of Middle School students. Their English was remarkable, some were fluent. They had a good knowledge of tobacco issues, a useful meeting in which both sides learned a lot.

In the evening, the delegates were transported by a fleet of buses, escorted by a police car, to a theatre. By 8:30 p.m. we were all seated in the front rows of the theatre. We had to wait another hour while the rest of the hall filled with locals, before the show began. Plastic bottles of distilled water were distributed to keep us cool.

The show was worth waiting for. It was all singing and dancing of folk tunes, with colourful costumes and brilliant lighting. Interestingly, there were several scenes in which performers dressed as PLA soldiers danced and sang. The stars were the compere, a very polished host, singer and musician, and a hugely jolly Mongolian singer. The company had played two years previously in front of President Jiang Zemin.

Saturday, August 19
With the main conference having been completed on Friday, the next two days were scheduled for site visits. By 8 a.m., we were seated in one of a fleet of six tourist coaches. Two police cars preceded our cavalcade. We travelled on an excellent two-lane highway with little traffic. Even so, the lead police car persisted in driving down the centre of the road, forcing oncoming traffic to slow down and go onto the hard shoulder. Woe betide any

lorry on our own side of the road that did not get out of the way; the police car would drive alongside, the driver waving an arm and no doubt hurling abuse.

The road ran south and east down a wide valley, initially all desert. Ranges of rocky mountains reared up on both sides, topped with snow to the north, the Tianshan Mountains. At a point where the valley narrowed to about five miles, we passed through a huge windfarm for the generation of electricity. Hundreds of tall silvery masts carried long-bladed rotors, a few swinging lazily in the still air. It had been built with aid from the Netherlands.

Further along, we passed a salt lake, and further down came to a grassy valley where we saw herds of sheep and goats and horses, cows and a few camels. Turning right, we followed a river through a narrow defile between rocky mountainsides, emerging into a sandy desert, the edge of the Taklimakan desert. As we descended further, we came to fields of grapevines, dotted with rectangular brick buildings each side having window spaces. These were the barns where grapes were hung to dry, producing raisins.

Our first stop in Turpan was at the local government office, a smoke-free establishment. On the walls anti-smoking posters were displayed, including one of President Jiang Zemin at the opening of the World Conference on Smoking Control held in Beijing in 1997 — welcoming Judith to the conference! She delightedly pointed this out — and was henceforth treated with very great respect.

Having made our 'official' visit, the rest of the day was spent sightseeing.

We stopped at the main square, where we were given strict instructions about the time to return to the buses, and let loose to admire the flowers, fountains and the events arena. Judith and I spotted the office of the China Tobacco Corporation distribution centre, invited ourselves inside and took photographs of the 53 varieties on offer, leaving behind a polite but rather perplexed staff. It was too hot to linger in the sun, so we returned to the bus at the appointed time, and then had to wait for stragglers, a feature of the rest of the day. The city centre buildings were modern and unattractive.

Next stop was the Burning Hills, a range of red sandstone hills that were no doubt a burning flame colour at sunset, but at midday were pale in the shimmering heat. Burning they certainly were in a temperature sense, it was over 40 degrees Celsius, the hottest place in China. At the stopping place were groups of Uighurs dressed in traditional clothes, willing to dance or have their photos taken, for a price; tourists could sit on camels and have their photos taken. We were intrigued by the fact that the most popular hat on offer was a stylish straw cowboy hat, with a 'Marlboro' hatband. Apparently, they had come onto the market the year before. Not far down the same road, we would have come to the lowest point in the Turpan Depression, 155 feet below sea level, second only to the Dead Sea.

On our way back into town, we stopped at the famous Emin (Sugong) Minaret, built in 1775, of sun-baked bricks, the surface laid in intricate patterns. It was 40-feet high, tapering for the upper two thirds. The large mosque at its foot was a modern construction, so far undecorated. The surrounding valley was covered with vineyards. A further short drive took us to a narrow valley situated between high, barren hills of shale. In contrast, the valley floor was lush and green with vines fed by a sparkling clear stream.

We walked down a wide passage overhung with a trellis of vines and lined at the sides with stall after stall selling raisins of various sizes and colours and other dried fruits, with other stalls selling knives, brightly coloured shawls and wines. We ate lunch at a restaurant beside the river, then strolled round the covered walkways. The winery was not open for viewing.

Back in our buses, our departure was delayed by half an hour by two women shopping, oblivious of time, finally collected by our irate police escort.

Our last stop was at the ruined city of Jiaohe, 20 kilometres west of Turpan. It had been the capital of the Kushi Qian state 2,000 years ago and had been burnt down by Genghis Khan at the end of the 13th Century. The city had been built in an excellent strategic position, on an island between two rivers with high bluffs on either side. Many of the mud brick walls were still standing. In our allotted 20 minutes, we saw a good deal, but then were irritated, as were the rest of the party when the last busload of passengers rolled up nonchalantly half an hour late.

By now, we were at least an hour behind schedule so missed out on the last item on the schedule, a visit to the Karez wells to inspect an underground irrigation system used for centuries at the oasis. By the time we reached the hotel after the 80-kilometre drive back, it was dark, and we were all tired. We ate and retired to bed.

Sunday, August 20
Another early start found us ready to set off in our bus cavalcade at 8:30 a.m. This time we headed out of town in a northeasterly direction, to Fukang, an agricultural centre built by the Han Chinese, where we visited the secondary school, built 46 years before. This time the bulk of our party was confined to their buses. Only the VIPs including us, were invited to walk down the avenue leading from the road to the school buildings, welcomed by the school band and a line of smartly uniformed children on each side of the road. A deputation from the school greeted us

while two movie camera teams recorded the occasion. We then inspected the immaculately neat grounds and admired the large anti-smoking mural. The walk back to the bus was delayed by yet more photography.

Business of the day being completed, we headed for the hills, to the Heavenly Lake (Tianchi) resort in the Mount Bogda area of the Tianshan Mountains. The road from Fukang quickly climbed away from the plains into a narrow valley; at the riverside were Uighur settlements, groups of tents called gers, and horses. As a privileged group, we were allowed to drive past the main car park to the lakeside itself, a steep climb up a wooded slope. The green waters of the lake were set off spectacularly by the surrounding forested slopes, and further back by towering snow-capped mountains. I was reminded of Lake Louise in Canada, similarly a glacial lake trapped behind a moraine barrier.

It was the last Sunday holiday before the start of school, so the place was packed with people. We queued to take a short boat trip on the lake; instead of admiring the view, we had to spend the time posing with locals while they had their pictures taken. Richard Peto was with us and put up with it all with a good grace. Disembarking, we walked slowly up to the Kazakh village above the lake. Inside a group of gers, we saw they had felt walls being adorned with colourful decorations. Judith was concerned that she might have a reaction to the altitude, 1,900 metres. All went well, but it would have been easier to take the ponies on offer. At the village, we watched a man preparing a goat for cooking. Having slit its throat, he made a hole in the skin further down and blew into it, separating the skin off the body, making the skinning process much simpler. We had heard of this technique from others in our party. They reported that, in their case, the goat was gently pacified by stroking, and its throat cut without external loss of blood. The blowing-up process and skinning was accomplished with extreme gentleness by the herdsman, stroking and talking to the goat during the procedure.

By the time we had walked down the hill to the foot of the moraine where the hotels and restaurants were situated, we had regained our appetites, and enjoyed an excellent lunch. Our drive back was enlivened by a videotape of a performance by the theatre group we had seen, made before a gathering of heads of state.

We had bought a whole pack of picture postcards at the hotel, but they could not give us any stamps. So, in the afternoon, I set off to find a post office, and to explore some of Urumqi on foot. The main street was like any other rapidly developing Han Chinese city. The latest buildings were handsome glass and concrete high-rise structures, but they stood out from a mass of undistinguished low-rise buildings. The major department stores were like the China Products Stores in Hong Kong. In the cool of the late afternoon, the wide pavements came alive with throngs of people, hawkers selling their wares and games of chance. I came back with two bottles of Xinjiang wine, but no stamps.

What we did miss was the native Uighur night market, at Erdao Bridge. I gather it was a maze of stalls, brightly lit, and with an exotic array of native craftwork, prominently featuring knives, plus goods brought in from neighbouring countries, Pakistan, Afghanistan and Mongolia — a delight for the bargain hunter.

Monday 20th
Regarding the trip back to Hong Kong, my main memories were of the crowds at the Urumqi airport, all with boxes of grapes or bottles of wine; and an announcer over the loudspeaker system whose clarity in English was the best I have heard anywhere. We viewed the vastness of the desert before reaching the Shaanxi

plains. Then there was the wait at Guangzhou Airport before we could board our Dragonair flight back to Hong Kong.

The Han and Muslem Uighurs did not mingle. One of our Han guides, a Public Health worker, had been living in Xinjiang for years but could speak no Uighur. About 50 years ago, more than 90 per cent of the population of Urumqi were Uighur; now they were in a minority. The same process was taking place in Tibet, the Han gradually becoming numerically dominant, not just militarily and commercially, and teenage Tibetans adopted non-religious Han-cum-Western lifestyles.

Xiamen 2002 – Island of No Cars
Our Hong Kong friends, Moyreen and Brian Tilbrook, had booked a cruise to Xiamen, a port city in Fujian Province. On a last-minute whim, we joined them on SuperStar Leo, the flagship of the Star Cruises line. It was a giant boat, 268 metres long, with 13 decks and 14 bars and restaurants. It carried about 2,000 passengers and 1,100 crew and travelled at a speed of 25 knots.

From the top deck, we watched Hong Kong harbour disappear behind us, its evening lights ablaze. By noon of the next day, we were in sight of land – Quemoy and Matsu, two islands held by Taiwan – on our way to berthing in Xiamen, formerly known as Amoy. We were almost alone in disembarking to have a look at Xiamen – almost all the other passengers were gamblers and never left the ship. No gambling was allowed in Hong Kong except at Jockey Club races.

Xiamen has been an important seaport for centuries. The Portuguese traded there in the early 1500s, then the Dutch, British and French. It was closed to foreigners by the Qing dynasty in the 1750s, until it was forced open by a British naval force and army in 1841 and was declared a Treaty Port. We visited the island of Gulangyu, a pedestrian-only island off the coast of Xiamen. It had architecture that had remained much as it was for the last century and a half, with old colonial homes and an old town. No petrol or diesel engines were allowed on the island, so strong men pushed and pulled heavy carts through the narrow streets. We all gave a hand to three men straining up a hill with a cart loaded with bags of cement, to their amazement and smiles.

We climbed the southernmost hilltop to a museum — a beautiful single-storey building, whitewashed, surrounded by gardens and shaded by tall eucalyptus. On the way back to the ferry, we passed the Moon Garden, surrounded by a wall ornamented with deep blue-coloured tiles. On the headland, on top of a huge rock stood the statue of the 17th Century hero, Koxinga or General Zheng Cheng-gong, who drove the Dutch out of what was then Formosa, now Taiwan. He also fought for the last Ming Emperor against the Qing invaders.

Beijing 2012: From Temple Hotel to The Peninsula
This was a family holiday. Our elder son Andrew, his wife Beverley, daughter Kate, then aged twelve, and son Robbie, ten, joined us in Beijing, after they had visited Xi'an. Andrew had requested authentic Chinese accommodation, after enjoying an excellent courtyard hotel in Xi'an. The one in Beijing was in a poor district, down a grubby, narrow side street. The hotel had been built around an ancient temple of three courtyards surrounded by two-storey residential buildings. The courtyards had gardens, a pool with golden carp, and several 10-foot-tall stelae riding on ornamental turtles. Our rooms were big enough, with the usual amenities of television, telephone (antique), hair dryer, fridge and air conditioner and ensuite shower rooms with very hot water; but they were sorely in need of a repainting and dusting. With reluctance, and only at our request, the staff swept the rooms and removed bucketloads of dirt.

Since it was the first visit for Beverley and the grandchildren, we headed north to the Great Wall, via the Ming Tomb valley. The Wall could not have been more different from our visit in 1976, when we were the only visitors. It was absolutely packed and often we had to wait to proceed. During one of these waits, Judith practiced tai chi on the wall, much to the astonishment of local tourists. We also visited Tiananmen Square, the Summer Palace, Kunming Lake and the building where the young Emperor Puyi was confined by the Dowager Empress. We walked to the top of the man-made Hill of Longevity behind the palace where we found a Buddhist temple and a white stupa. The guide told us the Summer Palace was burnt down by French and British troops in 1860 and again in 1900. The Dowager Empress Cixi Taihou rebuilt it, using money meant for the navy, before the declaration of the Republic in 1911.

We circumnavigated the lake in a Dragon Boat motorised ferry, under the 17-arch marble bridge leading to Nan Hu Island. We then hired a paddle boat with seating for six and worked our way round the island and under the arches of the bridge. It was hard work on the thighs. The adults did most of the paddling, with the youngsters doing the steering.

The bus took us back into town for a delicious Chinese meal at a restaurant near a theatre where we watched an excellent acrobatic show. The audience applauded little and rose to leave even as the players came out to make their bows. We knew this was the Chinese custom, but it still distressed us; we applauded loudly to make up for it.

The grandchildren had behaved very well through three days of sightseeing, now it was their turn—the 2008 Olympic Park. Inside the swimming Cube was the Waterworld entertainment complex. There were water slides galore, the three most extreme closed to those older than 60, thank goodness. On the last night, since we were tiring of our very basic living quarters, we all agreed on a luxury evening at the Peninsula Hotel for dinner — a very fine ending to our visit in Beijing.

Harbin 2015, February 5-8

I suggested this trip to Judith as a spin-off after one of her scheduled conference meetings in Beijing from February 1-4. She readily agreed. We had both been enthused by reports from friends who had been there for the Harbin Winter Ice Festival lasting from January 5 to the end of February.

I flew from Hong Kong on Cathay Pacific, arriving at Beijing Airport Terminal 3. I followed the crowd out through health, immigration, and customs. With only a backpack, I did not have to wait for luggage — I was wearing all my heavy mountaineering clothing. A shuttle bus carried me to Terminal 2, about seven kilometres and 20 minutes away. Judith was waiting at the check-in counter, having left town by car an hour before. We had a couple of hours to kill before we could check in to our China Southern Flight departing at 4:40 p.m. for Harbin, so we found a Panopolis coffee shop that served excellent drinks and food and spent the time there.

The flight to Harbin took an uncomfortable two hours in a packed economy class; a tasty hot meal helped to pass the time. At Harbin airport, we were met by a Shangri La Hotel staff member, car and driver, booked by Judith, worth the 530 yuan, in anticipation that we would arrive well after dark in a temperature of -20 degrees Celsus with 45 kilometres to reach a hotel in a city of a million people. Just out of the airport, we passed a brilliantly lit ice construction, an appetizer to whet our anticipation. In the city the traffic was heavy, so the journey took nearly an hour.

The hotel lobby was spacious and the staff efficient and

welcoming, so we were soon in our room on the 18th, the top floor, overlooking the Songhua River. The river was frozen, about half a mile wide covered in snow, lit by the highway bridge running across it.

Having unpacked, we set off to explore the hotel, still in our heavy clothing, and went into the Ice Bar and Restaurant built entirely of blocks of ice; chairs of ice were covered with fur cushions, the ice shelves behind the ice bar held bottles of spirits; a small birch-bark tepee had a fire burning inside, and a suit of clothing of a hunter was hanging on the wall. We sat and had drinks at one of the ice tables, and had our picture taken by excited Chinese holidaymakers. In the restaurants were round tables set for Mongolian hotpot meals, but we did not feel hungry so we retired early.

Next morning, we drew back the curtains of the picture windows and looked out over the vast expanse of river and flat plain beyond, white with snow, trees black. A few people were already walking over the frozen river. There was a huge buffet for breakfast catering to all national tastes. I enjoyed a traditional 'full monty' while Judith had an omelette. Coming out of the dining room we chatted with an Australian couple living at Stanley in Hong Kong; they were just concluding their holiday and were full of useful information. Later, we met up with them at the hotel entrance and joined them for a walk down the steep bank and onto the river.

We passed an area where the snow had been cleared down to smooth ice and watched some old men using a whip at the end of a stick to spin heavy metal tops. Elsewhere were children skating and sledging, ice yachts, sleighs pulled by horses, ornate floating landing stages by the riverbank and heavy river sightseeing boats in an icy grip till spring, and smaller fishing boats lying on top of the ice. We returned to the hotel for lunch and to prepare for our visit to the Sun Island Snow Sculpture exhibits; the other couple walked on down river to catch a cable car that crossed over to the north bank to an ancient Russian-looking mansion.

We lunched in the main restaurant, then after a rest we put on all our Arctic gear, hired a taxi for the afternoon and set off at 1:30 p.m. across the bridge to Sun Island Snow Sculpture Park. The very pleasant and helpful taxi driver dropped us off at the gate and promised to wait for our return.

The snow sculptures were amazing, imaginative, varying in size from ten feet high for the competition entries to 50 feet high for the major monuments. We saw groups of workmen freshening the surface of a sculpture that, facing south, had started to show surface melting and staining. Other workers were just starting to shape a huge block of compacted snow blocks. One sculpture had a theme of 'apple' with Adam and Eve in a garden, Isaac Newton whose falling apple gave him his gravity insight, and a huge apple with a bite out of it. Another group featured major buildings, castles, towers and churches. Tree trunks were covered with colourful plastic wrappings; pussy-willow bushes had red or green catkins. Large play areas had slides, sledges pulled by dogs or goats, four-wheel snow buggies on a racing track. Stalls sold kebabs.

We did a circuit covering the entire area of four square kilometres before returning to the entrance gate, buying two baked sweet potatoes, oven hot and delicious; one we ate, the other we gave to our driver. By now it was 4 p.m. and some sunshine was still coming between the clouds. We drove a kilometre to the entrance of the Ice and Snow Fairyland, carefully noted where the taxi was parked in the huge car park filled with cars and buses and set off, again comfortable in the knowledge that our taxi driver would be waiting for us. We had been advised that getting transport back across the river to the city was problematic because of the crowds.

The timing was perfect in that the light was fading, and the coloured illuminations had just started to come on. The buildings and statues being made of ice were translucent, so coloured neon lights buried in the ice lit the structures. The lights changed colour, too, so the scene was dazzling in different brightly coloured hues. Among the many structures was a series of igloos containing drinking bars, an outlet for the Heineken beer advertised near the entrance. One series of giant ice wall rooms held oversize ice furniture, tables, chairs and baths. A carousel had ice horses for children to ride on. An artificial hill had steps leading to the top and a slide for descent, leading down to an ice rink for skaters and an ice maze. There was a large monument to the year of the goat. One enclosure had 20 very finely wrought ice sculptures — exhibits of an international sculpture competition. By 6:30 p.m., we were both satiated with colour experiences, hands really chilled, warm otherwise and happy to return to the warm taxi for the drive back to the hotel.

Next morning, there was a light mist and colder air at minus 14 degrees Celsius, so we had a leisurely start and did not go out till midday to explore the city. A taxi took us to our first objective, St Sophia Church, the only Russian church not to be destroyed by the Chinese, and now a museum, packed with Chinese tourists. From the outside, it looked elegant with tall onion domes and intricate stonework; inside, it was gloomy, badly lit by ornate chandeliers, the walls' drab paint was peeling. Black and white photographs depicted the history of the city from the time it was a fishing village through the time of a great trading port populated by Russians, to the present. It was difficult to visualise the church when it was in its heyday with rich decorations, icons, gold ornaments, and candles.

By the time we came outside, it was snowing, a very fine

snow, like frozen mist droplets. A very large ornate wrought iron structure was in the square outside the church, function unknown. We hurried down Shangzhi Avenue to the north and across one block to the west to get onto Central Street and to find a Western food restaurant, and warmth. It was full and not taking any bookings till 4 p.m. We moved on, very soon seeing a sign pointing down a stair to Restaurant Tatoc. At the entrance we were greeted by a young, beautiful, blond Russian in Russian dress. We had struck gold. The restaurant had been established in 1901 and served authentic Russian food, with excellent service. We had a very leisurely meal of borsch and beef stroganoff in comfortable warmth, waiting until it was getting towards dusk when the ice lanterns at Zaolin Park would be lit.

The Park was just one block to the east but entailed crossing a main road packed with cars and buses, none of which took any notice of the zebra crossings. But the Park was closed. We walked from one entrance round to another, also closed. Gradually people started to gather, and, at 4 p.m., the gates were opened. We went in free on the basis that we were older than 70. The lighting not yet being switched on, we headed straight for the nearest café, in a building made of blocks of ice, the inner walls draped with a thin cloth. Here we had hot drinks, warming our frozen hands on electric radiators, and Judith struck up a conversation in Mandarin/English with a cafe worker. After an entertaining half an hour, the lights came on so we wrapped ourselves up again and ventured forth.

The Park, covering two city blocks, was thickly planted with trees and had a couple of small hills. The wide paths were lined with ice lanterns (made very simply by putting a bucket of water out to freeze, tipping out the block of ice, coring out the centre and planting a light in the cavity). One area was enclosed by glass walls to display some beautifully crafted figures lit in bright ever-changing colours. A slide constructed of ice led down to an icy play area for children.

To get back to the hotel, we took a taxi. The one that stopped for us had a man sitting alongside the young man driving, a friend we thought, but it turned out he was another passenger, which explained why the taxi shot off in the wrong direction for us, heading to where the first passenger wanted to go. The taxi then headed straight for the Shangri La but stopped again to pick up a woman who sat on the front seat with her child in her arms, no seat belts for anyone. Despite the warmth of the taxi, there was ice on the inside of the windows. The driver spoke some English and had taken tour groups to Hong Kong; he also sold insurance — a slick operator. His ambition was to see Australia.

Through the day, we had been getting urgent messages from Reina, our travel agent in Hong Kong, to say that our morning flight to Beijing the next morning would be two hours late and we would miss our connection to Hong Kong. The man at the hotel business centre had confirmed our seats but had not told us of the delay. The heavy smell of alcohol on his breath may have been the reason. We had to re-book a flight leaving at 9 a.m. on China Southern, which would mean getting up at 5:30 a.m. and waiting for five hours at Beijing.

In the evening, Judith went down to the spa for a foot massage. I failed to find any watchable TV, so I started reading Kate Adie's book about the part played by women during the 1914-18 War, which was fascinating.

On Sunday morning, we were up in time for a hurried breakfast before leaving for the airport. In daylight, we marvelled at the immense housing developments, clusters of 30-storey apartment blocks being built or completed and lying empty. Our flight left on time, after it had been de-iced by fire truck spray using special fluid. The plane was packed, how Reina had managed to get us booked at the last minute I do not know — the Chinese New Year Holiday rush had already started.

At Beijing, the first two hours of our wait we spent in a coffee shop, until the airline counter opened, and we could check in, and move on to the business lounge.

It was good to be back in Hong Kong. It had been a long way to go for two days of sight-seeing, but so worth it. Harbin is a unique city about which we had heard much from our Russian friends in Hong Kong. The Ice Festival itself was a spectacular, once-in-a-lifetime experience.

Beijing APACT Conference September, 2016
The three-hour flight to Beijing was uneventful. I whisked through immigration due to Judith's APEC card. A hire car driver was waiting for us and drove us to the V-Continent Hotel in the North Star complex near the Olympic Games area. We went down for the hotel buffet of Asian food, 330 yuan each, which we almost justified. Back in our room, we watched part of a submarine war drama, and then, more happily, *Shanghai Knights* with Jackie Chan and Owen Wilson.

Thursday September 22
We did not awaken until Judith's alarm went off at 8:30 a.m. We reached the breakfast room with half an hour to go before it closed, and met Geoff Fung and Ann, and Michael Erikson, Judith's Tobacco Atlas co-author. Judith spent much of the day at the Bloomberg partners office, while I went for a walk, both returning to the hotel at 4:15 p.m.

For my walk, I headed north, around a fine piece of open grassland, just right for a cricket pitch, and north again to a pleasant park of trees, ponds, walkways and many families with children.

I walked north and west, crossing a major roadway to get into the Olympic Park. A loudspeaker was putting out an orchestral version of Gershwin's *Rhapsody in Blue*. I continued up the western shore of the Dragon Lake, a wide expanse of water only a few feet deep, lined by high reeds, walkways shaded with trees; at intervals, stairs led down to toilets and underground car parks. On the western side of the path, I passed the Bird's Nest Olympic Stadium, sports grounds, a sunken shopping area, and, near the top of the waterway, a hill with a group of immense, elegant towers opening up at the top as viewing platforms. Across the 5th Ring Road was an immense area of landscaping with all sorts of trees lining a large lake with many islets and a range of higher ground leading to the Land of Heaven, situated on the North-South axis that runs right through the centre of the city of Beijing. I started by following the red running track for Beijing Marathon runners that wound westward along the southern shore of the lake.

I passed drinks outlets and running shoe shops and the main South entrance to the forest, a memorial to the Olympics with a plaque in three languages; it was the speech in 1892 when Baron de Coubertin enunciated the principles of the Olympic movement. Further on, I stopped to buy a bottle of Coca-Cola and a bottle of water, then climbed north and east again up the west flank of the ridge through areas of streams tumbling down rocky valleys, almost deserted, and on to the highest point, Land of Heaven. It had a view south right down towards Tiananmen Square hidden in haze, and north over the wooded North Forest.

A stone-paved trail led back down the hill towards the lake. Orientation was always easy because of the very tall group of observation towers to the south. By the lake, I walked from island to island over little bridges, past gorgeous vistas of water covered in lilies, borders of rushes in flower and overhanging weeping willows; Monet would have been ecstatic.

I left the Forest by the Southeast gate and walked back down the western edge of the Dragon Lake, or Yang Shan River where workers in row boats were scooping up rake-loads of weed.

Down by the Bird's Nest stadium, I came within earshot of the music, now *Ode to Spring*. I carried on round south of the stadium to where the Dragon's tail ended at the huge pedestrian concourse that runs between the stadium and the Cube aquatic centre, with a view of Land of Heaven hill on the northern horizon. By now weary after walking for more than ten miles, I was glad to turn towards the V-Continental hotel, a shower and a rest.

The construction of the Olympic Park started in 2003. A large area of northern Beijing had been flattened to make way for the Park. The main buildings were the oval Bird's Nest National Stadium and the square Cube Aquatic Centre. Many more buildings and landscaped parkland combined to make an enormously impressive, modern venue, worth the US$40 billion it was reported to have cost. The country has come a long way since I first visited 40 years earlier.

Dinner was at 6:30 p.m. in the same Asian restaurant in the hotel, joined by the ebullient Geoff and his co-worker Anne. We were also joined by Mike Daube from Australia who started with ASH (Action on Smoking and Health) UK in 1973, and later Damien O'Hara, a smoking cessation counsellor from Canada. He was brought up in Hong Kong — his family was under the care of Peter Drummond Smith and myself at Drs Anderson & Partners. Also introducing themselves was another conference attendee, Harvey Gimbel and his wife Ann from Loma Linda University, California. It was a good evening.

The Beijing trip about which I had felt misgivings was already a success. Small negatives were the facts that I could not get onto my Gmail account in China, and that censorship of BBC TV blocked some of the reporting of event in HK.

Friday September 23
Judith and I did 'Eight pieces of cloth' Tai chi exercises before breakfast. After breakfast, we registered for the conference, with an extended hassle because our HSBC Visa cards did not work, so we had to find and pay in cash, which took all morning, with visits to various banks and cash outlets, leaving us shorter than we had planned. We had lunch in the room—bacon sandwiches brought from breakfast. At 2:30 p.m., I carried a parcel of books to the next hotel where Judith was attending the Asia Pacific Conference on Tobacco. She returned with gifts, a Chanel silk scarf, a box of cookies from The Brothers Hotel in Taiwan and a blue elephant soft toy. I had spent an hour in the North Star Park walking and sitting under the weeping willows looking at the reflections of other trees in the water of the lake.

For dinner we were with 30 other VIPs, all members of the APACT Committee at a Peking Duck Restaurant. The usual starters were augmented by duck tongues, duck hearts, duck feet and duck soup. Then came whole glazed roast ducks. A half dozen were expertly carved by the tableside, the slivers of duck meat and skin were now ready to be placed on wafer thin pancakes along with chopped chives and dark sauce, wrapped up in the pancakes and eaten by hand–delicious. The meal ended with fresh fruit. Toasts in red wine were celebrated before and at the end of the meal.

Saturday September 24
The first full day of the conference in the International Conference Centre started at 9 a.m. and went non-stop till 5.30 p.m., with only an hour break for lunch. Judith and T.H. Lam, both from

Hong Kong, were the commentators for the opening ceremony. In the afternoon session, Judith and a Professor Wang were the co-chairs. Judith performed very well on both occasions, speaking clearly, concisely and with enthusiasm.

In the evening, a presentation was made by economist Rose Zheng, Director of WHO's Collaborating Centre for Tobacco and Economics, and Professor of the School of International Trade and Economics (SITE) at the University of International Business and Economics. We had another gigantic meal, this time of southern Chinese food, at least 20 courses. We were the guests of the Gates Foundation China Office headed by Prof Lin.

Also present were Professor Hu Teh-Wei and Professor Hu Dayi, President of the Chinese Association on Tobacco Control, and five other staff members. Professor Hu is a cardiologist and lost 22 kilos on a diet and exercise regime, in a cohort of 300 people linked by a mobile IT fitness monitor. Premier Xi's exhortation not to have lavish meals has fallen on deaf ears.

This was no longer the city of Mao suits and bicycles. People were dressed fashionably, some women wore make-up. The roads were filled with cars and motorcycles. Glittering new buildings dominated the skyline.

Chapter Ten
A Happy Retirement:
Family, Gardens, Golf and Travel

The greatest pleasure on retirement was to hear my telephone ring and know it could be a call from a friend—never again a call to attend a patient. The next greatest was to be able to take my time getting up in the morning and not have to leap out of bed, half awake, to start the day's work. I was able to lie back and wonder: "What shall I do today?" Boredom has never been an issue. I have always had something interesting to do. At home in Hong Kong, there is the half-acre garden. I enjoy gardening, spending an hour or so each day tending to it, especially in the winter months when there are no mosquitos. I plan what to grow, where to plant it, and to trim the excess growth, a constant commitment. Nowadays I enjoy the assistance of Filipino

Riftswood garden

helper Billy—full name Belino Mallare—a hard worker, smart and tidy. He has helped me to upgrade the garden to where it should be. Billy's wife Melda is equally neat and hardworking, with a pleasant smile. Before they joined us, we were helped by their older relatives, Oscar and Lucy Abenoja. When they retired in 2011, I wrote to them as follows:

TO: Mr Oscar Estioco Abenoja and Mrs Lucresia Mallare Abenoja

October 2011

Dear Oscar and Lucy,

This letter of appreciation is written to thank you for the many years you have spent in our household. Oscar, you joined us in 1975 when you were 30 years old. Your sister Flor was already working for us; in 1981, she left for Canada and your wife Lucy joined us. Since then we have appreciated your hard work, dependability and honesty.

You have both been indispensable, particularly when Andrew and Richard were very small. Oscar, you have done wonders for the garden, the many home-grown organic vegetables, fruit trees and flowering shrubs and bushes are testimonials to that. You have managed the pool maintenance and cared for our succession of cars, becoming a very safe chauffeur who has driven us many thousands of miles, and looked after our dogs—who will miss you also.

Lucy, you have done all the housekeeping and cooking, leaving us free to continue to develop our careers. Your cooking is second to none.

You have brought up two fine daughters who are now into successful careers. We were glad to help you with their education expenses and are pleased to see how worthwhile it has proved to be.

This last summer you have had an uncomfortable time, coping with discomfort and responsibility while the house has been completely refurbished. The result has been very good. Thank you.

We are sad to see you go but happy to think that you will have many years of well-deserved retirement back with your family in the Philippines. All our family, including children and grandchildren, are very fond of you, so we hope that we will all meet again when you return to visit your daughters in Hong Kong.

Best wishes,
John and Judith Mackay

Membership of the Hong Kong Gardening Society has been a spur to our work. Several times I have opened the garden to other members. In preparation for these visits, we must do much extra work. During the last visit, I identified and labelled more than 200 different plants. Inspiration and new ideas have also come from visiting other gardens in Hong Kong, tours to neighbouring parts of China and a longer visit into Yunnan Province. In the southwest, Yunnan accounts for only 4.1 per cent of China's land area but contains 19,333 species or more than half of the country's higher plants. It is also home to the most plant species endemic to China.

Golf has been one of my other chief pastimes. Back in 1968, I joined the Royal Hong Kong Golf Club at Fanling and the Clearwater Bay Golf and Country Club in 1981, shortly after it opened. The latter club is a short and pleasant drive ten kilometres down to the end of Clearwater Bay peninsula. Fanling is 36 kilometres away, near the border. The first Cup I ever won was the Super Seniors Trophy for over-60s at Fanling in 1998. Since then, I have won many other prizes on the Seniors' Circuit, playing with the Hong Kong Club Golf Section, and with the Rotary Organisation in Hong Kong.

The Seniors' Circuit was started in 2000 to give people aged 55 or over a chance to play all the courses in HK and across the border, at group rates. It started with only a few golfers; so my prize winnings almost covered my expenses. But the numbers expanded quickly to 200 and more. Competition became ever more severe and prizes more difficult to win.

The Hong Kong Club golf group was more relaxed, as many as 20 competitors at a time out to enjoy themselves rather than to compete, and several prizes for each event. With this group, Judith and I went on several visits into China, including the Mission Hills complex of twelve courses just across the border, and once to Hainan Island, which has another ten Mission Hills courses, all designed by different internationally famous golfers. I was part of a team that went to Singapore to play against three clubs there.

As it was my first visit to Singapore, I spent my spare time sightseeing. I got up early one morning and climbed the highest point on Singapore Island, Bukit Timah. Rising 532 feet, it was not a challenge, but it added another summit to my list. In one golf match, I had to drop out after nine holes because of an episode of atrial fibrillation. I enjoyed the outing, being with friends, playing new courses. As I don't drink alcohol, I chose not to join the late night revelry.

By 2015, my various accidents and illnesses, detailed later in this chapter, had reduced my golfing performance to the extent that my handicap had risen from around 14 to over 24. This makes me ineligible for major club competitions. Judith and I continue to play casual rounds with friends, and with our boys when they are in Hong Kong and when we are in the UK. Both Andrew and Richard are good golfers. I took part in the annual competitions of my Rotary Club and often won prizes. My most recent outing was the 2018 Rotary District competition with eight other members of my club. It was held on the coldest day of the year, in January, at Fanling, in torrential rain. My partner and I battled on to complete the round, some others gave up, but we won no prizes.

Back in Scotland, I play in the summer with a group of 'Amblers' at the Bruntsfield Golf Course in Edinburgh. This jovial band of middling to poor golfers turns out every Wednesday, come rain or shine, then enjoy a large lunch together at the club. One summer, with Judith, I joined the annual Amblers outing to a course at Milnathort in Fife, on a windy day with rain all morning. Judith and I both won prizes – a creative piece of scoring, possibly to welcome newcomers to the event.

Another, more serious event in Scotland is the Royals Trophy between teams of golfers from the Royal Hong Kong and Royal Calcutta golf clubs. The match was started by Joe Hardwick who had been a senior golf professional at both clubs; we all fondly remembered him. Two other golfing societies are based at the HKGC at Fanling. The Fanlingerers was started to raise money for war-blinded veterans of World War I. It had an annual match in Hong Kong and another in Scotland. As the numbers dwindled of both those blinded in World War I, and of the Fanlingerers, the society merged with the China Golfing Society. The Hong Kong meeting of the society raises money for Cheshire Homes. This charity was set up in Britain in 1948 by Leonard Cheshire, a former pilot of the Royal Air Force, to care for elderly people in the last stages of their life. Since then, it has established such homes in many parts of the world. In addition, the 200 or so China Golfing Society members living in the UK hold frequent meetings.

As a graduate from the medical school at Edinburgh I was

able to join the Edinburgh Medical Golfing Society in 2005. Matches are held every year at Luffness in the summer and Elie in the autumn. In 2006, I won the cup for the best net score. I was appointed the Captain for 2013, and donated a silver quaich, inscribed 'Edinburgh Medical Golfing Society', for the winner over the two meetings annually. The meetings were very social, a large lunch, a round of golf, and a large dinner to follow.

Climbing Mountains
Since my childhood, I have always been attracted by mountains. I started to climb as a young man growing up in Scotland and then during my summer experiences at hill stations in India. After retiring in 1993 from full-time work at the early age of 58, I was young enough to fulfil my ambition to climb the mountains that were accessible to a mountain trekker. Since then, I have climbed the highest peaks in 25 countries. The second volume of this autobiography gives full details of my climbs.

The Handover
In 1842, with the Treaty of Nanjing ending the first Opium War, China ceded Hong Kong Island to Britain. In 1860, a second 'Unequal Treaty' forced China to cede land on the mainland as far as what is now Boundary Street. In 1898, a further agreement leased the New Territories, 952 square kilometres in the south of Guangdong Province. Claude MacDonald, the British representative who signed the treaty, believed 99 years was "as good as forever" and that his government would never give it back. But, in 1984, the Joint Declaration between Britain and China agreed that, when the New Territories lease expired in 1997, the sovereignty of the entire colony would revert to China. Without the New Territories, the ceded Hong Kong Island and tip of Kowloon would not have been viable. The day of the

handover was historic in many senses—the final withdrawal from China of the strongest colonial power of the 19th Century and Britain's loss of its last major colony in the world.

It was a grey day in every sense of the word. Judith and I watched on television as the Union Jack was lowered at the Governor's house to the melancholy sound of a military band playing the bagpipes. The last Governor, Chris Patten, his wife and two daughters were in mournful attendance. We watched as the flag was lowered again to be replaced by the Chinese and Hong Kong flags at the Handover Ceremony in the Convention Centre on the harbour waterfront in Wanchai. Prince Charles had the unhappy duty to be present at the loss of Britain's last major colony, or rather dependent territory, the designation used at that time. Representing China were senior officials, including President Jiang Zemin and Prime Minister Li Peng.

The night before the Handover, Judith and I attended a concert performance modelled on 'The Last Night at the Proms' at the Royal Albert Hall in London. This last night is the culmination of an eight-week summer season of classical music and is broadcast by the BBC to a nationwide audience. The proms was founded in 1895. The orchestra played all the tear-jerking favourites, such as Elgar's Nimrod; we all wore party hats and sang *Land of Hope and Glory*. The proceedings were interrupted to applaud the appearance on stage of Sir Richard Branson, who had funded the concert and whose Virgin Airways flew the London-Hong Kong route.

On the night of the Handover, we were at the Hong Kong Club and attended a huge party. To escape the noise and revelry for a moment, I went outside and found a crowd in Statue Square, listening to speeches by Martin Lee QC and other members of the Democratic Party from the balcony of the Legislative Council building. It was rousing stuff. Through a megaphone, the speakers announced that the Basic Law had laid down a progression to democratic elections with universal suffrage, and that they, the Democratic Party, were determined to bring this about. More than 24 years later, it still has not happened. In 2021, an election for the Legislative Council took place under a new constitution with only the candidates assessed as loyal to Hong Kong and China permitted to take part.

We watched on huge television screens as Her Majesty's Yacht Britannia carried the royal party and former Governor Patten away from Hong Kong for the last time. On the stroke of midnight, 4,000 members of the People's Liberation Army drove across the border in 417 vehicles, including 21 armoured personnel carriers. There was no opposition and scant crowds on a wet night. The PLA also brought in four fast patrol ships and seven helicopters.

This was a very emotional time for a British person like myself, watching the Union Jack coming down forever; Hong Kong was a dependent territory of Britain no longer, but a Special Administrative Region, SAR, of China. I knew that, at any time, I could return to Britain if Hong Kong became a 'difficult' place in which to live. Judith and I were confident that the change of sovereignty would be smooth, and so it has proved. For many Chinese residents, emotions ran much deeper. They had left China to make a new life in Hong Kong and now were faced with the prospect of having to move again. Many did emigrate.

The People's Liberation Army, PLA, established its headquarters at Tamar, which had been a Royal Navy base for 100 years. It also took over other establishments on Stonecutters Island, Stanley Peninsula, Sek Kong airfield and sites near the border with China that was now simply a boundary. One of the new properties of the PLA was the Gun Club Hill Barracks on Gascoigne Road in Kowloon. It is the site of the United Services

Recreation Club, which was founded as a military club in 1911 and later had a mixture of civilian and military members. While the PLA owns the site, it has not intervened with the club's activities nor shares in its profits. It is open to PLA officers.

Since 1997, members of the PLA are very seldom seen outside their barracks. People believe that they are ordered to remain inside and receive modest pay that would buy very little in the shops of Hong Kong. The biggest losers have been the bars of Wanchai. For decades, British squaddies were among their best clients. On National Day, the PLA drill team puts on impressive exhibitions at the Hong Kong Stadium and it holds an Open Day once a year on Stonecutters Island.

Ghost Town
I had retired by the time the epidemic of Severe Acute Respiratory Syndrome (SARS) hit Hong Kong in February 2003. It was a frightening time; at the beginning, the causative agent was unknown, nor did we know the mode of infection or the proper treatment. I attended one meeting in which the senior government and health officials were agonising over what to do. Dr E. K. Yeoh, Secretary for Health and Welfare, was torn between publicising the problem and creating a general panic or holding back in the hope the epidemic would soon be under control. Hong Kong became a ghost town; the few people on the streets all wore protective face masks. The World Health Organization declared Hong Kong a 'No Go' zone for tourists, so the hotels and airlines were empty. Many doctors treating the infection became infected themselves. I avoided going into town and stayed in the relative safety of our house in the countryside. The WHO declared the outbreak contained in July 2003. In Hong Kong, there were 1,755 cases, including 299 deaths; it was the second-highest death and case toll after the Mainland of China.

A DOCTOR'S LIFE IN HONG KONG

The economy was badly affected by the loss of tourists and took months to recover.

In January 2020, a strongly related corona virus acquired from an animal host started an epidemic in Wuhan. It was the beginning of the 'Golden Week' Chinese New Year Holiday, when tens of millions of people return to their homes places aboard crowded trains—the ideal conditions for the spread of the virus. It came rapidly to Hong Kong and round the world. Again, Hong Kong was devastated economically.

Judith, Sons and Grandchildren
Since 1984, when she left hospital medicine as described in the last chapter, Judith has worked in public health, particularly in tobacco control policy. Her career includes being a Senior Policy Adviser to WHO on Tobacco Control. She has worked as a consultant with the Vital Strategies part of the Bloomberg Initiative, and also with the Bill and Melinda Gates Foundation in China, Qatar and Indonesia.

2008 Buckingham Palace: Judith's OBE

Since 1990, we have been the two directors of the Asian Consultancy on Tobacco Control (ACTC). Judith has written or co-authored twelve Health Atlases between 1993 and 2015, when she handed over the authorship to the next generation. She continues to be invited to advise national governments on tobacco control strategies. She has received many honours, including the Hong Kong Silver Bauhinia Star, Britain's Order of the British Empire (OBE) from Queen Elizabeth, many awards from China and a royal medal from Thailand. She has a curriculum vitae that runs to many, many pages. I enjoy and admire all her successes and count myself lucky to have such an accomplished and loving partner. In 2020, when her contract with Vital Strategies was not renewed, she embarked on a short assignment with Johns Hopkins University. She continues an ongoing project with the Global Centre for Good Governance in Tobacco Control (GGTC) and the WHO's Framework Convention on Tobacco Control Knowledge Hub, exposing tobacco industry tactics. She says she will be working until she is 100 years old.

Andrew always wanted to be a doctor. He finished his pre-clinical training at Cambridge University and went on to Glasgow University to complete his clinical course. He had wanted to study at Edinburgh University, like his parents, but Edinburgh had a quota of only two places for 'overseas' students as Andrew was labelled, and these places had already been taken with deferred entries. In 1990, Judith and I went to his pre-clinical graduation ceremony at Cambridge, and in 1993 attended his final graduation in Glasgow in the beautiful Bute Hall. We were proud parents indeed. Andrew decided to become a doctor in his early teens. He may well have been influenced by the enthusiasm Judith and I showed for our careers but we did not push him into Medicine. He was bright, competitive, a leader, so we had no doubt he would succeed. As indeed he has.

He chose to do his pre-registration year at Christchurch in New Zealand. We visited him there during the New Zealand summer in January 1995. He was with a large group of graduates who had, like himself, come from the UK; they replaced an equivalent number of New Zealand graduates who chose to go to Australia or the UK for their pre-registration year. He was clearly having a great time. One evening we all went to an open-air concert in a park at Christchurch. We sat on rugs spread out on the grass, ate well and drank excellent New Zealand wine and listened to fine operatic singing. Together we explored Christchurch, played golf, drove over to the west coast and lunched at the fine country estate of a Hong Kong friend. Tragically, since then, Christchurch has suffered two earthquakes, which damaged much of the city.

After he returned to Scotland in 1995, Andrew achieved his key objective by being accepted by a leading General Practice in Edinburgh. In 1998, he married Beverley Mee, a doctor who had qualified at Edinburgh University and trained in General Practice. Together they bought a small ground floor flat in Montgomery Street below Calton Hill in the centre of Edinburgh. In 1999, with parental help, they bought a large house with a magnificent garden in Haddington, a lovely town with 10,000 people, 27 kilometres east of Edinburgh. In 2018, Andrew was elected a Fellow of the Royal College of General Practitioners, in recognition of his many years of work, research and teaching abilities.

Our first grandchild, Kate, was born in 1999 and our second, Robbie, two years later. Because of Beverley's diabetes, both berths were induced prematurely, giving everyone anxious neo-natal weeks. Fortunately, the two children had no long-term problems. They attended primary school in Haddington, and secondary school at Loretto; it is a private boarding school on 85 acres, founded in 1827 in Musselburgh, eight kilometres east of Edinburgh. Despite her difficult start in life, Kate has turned out to be exceptionally bright; in 2017, she earned a place at Cambridge to read medicine. She qualified as a doctor in 2023. Robbie, too, is doing very well; he was a prefect in his last year at school. In 2020, he achieved three As in his subjects in his GCE examinations; he was accepted by Bristol University to read Electrical and Electronic Engineering.

Our second son Richard followed Andrew to Cambridge University. He completed a degree in Natural Sciences, then went on to Brunel University for a degree in Environmental Law and Management. His first job was as Environmental Officer for Cambridge University. In 2002, he married Kate Allan, his partner for ten years; he resigned from his job to take a world tour with her. Sadly, the marriage lasted for only a year. Subsequently, he wrote two books, worked in London for an environmental consultancy. Now he is with Mott MacDonald, Civil Engineers, living and working back in Cambridge. In 2007, he married for a second time, to Emily Vollans; they were happy for many years and blessed by the arrival of Ellen in 2010. Unfortunately, in the last few years, the marriage did not go well. Emily was very focused on her own start-up IT company; in 2016, she insisted on separating. At Christmas that year, Richard came to join us in Hong Kong on his own, not with the rest of the family as planned. It was a potentially unhappy time, but we made the very best of it for him. Since then, Richard has recovered much of his élan and lives in a splendid new eco-house in Cambridge. This is an environmentally low-impact home designed and built with materials and technology that reduces its carbon footprint and its energy needs. He shares care of his daughter Ellen with his former wife Emily. Richard brings Ellen with him when he comes to us for holidays.

Illness

In 1998, I developed episodes of palpitations and loss of energy. I went to see former colleague Philip Wong, an interventional cardiologist, who carried out tests, including a Holter 24-hour monitor; they showed I had a Sick Sinus Syndrome—the heart beating variously much too fast, or much too slow. He started me on medication; when progress was not impressive, he advised I should have a pacemaker. I hated the idea and sent an urgent message to Dr Hugh Miller, then a consultant cardiologist at the Royal Infirmary in Edinburgh, a classmate of Judith's and previously in Edinburgh a senior colleague to Philip Wong. In the nick of time, while I was in Philip Wong's office, he phoned back and talked over with Philip my history; he advised that I continue on a different medication. Gradually, my heart returned to a normal rhythm, thank goodness.

In 2009, I started having short episodes of palpitations, which made me extremely weak. I returned to Philip Wong and learned I was having paroxysmal atrial fibrillation. Over the next two years, the episodes became more frequent despite medication; they seriously limited my ability to exercise and play golf. In the summer of 2011, while I was in Edinburgh, the fibrillation became persistent. The local GP advised me that it would take months for me to see a cardiologist working with the National Health Service, so I continued medication and returned to Hong Kong for treatment. Philip Wong and a second cardiologist recommended I undergo an atrial ablation procedure. An electrical probe is inserted into the heart to selectively burn the lining round the pulmonary arteries in the left atrium; this cuts off the abnormal focus of the electrical activity that causes the fibrillation. The operation in November 2011 at the Adventist Hospital took more than six hours. The next morning my heart was in atrial flutter. The doctors were happy that the fibrillation had gone and informed me that an electro-cardioversion would be necessary to bring back sinus rhythm. The next morning I underwent a successful procedure. My three days in hospital were not something I ever want to go through again.

The combination of prolonged anaesthesia and heavy

medication left me unable to drive a car, or even to write properly, for some months; it is still affecting my balance and the strength in my legs. I continued the medications designed to slow the heart and inhibit irregular beats, and to prevent blood clots forming. In April 2013, one year after the first operation, I was diagnosed as having atrial flutter; the best first line treatment was another ablation. This was carried out successfully on May 2 at the Adventist Hospital by the same two doctors. A lighter anaesthesia lasting just two hours has led to a faster recovery of general function and a completely regular heart rhythm.

More than a million people in the UK have atrial fibrillation (AF); many experience no noticeable discomfort, many do not take medication and few of my age have the ablation surgery. My reaction to the arrhythmia was more marked, because I have naturally low blood pressure and a slow heart rate, leading to more noticeable dizziness and fatigue. The medical consensus now in the UK is that ablations should be considered earlier than they used to be.

In 2014, I had a fall resulting in acute chest pain and shortness of breath. This was a disastrous accident because it took place in the desert 300 miles south of Amman, capital of Jordan. I did not realise, initially, how bad the situation was. So I continued sightseeing in Petra, travelled to the Dead Sea for a swim, and spent a day viewing the Citadel in Amman. By the next morning, I realised that I could not keep going; I had an X-ray of my chest and saw the damage—two broken ribs and a collapsed left lung. Through Judith's contacts in the Amman conference she was attending, I was entrusted to the best chest physicians and surgeons in the city. I spent two days in hospital and came out with a fully expanded lung and one-way valve to keep it so until I could return to Hong Kong. Before departing, we joined the other conference delegates for their farewell dinner at a superb restaurant; the guest of honour was Princess Dina Mirad, patron of the King Hussein Cancer Foundation in Jordan.

In 2015, while in Edinburgh, I had a transient loss of power and control of my left arm. Doctors diagnosed this as a Transient Ischaemic Attack, (TIA), and treated it with an anticoagulant and a statin.

Dr Philip Wong, colleague, friend and my cardiologist for 20 years, died of lung cancer in 2021. This was a great loss to me and the medical community.

Episodes of AF became more frequent and difficult to control on different medications. In 2022 I had to accept the fact of permanent AF. I feel well and enjoy leisurely golf outings, but accepted that competitive golf and my mountain trekking days are over.

Keeping in Touch
After retiring from clinical medicine, I retained my membership of the British Medical Association, so that I could keep in touch through the pages of the British Medical Journal. I also maintained my Fellowship of the Royal College of General Practitioners, but I resigned from my Fellow Emeritus status with the American College of Chest Physicians. In Hong Kong, I retained membership in the Hong Kong Medical Association, and with the Hong Kong College of Physicians. In 2016, the College gave me an Honorary Fellowship, for the years I had contributed since the inauguration of the College, and particularly for my editorial work with the college's medical Journal, 'Synapse'. In 2017, I was honoured with Fellowship of the Royal College of Physicians of Edinburgh — coming full circle, having qualified in Edinburgh.

Judith had already been presented with an Honorary Degree from Edinburgh University; it was at a very impressive

JOHN MACKAY

2015 Honorary Fellow, HK College of Physicians

2023 Royal College of Physicians of Edinburgh, Fellowship, Signing of the Roll ceremony held at the Usher Hall, since the McEwan Hall was being refurbished.

Golden Wedding Anniversary
2017 was a gala year of celebrations. Judith and I feted our 50 years of marriage at a luncheon in the Balmoral Hotel in Edinburgh — it was the very same room in which we had held our wedding reception, in what was then the North British Hotel. Sixty people came, all wearing something gold. Judith and I had bought gold-embroidered jackets, very flamboyant, from Stanley Market, and I had a gold-coloured cravat. Guests brought photographs from the past they shared with us.

It was a great success. The huge buffet was all British produce, even the 'Champagne' was an English sparkling wine — our way to acknowledge the recent Brexit agreement with Europe. The table plan was a top table of immediate family, one table of 1961 Edinburgh University graduates, one of 1966 graduates, one of Yorkshire 'Roses,' one of Scottish 'Thistles', and one of Hong Kong 'Bauhinias'. I recited a poem and Judith gave a short welcome talk. At the end, guests took away the leftovers, Hong Kong-style.

The next day, we had another large lunch, at our home in 10 Garscube Terrace for all those who had come a long way. They included Judith's niece Anne and husband Jim Ahlman, and Judith's nephew Bob Westgate with his wife Fiona and six of their family from the US. The occasion showed the virtue of our commitment to keeping in touch with our family and university friends. Visits, letters and Christmas cards all had helped to keep relationships alive.

In August, Judith and I took the family to Cuba for a Golden Celebration; Andrew, Beverley, Kate, Robbie, Richard and Ellen came with us. We planned a schedule to suit ages seven to 80;

it worked out very well. During the first days in Havana, we did sightseeing tours and spent time at the hotel swimming pool. One day we walked to Castillo de la Real Fuerza built in the 1570s and housing a fascinating collection of water craft, from dugout canoes to great galleons, and collections of booty discovered from shipwrecks. We then queued for a long time in the heat to get into the Museum of the Revolution housed in what used to be the governor's palace. Again, a fascinating historical presentation of the history of the Republic, liberation from Spain, from Batista's dictatorship and Castro's rebellion. Outside the palace were displayed armoured vehicles, a tank and a ground-to-air missile that brought down a US plane.

That night we dined on the 9th floor, top of the hotel La Torre de L'Oro, where an especially good meal was enhanced by excellent performances by two opera singers, tenor and contralto, with piano accompaniment, a reminder that Cuba had centuries of occupation by a cultured elite Spanish society. The sunset was spectacular.

Then we took a drive 370 miles to the south coast to visit Trinidad, a UNESCO heritage site that is one of the best preserved cities in the Caribbean. To be more part of the community, we stayed in a Cuban guesthouse. We took a bus tour to the east of Trinidad, stopping at a hilltop, Mirador de la Loma del Puerto, providing a panoramic view across the valley, Valle de los Ingenios, backed by the Sierra del Escambray mountains. The valley was a bountiful sugarcane growing area with many plantations and sugar mills, and a train to carry the produce to the port of Trinidad at Ancon. The next stop was a plantation, San Isidro de los Destiaderos, built in the 1830s; it was very prosperous at one time but was abandoned when sugar became unprofitable after slaves were freed in 1886 and sugar beet production in Europe began in 1890.

We travelled east along the south coast, then north on the far side of the Escambray Mountains, through Sancti Spiritus and Santa Clara on the central plateau. Then we took a winding road to the northern coast, finally traversing an amazing 47 kilometre causeway that links off-shore islands, ending at Caya Santa Maria for a beach holiday. We swam, sailed, went scuba diving and built the biggest sand castle on the beach. Finally, we returned to Havana for the flight back to the UK. It was a fascinating trip. Two weeks after we left, two typhoons devastated Havana and the north coast of Cuba. We were so lucky.

Back in Hong Kong, Judith and I celebrated a Double 50th — her arrival in HK and our wedding in 1967. We held an evening reception at the Hong Kong Club for 120 people; we had champagne and a buffet, with decorations of golden balloons recycled from our reception in Edinburgh and scarves recycled from my trekking expedition at Simikot in Nepal. Everyone wore something gold, ranging from jackets and scarves to socks and a golden wristwatch; one guest brought and donated a broken golden cigarette lighter from his youth, long discarded since he stopped smoking! A continuous loop of family photographs ran throughout the reception, expertly put together by Judith. She and I both gave short welcoming talks. The party was a great success.

The two parties, in Edinburgh and Hong Kong, reflected the two worlds in which we have lived and the circle of family and friends we have in both. The Hong Kong gathering illustrated how far we had come from a social life in a 1960s expatriate bubble, to our working and leisure life within a very mixed community 50 years later.

Four-Masted Sailing Ship
Judith and I did not leave Hong Kong again until May of the next

year, 2018, to spend three months in the UK. We met family and friends, staying most of the time in Edinburgh, with five days in Fortrose on the Moray Firth with my sister Eleanore and her husband Les. Our son Richard and Ellen stayed with Carolyn Wilson, Eleanore and Les's daughter, and her family. Juanita, my brother Donald's adopted daughter, and her daughter Amira spent a week with us in Edinburgh. It was a great success.

In August, we returned to Hong Kong for a brief turnaround, before going to Bali in Indonesia for an Asia Pacific Conference on Tobacco meeting, at a gorgeous beachfront Hilton Hotel. The day the conference ended, Judith and I boarded the Star Clipper, a four-masted sailing ship for a memorable seven-day cruise around neighbouring islands. Each day we woke up at a different island, spent the day swimming, looking at coral, or venturing inland. Once we were driven to the edge of the caldera then walked to the top of Mount Bromo volcano, 2,329 metres above

2018 Star Clipper off Bali

sea level, in East Java, and once we hiked up to see the waterfalls on Sambawa Island. On the one day we spent at sea, the ship offered many activities. Judith was brave enough to climb a rope ladder up the main mast, the oldest person on board to do so. I contented myself by admiring my brave wife and walking along the bowsprit and onto the safety netting below it. The food was exceptional—each day different, with cuisines to suit any taste. The Captain, Sergey Tunikov, revelled in his job. An athletic 50-year-old dressed immaculately, he ran the ship with authority and led the dancing in the evenings. With all its 16 sails unfurled, the ship was a striking and romantic picture.

My return to Hong Kong was spoilt when I tried to renew my driving licence and was turned down by the insurance company because I was over age 70. However, a new medical certificate to say I was fit to drive convinced the insurers to renew. The sad prospect is coming closer when I will not be able to drive. In Hong Kong, this is an irritation, not a hardship because the public transport system is excellent; here Judith and Billy can drive me. In the UK, it will be more of a problem.

The year 2019 was an exceptional one for travel. In December, Judith and I spent ten days with all the family touring Jordan. It was a successful and fascinating trip that combined visits to Petra and other historic sites, camping in the places where Lawrence of Arabia lived, Wadi Rum, swimming in the Dead Sea and visiting Biblical sites and Jerash in the north of the country. After the holiday, we all flew back for Christmas in Britain with Andrew and family, and Richard, at Greenknowe, Haddington. This was our first Christmas in Britain for 20 years, one to remember. A serious downside was that Judith was unwell, suffering from influenza; she was only just fit enough to fly back to Hong Kong. The celebrations were punctuated by intense activity as Judith and I completed the sale of our Edinburgh house at Garscube

Terrace, and moved furniture to a new flat at Riversdale Crescent, also in the Murrayfield district of the city.

Selling the Garscube house was a very difficult decision. We had owned it for 40 years, filled it with furniture and artwork and nurtured the garden. It was a lovely, elegant, large, three-floored house in a prime residential area. But it was too large for two people. We accepted the advice of friends: "move now before you have to." In the moving, Andrew and Richard were a great help. Andrew took the few large pieces of good furniture, large trunks of family memorabilia and gardening equipment into his house in Haddington. We look forward to settling into our smart flat on Riversdale Crescent; it is ideally situated and equipped for an older couple, with lifts, an underground car park and it's closer to shops than Garscube Terrace.

But another question was when we would be able to live in it. Since January 2020, we lived in Hong Kong, unable to travel to the UK because of the coronavirus pandemic that had virtually shut down international travel. Unfortunately, we had been unable to see our children and grandchildren here or in Britain for nearly three years. We have enjoyed keeping in touch by getting together on Skype. Neither has Judith been able to attend conferences in person nor have we been able to make foreign trips. Initially, in 2020, in Hong Kong the daily infection rate was in single figures but it quickly became worse. Judith and I spent 90 per cent of our time at home and in the garden keeping busy. Golf courses, entertainment venues were closed, restaurants open only until 6 p.m. Only two people at the same table permitted.

Because of the government's swift action on contact tracing and isolation, border controls and vaccination drives, the situation was under control by mid-2021, and at the end of the year remained so. By then, Hong Kong had nearly 12,600 cases and 213 deaths; this compared well with nearly every country in the world. The virus has badly hit the economy of Hong Kong, as elsewhere. Things were worse in Britain, with more than twelve million cases and 150,000 deaths and a bigger blow to the economy. The government was having to make difficult decisions following Brexit, its decision to leave the European Union.

In 2023 a wave of new infections of the Corona-19 emerged, deaths rose to more than 10,000. The Hong Kong Government, like that of China, has been very exacting in its control policies. The rest of the world has opted to open up borders and try to get back to normal international commerce and tourism. As soon as travel restrictions were eased in Hong Kong, we returned to Britain for a three-month summer holiday. At last we saw our family again–and caught Covid.

Contributions

My contribution to the welfare of Hong Kong has largely been through my medical career and membership in medical societies and non-government organisations (NGOs). Drs Anderson & Partners, as provider of medical facilities to many engineering companies, had a role in supporting construction of the first cross-harbour tunnel in 1972 and the Mass Transit Railway. During its construction, workers endured hyperbaric conditions — high air pressure environments during underground tunnelling to keep the water out. They were required to have regular health tests.

One of my other duties was weekly visits to the medical clinic at the High Island reservoir in the Sai Kung country park. This massive project involved not merely building two huge dams, but also constructing conduits to channel water from the hills into the dam; in addition, there was tunnelling and laying of pipeline to take water from the dam to a water purification plant at Shatin. The spin-off benefit for me was a pass for access to the Sai Kung wilderness that was being opened up by new roadways. The only one who complained about this development was the head of the Outward Bound School, the redoubtable Jack Tucker; he regretted the loss of wilderness for his school activities. I made a point of being one of the last people to motor a boat into the bay before it was closed off by the High Island dam.

A related contribution was my time as a blood donor. This ended in 1986 when donors from Britain were barred because of the epidemic of Mad Cow Disease, a rapidly fatal disease of the brain that can affect humans. I still contribute monthly to the Hong Kong Red Cross Society to help their excellent work.

For many years, I have also made monthly contributions to UNICEF, the United Nations International Children's Emergency Fund, which is active in Hong Kong, the rest of China and the world. Sadly, there is never an end to appeals for help.

The World Wide Fund for Nature has an active branch in Hong Kong. Since 1983, it has managed the Ramsar Mai Po Nature Reserve, an important wetland area for migratory birds; it was recommended for conservation by Sir Peter Scott in 1964, and visited by Prince Philip, Duke of Edinburgh, in 1986. It now also manages a nature reserve at Island House in Tai Po, previously the residence of the Colonial District Officers, and a marine centre near Hoi Ha in Sai Kung. I have supported WWF directly and by sponsoring teams taking part in the Annual Big Bird Race — a competition to identify the most bird species in a single day.

I also contribute to OXFAM, the Oxford Committee For Famine Relief, formed in 1942 to provide relief food to Greece during World War II. Oxfam Hong Kong started in 1976, Oxfam International started, and I became a partner, in 1995. Since 1986, the fundraising highlight each year has been the Oxfam Trailwalker, a 100-km race for teams of four, over the hills of

Hong Kong from east to west across the New Territories on the MacLehose Trail. I have supported one team for many years, headed by a family medical friend, Dr David Kwan, who had worked with Judith at the United Christian Hospital in the 1980s. I have walked the whole trail, in stages and so I know how tough it is. The fastest competitors have run the trail in twelve hours. Over the years, the Trailwalker has raised HK$600 million for WWF.

Friends

Friends of Hoi Ha (FOHH) was started by a 'Dynamic Duo', David and Nicola Newbery, who live in an idyllic village on the north coast of Sai Kung Peninsula. They, Judith and I and others campaigned for preservation of the Hoi Ha area. FOHH has been hugely successful in leading the campaign resulting in the Government creating a marine preservation zone for the bay; it contains many corals and has therefore become a breeding area for marine life.

Friends of Sai Kung is a larger organisation that we help. It aims to limit overdevelopment and destruction of one of the most beautiful areas of Hong Kong, the Sai Kung Peninsula.

Friends of the Earth (FOE) was founded in 1971. The Hong Kong branch was founded in 1983 by a group headed by Linda Siddall and Henry Litton, Ruy and Karen Barretto, John and Nancy Rhind and others, including me. The impetus was the proposed construction of a nuclear plant at Daya Bay in Guangdong province, 50 kilometres northeast of the urban areas of Hong Kong. It was to provide electric power to Hong Kong and neighbouring areas of China. The project had been proposed by Lord Lawrence Kadoorie, chairman of the Hong Kong China Light and Power Company; it was agreed to by Chinese leader Deng Xiaoping and endorsed by British Prime Minister Margaret

Thatcher. There was a huge negative reaction in Hong Kong because any accident at the proposed plant would bring nuclear fall-out down the prevailing winds to Hong Kong.

A major meeting was organised by FOE (HK) to debate the issue, with two Members of Parliament from London, one for and the other against. One of them stayed with us, the other stayed with the Henry and Linda Lytton. Linda vowed that, if the project went ahead, she would have to leave Hong Kong. It did: and she moved to Perth, Australia. When Linda resigned as chairperson of the FOE Board, I was elected Chairman, to be followed by Christine Loh. FOE projects in which I was involved were planting trees in the New Territories hills, and demonstrating against a proposed development in the pristine fresh water wetland, Sha Lo Tung Valley.

From its tiny expatriate beginning, the organisation has grown to 12,000 members in Hong Kong. It does great work campaigning for clean air, reforestation and recycling of waste. Ms Mei Ling, who campaigned in Hong Kong and China for FOE, was named in the United Nations Global 500 Roll of Honour on World Environment Day 2000.

Trees For Life (TFL) is a charity founded in 1989 in Scotland, dedicated to restoring the Caledonian Forest. I first met the founder and inspiration of this project, ecologist and wild-life photographer, Alan Watson Featherstone, at its headquarters in Findhorn, Moray, in Scotland. Only two per cent of the original forests remain in Scotland, so the project has a long way to go. It has planted more than 2 million trees already. Animals that used to live in the forests, like red squirrels and beavers, are being reintroduced successfully. In 2004, I was involved with planning Alan's visit to Hong Kong. He gave a number of inspirational talks, and took pictures of mangroves to add to the wonderful calendar that TFL sends out each year. The many people involved in this work can quote to you what was said by Nelson Henderson, a famous Scottish rugby international. "The true meaning of life is to plant trees under whose shade you do not expect to sit."

Chapter Eleven
March 1999
India Revisited:
A Nostalgic Journey of Rediscovery

In March 1999, my brother Donald and I made a nostalgic journey of rediscovery back to India where we had lived for nearly six years as children during World War II. In late 1939, to escape the war in Europe, my mother travelled with Donald and me to join our father in India. We stayed there until the end of hostilities in August 1945. Then, it was a British colony. In 1947, it became an independent republic.

My father joined the Indian army in 1919, having served in a British regiment in France in World War I. He retired as a Brigadier in 1947, just weeks before the end of British rule and the division of the country into Pakistan and India. The Japanese had entered the war in December 1941. When they conquered Malaya, they interned my uncle Culbard, an officer with the Chartered Bank. He had sent his wife and two children to Australia, where they spent the rest of the war. My uncle Rowand was an accountant with the Burmah Oil Company. He lost all his possessions to the

Japanese, but escaped with his wife Gwen and son Alastair, who joined us in India for some of the time from 1942.

Donald and I planned the 18-day trip in 1999 to revisit the places where we had lived during those wartime years and retrace some of the routes we had travelled. We chose to stay in Delhi, Simla, Darjeeling and Kalimpong, all places where we had lived with our parents during the war. We selected March as the best month to go — before the heat of the summer on the plains, before the monsoon, and after the coolest part of the winter. It was Donald who chose the tour agency and itinerary, in consultation with me.

Donald and I were both very keen to make this trip, to rekindle the memories of what had been an amazing part of our childhood, memories that were beginning to fade. Importantly, we wanted to spend time together having lived most of our adult lives on separate continents, Donald in Africa and the West Indies, myself in Asia.

The trip was a huge success. We had found all the places where we had stayed half a century before. We had savoured again the sights, fragrances and music of India. I had enjoyed the time spent with my brother and also felt sure that he had enjoyed being with me. During the next years we became even closer during the regular visits Judith and I made to Donald and Jo in Cornwall.

Donald and I had planned another trip together to explore Mayan civilization ruins, but it never happened, and will not happen: Donald died in 2013 after a stroke. He was aged 80.

1980 Donald's OBE Buckingham Palace

JOHN MACKAY

Prologue

Several events just before my departure conspired happily to prime me for the trip. On March 1, I arrived in London with Judith, after attending a conference in Las Palmas, the Canary Islands. The next day I followed a procession of 200 Hari Krishna devotees, singing and dancing down Oxford and Regent Streets; they were dressed in weird costumes and carried a shrine containing a religious effigy. That evening I deepened my Indian orientation with an excellent dinner at our son Richard's favourite Indian restaurant in Cambridge. The following day I enjoyed another fine Indian meal at the Bengal Lancer, with my cousin Barbara Thomson, just up the road from her house in Raglan Street, London. Finally, on the day of departure, March 4, I met David Simpson, a friend and anti-tobacco activist, for lunch. He brought me a gift, *The Hill Station*, a novel by J.B. Farrell set in the Indian town of Simla a hundred years ago.

London: Thursday March 4, 1999

Donald and I met outside the Royal Academy to view the exhibition 'Monet in the 20th Century'. It was a wonderful display of his lily pond, Venice and Thames bridges series. Afterwards, we joined Judith at the residence of The Royal College of Physicians, where we had been staying for a few nights. At 7:30 p.m, we left for Heathrow, driven by Mannie, the Nigerian who drove a hire-car for Judith when she is in London. Our plane was a British Airways Boeing 747. Our economy class seats seemed narrower than usual. We left at 10:25 p.m. and did not get our meal until 90 minutes later — an uninteresting Indian vegetarian dish that was all there way on offer. Breakfast was yoghurt, a Danish pastry and tea, meagre fare compared with the meals on Cathay Pacific.

To Delhi: Friday March 5th

It was 12:45 p.m. local time when we arrived at Delhi International airport. We were met by Ravi Sandhu, Tours Manager of the Mysteries of India travel agency, plus a car and driver. The roads into the city were bad, surprisingly so because a country usually wants to make a flattering first impression. We were driven through the centre of New Delhi to our hotel, The Oberoi Maidens, in the old town not far from the Yamuna River. It was a grandiose, British Raj-style building, with four storeys and a palatial layout.

Our first stop after check-in was the hotel pool. The water was surprisingly cool; after a quick and refreshing dip, we were happy to sit out in the afternoon sun, drink tea and listen to the birds. There were the ubiquitous sparrows, crows, and pigeons, but also others more typical of India—kites, parakeets and peacocks. A family of monkeys stalked along the wall dividing the hotel from the park next door. There were few guests, all European. It appeared that the main tourist season did not start untill Easter.

We ate supper in the hotel coffee shop and were early to bed.

Delhi: Saturday March 6th

I slept poorly. The room and bed were comfortable but I was chilled by a draught from the air-conditioner. I was up at sunrise, 7:00 a.m. Always an early riser, Donald was up before me. Breakfast was a substantial buffet.

Our guide for the morning, Ashok, picked us up with a Sikh driver in an Ambassador, non-air-conditioned car. The first stop was close by the Red Fort. A huge gateway led through the immense red sandstone walls to a covered market place, to which the ladies of the court could go, but no further. Across the garden was the Diwan-i-Am, a public audience chamber of ornately carved red sandstone with wonderful Persian-style archways.

Walking past this, we found an inner garden, the private council chamber, the Diwan-i-Kas, where stood the peacock throne, and the royal chambers.

The buildings were of brick, faced with white marble, originally inlaid with semi-precious stones. With Persian carpets on the floor, it must have looked sumptuous. The buildings looked weather-stained and run down; the gardens could have been lovely if the fountains and water-courses had been flowing. But the Yamuna River is now a mile or so away, not flowing past the palace walls as it used to, and there is a critical shortage of water in Delhi.

Our next stop was the Jama Masjid, the largest mosque in India, at the edge of Old Delhi, within sight of the Red Fort. It was also built of red sandstone. The spacious, raised, prayer floor was surrounded by a cloister pierced by gateways on the north and east; it faced the mosque building to the west in the direction of Mecca.

From the mosque, it took us nearly an hour to travel the few yards to the main road through the crush of traffic leading to the Chandni Chowk, the market of Old Delhi. There were lorries, cars, motorbikes, three-wheeled motorcycle-driven tuk-tuks, bicycle-powered three-wheel pedicabs and porters hauling great loads on two-wheeled carts. The hooting of horns was incessant. The mood was not bad tempered, more philosophical; this was the daily routine. Every vehicle was overloaded. The maximum I counted was a group of nine schoolchildren on a pedicab designed for two passengers.

Not far away, we stopped at the Raj Ghat, a parkland area near the Yamuna River where national figures are buried. We visited the tomb of Mahatma Gandhi, a black marble slab on a plinth in the centre of a garden; it had a surrounding embankment enclosing 100 square yards. It was simple and serene. Many pilgrims were visiting to pay their respects. Indian music was playing. Indira Gandhi was buried in an adjacent area. She was Prime Minister in two stretches for nearly 16 years, until her assassination on October 31, 1984 by her own Sikh bodyguards. This was after the Indian Army laid siege to the Sikhs' holy Golden Temple in Amritsar to root out extremists and separatists.

We were driven to nearby Connaught Circle, to what I suspect had been the guide's objective all day — the tourist shops from which he made a commission. We were ushered into a carpet shop where we saw many beautiful pieces, including an intricately patterned silk carpet for £2,500. Donald was much taken with it, but realised that it would cost more than the price of our entire trip and gracefully declined even the final offer of £1,600. We were then taken to a jeweller's shop where again temptation was thrust before us but we resisted. By this time, we were ready to return to the hotel for lunch and a siesta. On the way, we passed a fleet of 30 lorries packed with farmers coming to a demonstration. That was all Delhi's traffic needed, I thought, a demonstration to block the already chaotic roads.

After a much-needed siesta, we had another swim and afternoon tea by the pool. Later we had an outdoor buffet and BBQ, with entertainment from a two-man group assisted by a tape-recorder. When the drummer was accompanying the taped music, it was fine. But, when the tape was switched off and the second man played his guitar or electric keyboard, the effect was terrible — he could hardly play either instrument. We concluded he must be a relative of the manager.

JOHN MACKAY

To Sikandra and Taj Mahal: Sunday March 7th
We were up before dawn, and down to breakfast at 7:00 a.m., having packed sufficient gear for an overnight trip to Agra. Our smart young Sikh driver picked us up at 9:30 a.m. in his Ambassador car, the workhorse of India's roads. It was 20 years past its prime as a design, based on the original Morris Oxford. It took an hour of steady driving to leave the Delhi conurbation and reach the rice fields of the vast Gangetic Plain. The road was a dual carriageway, with a raised central divide planted with grass and bushes, the bougainvillea in bloom.

Traffic discipline was appalling. The main problem was the slow lane which carried the occasional very slow vehicle, drawn by a water buffalo, a camel, or sometimes a donkey. There were also tractors pulling trailers with bamboo supports holding up canvas walls as high as a double-decker bus; they were bulging to twice the width of the trailer with huge loads of straw.

Because of this, no lorry or car in the fast lane would move into the slow lane, unless hooted at from no more than two feet behind its rear bumper. All the lorries were decorated with brightly coloured designs and lights, with 'BLOW HORN' written on the back. Cattle posed an additional hazard as they nonchalantly grazed on the central divide or sat chewing their cud—safe in the knowledge that, because they were sacred animals, no one would drive into them. Finally, and most bizarre was a lorry barrelling down the fast lane towards us—on our side of the road. I could only think that, fearful of being late for their delivery, the driver left the congestion on their side of the road and chose the fast lane on the other side.

After two hours of this 'who-dares-wins' progress, we were glad to stop for a rest at a tourist restaurant and outlet selling curios. Refreshed and nerves steadied, we set off again for Sikandra, home of the tomb of Akbar, possibly the best of the

Mogul emperors. He fought numerous campaigns to enlarge the empire but is considered to have ruled with religious tolerance and justice. His tomb reminded me of Angkor Wat, Cambodia. A perimeter wall enclosed a wide area of parkland. A raised causeway led to the central mausoleum, approached by a flight of steps. A lower floor had numerous crypts with graves of lesser personages. The second floor had a large central chamber containing Akbar's grave; side chambers contained more graves. The architectural style, we were told, was a mixture of Hindu and Muslim. The decoration was not elaborate.

Our guide for the next two days had joined us at Sikandra. He was the son and grandson of guides and took professional pride in his briefings. The facts sounded as if they had been learned by heart and came out as if read from a textbook, each syllable carefully pronounced. He said he also conducted tours in French. The drive through Agra revealed a large number of schools and colleges, some with the look of British public schools and reportedly famous in India. We stayed at the Trident Hotel run by a French company. It was a modern two-storey building set in a square surrounded by an attractive garden and swimming pool. The floors of the public rooms were laid with an elegant dark green marble and the furnishings were tastefully functional. It was to be the only modern hotel we stayed at throughout our trip.

We had a quick lunch at the hotel and then were picked up by our guide and car to go to the Taj Mahal just three kilometres away. We had to park one kilometre short of the gate, so the engine fumes did not damage the marble of the Taj. It seemed a good idea; but it did not work because an electric bus was not immediately available. We declined donkey or camel transport, and our guide piled us into a tri-car three-wheeled vehicle.

The red sandstone gatehouse led into a wide open square surrounded by cloisters; it was there courtiers and visiting nobles stayed during religious festivals. To the right was an imposing gateway of red sandstone decorated with white marble, before which we queued for a security inspection. Once through the gateway, we had our first view of the Taj Mahal, a building of amazing beauty, entirely of white marble. The central building, attended by four minarets, seemed to float at the end of the long pool that ran from the gateway to the Taj. On either side of the pool were strips of lawn dotted with ornamental trees; outside them, the paved walkway was raised above the level of the gardens, enclosing them by walls on three sides. The fourth side was bordered by the Yamuna River.

The marble of the Taj was intricately decorated with inlays of semi-precious stones in flower designs and quotes from the Koran. In the central, octagonal burial chamber was the gravestone of Mumtaz Mahal, the favourite wife of Shah Jahan, who died bearing his 13th child.

Shah Jahan is buried next to her. He had planned a lavish tomb on the opposite side of the river in black marble, linked by a silver bridge to the Taj Mahal. But his son Aurangzeb, who had killed both his own elder brothers, deposed him at the age of 68 and held him under house arrest in Agra's Red Fort for the last eight years of his life. He saved a considerable amount of money by burying his father beside his beloved wife. In Mogul times, the gardens had fruit trees whose produce were sold to pay for the tomb's upkeep. During our visit, the gardens were laid out in British style, with beds of flowers and shade trees. As a child, we visited the Taj and I remembered vague images. Seeing it again, I was even more impressed with its beauty.

The next stop was the Akbar Marble Arts Emporium. We were shown a row of craftsmen working on marble, chiselling out the recesses into which the precious stone inlays were meticulously fitted. We were told that they used the same techniques as their forefathers in the decoration of the Taj itself. They were apprenticed from the age of seven to ten, received no schooling and were retired at the age of 40 when their eyesight started to fail. One showed how the tip of his fourth finger had become deformed from years of working with chisels. The showroom downstairs was an Aladdin's cave of beautifully decorated white marble tables. I bought one small enough to carry home, with an intricate design of green flowers.

The Red Fort at Agra was very similar in construction and architecture to the one in Delhi—both were built by Akbar. Both had a great outer wall, the outer garden, the inner garden with the royal dwellings in highly decorated white marble and the walls at the rear of the palace towering over the Yamuna River. The captive Shah Jahan would have had the consolation that he could see the Taj Mahal from his apartment.

Our final stop of the day was a carpet shop where we were sat down and given the ritual cup of tea; ardent salesmen tried hard to get Donald and me to "fall in love with a carpet". Certainly they were very beautiful, woolen ones almost as fine as silk. The salesmen's cause was not helped by the fact that we were tired after a very long day and were interested only in getting back to the hotel. At dinner, the head waiter, an Indian, was very chatty; he told us of his entire career which included the Oriental Hotel in Bangkok and the Mandarin in Hong Kong.

Fatipur Sikri: Monday March 8
By 8 a.m., we were on the road again, through the streets of Agra and then the farming land to the west, to Fatipur Sikri. This was a city built by Akbar on a hill where a holy man had predicted that he would have a son; at that time, he had despaired of having a male heir. The city was used for 16 years and then abandoned for lack of water. The palace was on a huge scale, with a large building

enclosing a courtyard for his favourite wife, a Hindu who bore him a son and two other children, and very much smaller apartments for his Muslim wife and his Christian wife from Goa.

There was a stone pillar in the main square to commemorate his favourite elephant; it was trained to kneel on convicted criminals—a particularly nasty way to go. On the western side of the palace was a mosque, fronting onto a huge open-air prayer space. On the south wall was the tallest victory arch in India. A marble tomb marked the grave of the venerable holy man.

The buildings were all of red sandstone, intricately carved. As a child, I had also visited the palace but I remembered only a confusion of ruined walls on a hot day. We said farewell to our guide. He had been pleasant and knowledgeable, and deserved his golden generous gratuity.

The drive back to Delhi was pleasant while we were on country roads but, once we re-joined the Grand Trunk Road, it was back to the maelstrom. We had several near-misses, and two large lorries lying on their side on the road were evidence that not everyone was so lucky. Back in Delhi, we had a brief look at Claridges Hotel, very posh, before returning to the Oberoi Maidens in time for a swim and afternoon tea by the pool. We ate supper at 7 p.m. and packed, ready for a 5 a.m. start the next day.

To Simla: Tuesday March 9

We were up at 4:30 a.m. and into our Ambassador car, with a new guide, at 5 a.m. The drive through the old part of the city with the sparse night-time traffic was uneventful; we reached the railway station in just half an hour. The station was a grubby place, huge, with hundreds of people sleeping on the ground, and a raised pedestrian walkway connecting multiple platforms—a cross between Waverley Station in Edinburgh and a refugee camp. We followed our guide and porter, who carried our two suitcases one on his head and one in his hand, to platform four where the Himalayan Queen of Northern Railways was waiting for us. I took a photograph of the large diesel engine, and the large Sikh driver and his engineer who happily posed for me. We were in the only First Class carriage out of 10 carriages. We had cushioned reclining seats but they were battered, covered with plastic and not very comfortable. The train left on time at 6 a.m. and was into the countryside before the sun came up, golden, through the morning mist. The train travelled slowly, stopping at many stations, long enough at each one for passengers to buy food and drinks from platform vendors. At 11:30 a.m., we reached Kalka, at the edge of the plains, and changed to the narrow-gauge train that was to take us up the mountain to Simla. This train was even slower, and for good reason. It climbed increasingly steep mountainsides with gradients of as much as 1:33. There were 800 bridges and 90 tunnels in the 96 kilometres it took to climb 7,000 feet. In our compartment were two sets of newly weds; both brides had their hands and feet still decorated with designs in henna. They chattered the whole way, billing and cooing and giggling foolishly. On the train, there were only four other Europeans as the tourist season did not start until May. It was a chilly 9 degrees Celsius.

At Simla station, we were met by Shere Ali, our 71-year-old who took us to the Oberoi Clarke's Hotel on the Mall. This was a comfortable old hotel which must have been functioning in the 1940s. After check-in, we strolled along the Mall for half an hour before going back to the hotel for a good supper.

Simla: Wednesday March 10

I had a good sleep and awoke refreshed at 6:30 a.m. I had been warm in the bed farthest from the window. Donald cannot sleep or ride in a car without an open window. I needed stretching exercises to loosen up my muscles, stiff from hours of travel. I had no altitude sickness, headache or nausea at 2,130 metres. Simla would have had to be several thousand metres higher for me to feel any of those symptoms. From the window, I could see much of the town spread out on the mountainside. A seven-storey concrete skeleton of the planned Supreme Court building a couple of hundred yards away partially blocked the view. The better houses were at the top of the ridge; going down the mountain, the standard became progressively humbler. Those at the bottom had to cope with the refuse dumped by those above them. Most houses in the bazaar area were made of wood with corrugated iron roofs. Storey was piled on storey in a haphazard way that invited disaster from earthquake or fire.

Simla was the capital of Himachel Pradesh Province, and a popular holiday resort. But the shops, even on the Mall, suggested that customers were not wealthy. At the start of the 20th Century, the Mall was reserved for Europeans and their native sedan chair porters. During our visit, there was still segregation — only members of the legislature were allowed to drive cars on the Mall. This meant our taxi could not approach the front door of the hotel, but had to stop on the road below.

At 9:30 a.m., our driver picked us up to start our search for the house in which we lived during the summer of 1942. We knew that it was inside an army cantonment called Jutogh. Donald had a picture showing Dad standing in the garden of the house, with a church, largely hidden by trees, in the background. That was enough information for our driver. He took us straight there. The house was at the end of a short, tree-lined driveway with the church on higher ground to the left, behind a hedge. The metal bar gate was flanked by stone gateposts and low walls, all painted white. On the left gate post was a notice 'Jamal Lodge'; on the right was the name of presumably the last occupant, Colonel Patnaik. It had clearly not been occupied for some time; as the gate was on the latch, we walked in.

The drive swept in a half circle to the front of the house, with a garage on the left close to the garden wall. The house was a square bungalow with deep verandas at the front and back, and two small dormer windows at the front. The walls were white and the roof of red, flat, metal sheeting, pre-dating corrugated iron. Large bow windows on the other side of the house must have enhanced the living and dining rooms, looking out across a deep valley to a panoramic view of the Himalayas. To the right of the house, down a covered stairway, was a stone house with blackened and cracked walls, the kitchen. A short, covered passage connected this to the servants' quarters.

Memories came flooding back — of the flowers that used to spill over the circular bed in front of the drive. I remembered that I got up one morning to find that my fat little pony, Judy, which I rode to school each day, had produced a foal — quite unexpectedly to me. We called him Punch. The only sad memory was of seeing my mother, on the window seat in the sitting-room, weeping. She had just received a telegram telling her that her younger brother, Innes, had been killed in the war. He had been the last and the favourite of her four siblings. My mother's parents were already dead, and she was just 42. Donald remembered much more — going to the nearby village market to buy dog food and playing with the village boys in the concrete reservoir, one of them fell in and nearly drowned. He remembered being sent to a boarding school on the other side of town. As we prepared to leave, I saw that the man who had noted our arrival was talking to an army officer and gesturing in our direction. It was time to go. I was sad to leave a place that had revived such strong and affectionate memories.

On our way back into town, we stopped at what used to be the Viceregal Lodge and had become The Indian Institute of Advanced Studies. The driver set us down outside the impressive green wooden gateway and parked outside. Donald and I walked up a long wooded drive, with the bank on our left decorated with refuse from the buildings above. At the crest of the hill, the ground opened out, with a wide lawn on the left and The Lodge, a massive structure, on the right, facing south. It was built in 1884-88 in the 'Scottish Baronial' style, four storeys in grey stone; the first three were fronted by stone balconies.

A guide ushered us into the main hall, a dramatic area rising to the full height of the building and panelled in oak. It had three great display areas at the third-floor level; the cloth panels still showed the imprints of the array of guns and lances that had been there during the British Raj. The instruments of war had been removed to a museum in Delhi. We were allowed to look through glass doors into the vast banqueting room to the rear, and the ballroom at the western end of the hall at ground level. These areas were now a library and reading room. To the left of the entrance was a large reception room panelled in teak and having an intricately panelled walnut ceiling. To the right of the entrance was the council chamber where constitutional negotiations took place in 1945 between Lord Wavell, the Viceroy before Lord Mountbatten, Jawaharlal Nehru, Muhammad Ali Jinnah and other political leaders. Mahatma Gandhi was there as an observer. On display were many photographs of the participants. The talks failed, so we were told, because Jinnah insisted that all Muslims in government must be members of his Muslim League, not of the nominally secular Congress Party.

This failure paved the way for the separation of India into two separate countries at Independence in 1947.

The gardens were extensive. Wisteria climbing on the balconies were not yet in bloom, but already flowering were jasmine, azaleas, rhododendrons and daffodils. The indoor tennis court and croquet lawn looked unused. It was extraordinary that this massive and self-confident building, placed on a Himalayan mountain-top, had been seat of government of the Indian subcontinent for six months every year. On our way back to the hotel, on the wooded north side of the ridge, we saw our only deer. It was a sweet little animal of reddish brown colour with big ears. "Looks very succulent!" Donald said. For lunch, we chose the Indian option—no venison. At lunch and dinner, there were only two choices, one Indian, one European. Both were good. We were almost the only guests in the hotel. Perhaps, when it was fuller, they offered a more varied menu.

After our siesta, we set off again, walking up the Mall to the Ridge where Donald phoned home from the Telegraph office, then on to the Oberoi Cecil for tea. I was searching for what must have been there in the Simla of the past—a genuine Olde English Tea Shoppe. The Cecil was a recently completed, almost empty, five-star multi-storey hotel built around a handsome enclosed atrium. It did serve afternoon tea—Orange Pico, blended from the finest Darjeeling and Siliguri gardens—along with freshly baked, light-as-a-feather current scones with thick cream and strawberry jam. Bliss. Much refreshed and reinvigorated, we walked the three kilometres back along the Mall in the sunset, as monkeys climbed over the buildings foraging for food. For dinner, we ate the European option—very good, too. I started the book I had bought at a hotel in Agra, *The Far Pavilions* by M.M. Kaye, a romantic novel set in India after the Indian Mutiny. Three generations of Kaye's male relatives appear to have been in the

Indian Army, so the feel is authentic. It is extraordinary how first the East India Company and then the British army controlled such a vast country for so long

Simla: Thursday March 11
I was woken by the sound of monkeys running over the corrugated iron roof. After a breakfast of fruit juice, porridge, coffee and toast for me, and also, invariably, an omelette for Donald, we set off to climb Jakhoo Hill. At 2,455 metres, it was the highest point at Simla. We zig-zagged our way up through an area of cheap, council houses and then higher through pine forest and rhododendron trees. When we reached the top, we found an uninteresting temple to Hanuman, the monkey god. We were accompanied by many monkeys. The panoramic view compensated for the temple. To the south, we looked out over valleys and hills towards the plains; to the west, to Simla straddling its ridge; to the east to Sanjauli and its hill-top temple and to the north to the distant snow-capped high Himalayas.

We had walked up steadily without any breathing problems. Donald had been concerned with my exercise capacity after I had an earlier episode of sick sinus syndrome, but I think he was reassured after this outing. We descended along Jakhoo Road, along a shoulder of hill leading to The Ridge, past some fine old houses. We sat on the terrace of the Ashiana restaurant on The Ridge and had coffee before Donald set off to find the other house where we had lived in Simla. I went to look for picture post cards. There was a very poor selection on offer, the most interesting one being of The Ridge in snow.

We lunched back at the hotel. Donald reported he had found the site of the other house. It had been in the grounds of the Grand Hotel just east of The Ridge but had now been redeveloped. After our siesta, I walked to the telegraph office and telephoned

Saltburn in Yorkshire. I talked to Granny Longstaff; Judith was out. Reception was perfect. At 5 p.m., Donald and I went out again to explore the bazaars. Down the hill from the Mall was the Lala Lajpat Rai Chowk—narrow alleyways lined with little shops selling clothes, jewellery, groceries, pots and pans, spices and schoolbooks. All were geared for the local market, not tourists like us. The people were more interesting than the shops. Many worked for the provincial government, some were visitors from the plains, others were coolies bent double under heavy loads supported by a single thong around their foreheads or across their chests, some grey-bearded and old before their time; and schoolchildren. Simla seemed to have dozens of schools. The children were neatly dressed, boys in grey flannels, white shirts, ties and blazers, and the girls in uniform dresses. The Raj lives on. Judith rang back that evening. All was well at home.

Simla: Friday March 12
It was another fine day, cold enough in the morning to wear a jacket, but hot, shirt-sleeve weather in the afternoon. In the morning, we walked the three kilometres along the Mall to the city museum. It was set in a beautiful Raj-style house of two floors, with white walls and a red metal roof, set on the hill top next to the Viceroy's Lodge. It had a rich collection—stone temple carvings, metal statues of deities, photos of Buddhist stupas and monasteries, ancient weapons, swords, daggers, pistols, rifles and blunderbusses, mostly homemade. One room full of photographs and quotes of Mahatma Gandhi, and pictures of the 1945 Shimla conference and its participants. Another room was dedicated to modern art, of no appeal to me anyway: a collection of ancient coins, the most impressive being from Champa in the first and second century BC, using techniques of Greek origin.

I was particularly intrigued with the miniature paintings in Persian style from the Rajput kingdoms of Kangara and Champa. The ladies and nobles of court typically held flowers, wine cups or weapons for their portraits. After 1780-90, however, they are all portrayed smoking hookahs, presumably the height of sophistication at the time.

We walked back to the hotel, had a large curry lunch and then slept until it was time to go out for our evening stroll along the Mall, take photographs and people-watch. Children were amusing. Little ones in uniform with satchels on their backs ran down as children do, but with their arms outstretched in front, like a gesture of supplication, to stop their packs falling off. Hotels had names suggestive of Britain—Willow Brae, Crystal Palace and Rock-Sea. But we were 2,000 miles from the coast.

Monkeys were coming down from the woods in family troops; they were not aggressive, just looking for scraps and some were mangy. I watched one sari-clad woman creating a scene because a monkey was blocking her path. A relative throwing stones chased it away. Usually people just ignored them. Outside the government offices, a demonstration was taking place, seemingly a daily occurrence. This one consisted of about forty men sitting down and chanting slogans in response to their leader. They were surrounded by dozens of police with lathis, four-foot-long wooden staffs, officers with revolvers, and a few mounted police on what Donald said were fine Arab horses with extravagantly in-curling ears. That night we were in bed by 9 p.m., in preparation for an early start the next morning.

Back to Delhi: Saturday March 13

We were up at 6:30 a.m. for a quick breakfast, and ready at 7:45 a.m. for the porter to carry the suitcases down the road to the car, two cases on his head and another under his arm for

150 yards, for the going rate of 40 rupees (about 60p). We set off at once in the Tata minivan with Shere Ali at the wheel as usual. The estimated time for the 92-kilometre trip from Simla to Chandigarh was more than three hours. That was plenty of time to catch our train leaving at 12:40 p.m. for Delhi. We made it in two and a half hours.

Ali was fine driving down an open road. But whenever he came up behind another vehicle, he went berserk, hooting the horn and forcing his way past, despite blind corners, oncoming traffic or anything else. We were immensely relieved to reach the plains at Kalka and thankful for Ali's quick reflexes despite his age. The remaining distance to Chandigarh was on flat and straight roads, but not fast because of the heavy traffic. Much of the way was past the army's Northern Command headquarters.

We waited in the van for the next hour eating our packed lunch. This was a good decision. When we did go to the station, I checked out the First Class waiting room. It was a small room with 20 uncomfortable-looking plastic chairs against the walls. Six people were sleeping on the floor, and an unbelieving English tourist was videoing the scene on his camera.

The train, the Shatabdi Express, was grubby but the soft reclining seats were comfortable. The trip to Delhi, 270 kilometres away, took only three hours, with one stop. It was a stark contrast to our train from Delhi to Kalka that took five hours for only slightly further. For the first part of the trip, I sat next to an ex-Gurkha officer in the Indian Army; he became a professor at Waikato University in New Zealand. He had been on guard duty during the 1945 conference in Simla.

Lunch was provided on the train — curry, rice, pickles, a pot of yogurt, a piece of fudge and tea. It tasted fine, so I ate it all despite misgivings about hygiene. When we reached Delhi, the tour guide and the driver met us at the carriage door and drove us back to the Oberoi Maidens. After we checked in, we headed down to the pool for a swim and afternoon tea. There seemed to be a problem with the water supply because the pool surface was low and festooned with leaves; the attendant was netting them in a half-hearted manner. We joined the Saturday evening BBQ, sitting on the lawn, as far away as possible from the music.

To Darjeeling: Sunday March 14
Our tourist agency Mysteries of India car arrived promptly at 8:30 a.m. to take us to the airport. Our next destination was Darjeeling in West Bengal, where we had spent one summer as children. On our way to the airport we went via the Old Delhi army cantonment where we had spent a winter or two. It was a huge area with guards on the driveway entrances, so we gave up the idea of locating the house where we had once lived.

We flew Jet Airways, the biggest privately owned airline in India, in a new Boeing 737-400; it felt like business class. There was no smoking or alcohol; there was a reasonable meal during the three-and-a-half-hour flight to Bagdogra in Bengal, with one stop on the way. We flew down the Ganges Valley; the river was very low, judging by the wide sandbanks.

The airport was on the edge of the plains more than 400 feet above sea level and about 600 miles from the sea. The terminal building was old, to be replaced soon by a new one. Construction materials were all over the car park, so it was particularly difficult for driver Roshan to work his way out. He and the guide were young Gurkhas. We were given the option of going on the main road through Siliguri, which was longer and had heavy traffic, or by the old army road that was quicker but steeper. We opted for the second, the scenic route. Unfortunately, we did not have the option of going by the 'toy train', as we had done in 1944. The last monsoon had washed away part of the track and it had not been repaired. Soon we regretted our decision.

The road ran initially on an embankment over the floodplain, then crossed a bridge over a wide, dry, riverbed full of people gathering stones, gravel or sand for building purposes. Soon it was into the foothills, past a tea plantation named Margaret's Hope, and climbing ever more steeply. At the frequent hairpin bends, the protocol was that the car climbing should take the outside of the curve, whether or not that was on the left side of the road, and the descending car would take the inside. This sensible rule was understood by everyone, so it was safe, as we appreciated, except during a few very anxious moments. At intervals, we met lorries and jeeps coming down with loads of excited young men. They were waving the green flags of the GNLF, the Gurkha National Liberation Front, the leading contender in regional elections. The GNFL was founded in 1980 with the aim of a separate Gorkhaland state. In 1988, it gave up this demand after the creation of the Darjeeling Gorkha Hill Council. We climbed through rain forest vegetation, then bamboo and then into conifers. We passed through a straggling village of poor houses on a knife-edge ridge. There we joined the railway route. The rails ran above, then below, the road, and sometimes along the side of the road itself. At 2,000 feet, we hit a traffic jam caused by a mass of vehicles coming down from a political meeting of the GNLF in the next village. With the help of the police, it took an hour to get through the jam; the crowd was good humoured and patient, so there was no drama.

At first view, Darjeeling, population 120,000, was a depressing mass of shoddy buildings spread out on the hillside. The thick, dry-season haze obscured any view of Kanchenjunga that might have compensated. At the very top of the ridge, the Windamere Hotel was a pleasant surprise. We had come to India to rediscover our childhood, and the Windamere certainly helped. It was unchanged from what it must have been like in the 1940s, with its wooden walls, iron roof, spacious but primitive bathrooms, fans, no functional telephones in the rooms and certainly no TV.

A footpath led up from the driveway, through a colourful rock garden, to the reception area, offices and dining room. Across the passage was a two-storey wooden house. On the ground floor was the 'Music Room Lounge' with a piano that could not be played, Maisie's Tea Room, and a bar. Up a fine flight of stairs were bedrooms. The walls were covered with old photographs of the building of the railway, Darjeeling scenes at the turn of the century and seating plans for dinners honouring dignitaries such as the Governor of Bengal and sundry rajahs.

We were in the annex, a row of rooms just across the public path to the shrine at the top of the hill, and looking out on what was no doubt a wonderful view on a clear day. A corridor ran the length of the building at the front, doors leading off into small lounges. A second door led into the bedroom, with a bathroom at the rear. The high ceiling was of wooden boards painted white, with cracks showing between the planks — Donald thought they were to let the rat droppings through. At night, staff lit a fire in a small fireplace, by the time-honoured method of laying pieces of wood, soaking them in paraffin and lighting a match.

Dinner was served at 7:30 p.m. We had cream of asparagus soup, roast beef and Yorkshire pudding and two kinds of vegetable, a Tibetan noodle dish with cauliflower, carrots and turnip, and bread and butter pudding. It was a happy combination of the traditional English and exotic East. There were nine other guests who looked as if they were, like us, relics of the days of the Raj.

Darjeeling: Monday March 15

I was up at 6 a.m. to see if I could get a view of Kanchenjunga, 28,169 feet (8,586 metres). from Observatory Hill, just up from the hotel. Alas, the haze was just as dense as the day before. I heard that those who had taken the 5 a.m. trip to Tiger Hill had seen the peaks above the haze. We had decided not to join the tour because we had clear memories of having seen the snow peaks under perfect conditions in the past. We saw the great ice walls of Kanchenjunga rising up from behind the wide valley north of Darjeeling, with Everest an insignificant bump far to the northwest. Observatory Hill was heavily wooded with tall firs and cryptomeria japonica. At the top was a temple festooned with prayer flags. Long strings of them hung from every tree in colourful disorder. Monkeys played or sat grooming each other.

The hotel did well with flowers. I noted jasmine, camellia, coral azalea, roses, primroses, nasturtiums, zinnias, and fuchsia. Breakfast was full English, of course. A nice touch was the marmalade jars with beautiful floral decoration, from Worcester potteries.

The day before, when we had left the minivan, Donald had pointed out with some concern that its rear tyres were completely bald. The driver was puzzled that bald tyres should be considered a problem; every other vehicle on the road was running on threadless tyres. Nevertheless, this morning, the minivan had new tyres. The project of the day was to find our old house at Takdah. We set off down the road we had travelled the day before, then branched left onto the Kalimpong road for a few kilometres. There we turned right, down a very poor road of potholed tarmac for eight kilometres, through forests of fir trees and, later, tea gardens. Deciding we had gone too far; we retraced the road back to a huddle of houses at a T junction. Roshan found an old villager who confirmed that we had reached the right spot. It turned out that he had been the barman at the Tea Planters Club for many years, and certainly in the 1940s. Donald now recognised the surroundings and led us straight to our old house, on the hill just above the road. It was looking very smart, now part of a Green Fields school. It had been closely surrounded by tall firs but these had nearly all been felled and young trees were growing in their place.

There was another group of people looking at the house. We recognised two of them as an elderly English couple also staying at the Windamere. With them was the headmaster of the school and a couple of teenage girls doing a gap year as teaching assistants. The English couple was on an inspection tour for their organisation to check that all was well with the girls.

The Planters Club was a sad ruin. The roof was beginning to fall, the windows had all been taken out, and the interior had been stripped of all its fittings, including the floorboards; only the ornate metal fireplaces were left. Built in 1911, it must have been a great social centre in its day, with a large lounge and dining rooms, a billiard room, a saloon bar and a long verandah overlooking a wide lawn, tennis courts to the side, and through a border of trees, to the south down the Teesta valley.

Across the road, the playing field of Griffiths School had become an orchid nursery. Donald and I both remembered sitting very quietly in the bushes on the hillside above the field; we watched the schoolboys, armed with rifles and fixed bayonets practice running at stuffed sacks of straw. They shouted fiercely as they ran and plunged their bayonets into the dummy figures. It was wartime; the Japanese were not far away at the borders of Assam. Those boys might well be called up to fight when they left school. We were sitting so quietly that a cock pheasant walked right past us without noticing us. I remembered going up the road to the junior day school run by two Miss Hills. We caught butterflies and recalled the horrid black leeches that jack-knifed across the grass to get at you, and the hammer-headed horse leeches that were huge and scary. My cousin Alastair and his mother Gwen were there with us, Donald remembered, at a time when Mother went down to Calcutta to be with Dad.

We drove on down the road between the club and the school playing field to the village and tea garden of Rungli-Rungliot. Just before we came to the village, we stopped at a roadside shrine with brilliantly painted panels, and waited as a gang of tea pickers carrying their wicker baskets, passed by.

The village was just a string of houses and shops on either side of the steep road, and a flat area to one side where I remember going one market day. There was the body of a buffalo lying in the marketplace, its head still attached to the stake to which it had been tethered when the butcher had beheaded it with a huge kukri. We stopped at a teahouse for Donald's obligatory mid-morning cup. A lorry drove past with a gang of GNLF supporters waving banners. The drive back to the hotel took an hour. The bumping and lurching along the poor roads with the horn blaring had left me with a headache; after lunch, I had a siesta. Donald and I then had afternoon tea and cakes on the terrace, very civilised.

Afterwards we walked down to the Chowrasta, the equivalent to The Ridge in Simla. Thin, defeated-looking ponies stood with their heads drooping as they waited for people to take rides. The only building of antiquity left on the Chowrasta was a lovely old wooden structure that had become an upmarket library. Narrow lanes led off down the hill. A planters' club, built in 1868, was above the road on the left. I walked as far as the railway station to take photos of a couple of the 'toy-train' engines; they looked like museum pieces but were still operating. There were many trekkers/back packers, unlike in Simla.

I passed one building, the 'Hotel Nirvana', an appropriate name for Darjeeling. From street stalls, I bought a 'Mackay tartan' scarf of wool for 25 rupees, about 35 pence, and a plastic device that could draw hologram-type patterns.

A folk song and dance troupe entertained us on the terrace of the hotel for the hour after sunset. They put on a great show. The leader was a bearded extrovert who inspired his band with his energy and with his playing of a box-bellows accordion. He was accompanied by a flautist, a guitarist and a cymbalist and drummer, two female singers, a male lead singer who was a real troubadour, and four young dancers in a variety of brilliant costumes. There was a good dinner to follow, and then time to sit in front of the bedroom fire and read my book.

Darjeeling: Tuesday March 16
A heavy haze again obscured the mountains. At 6:30 a.m., I walked up to the top of the hill to take pictures of the Buddhist shrine, garlanded in prayer flags, then walked back to the hotel on the circular route round the hill.

At breakfast at 8 a.m., I ate too much, including fried eggs and trimmings, and felt uneasy for the next two hours. I made a mental note not to eat the cooked portion in future. Donald had, without fail, the omelette, with no after-effects. Guide Binay and driver Roshan arrived at 10 a.m. to take us on a city tour. First stop was a Tibetan refugee and handicraft centre. We watched wool being carded, spun, dyed and woven into carpets; elsewhere there was leather work, knitting, and wood carving. We drove past Tenzing Rock, on our way to the zoo; on it was a group of trainee mountaineers practicing rock-climbing. Nepali Sherpa Tenzing Norgay had been the first person to ascend Mt Everest with New Zealander Edmund Hillary, in 1953. At the zoo, we saw breeds of mountain goat, deer, leopards, and snow leopards, pheasants, and red panda bears, which are really a type of raccoon. The Siberian tigers were sleeping out of sight. The zoo was on a wooded ridge, with a large area in which the animals could move around, and it was well sign-posted. Still, it was sad to see them confined.

Next stop was the Himalayan Institute Museum. It contained a fascinating display of the Himalayan Mountains, the climbers and their equipment and the different routes they have taken up Everest. The Institute's main purpose is to train mountaineers. We had tea nearby at a cafe beside an imposing statue of Tenzing Norgay at the summit of Everest. We walked back to the hotel for lunch, a fine meal topped by a pudding of jam roly-poly. Our well-deserved siesta lasted until 3:30 p.m.

Armed with a sketchy road map of Darjeeling, we set off for the Botanical Gardens. It was a long way down the hill through areas of poor slums. The gardens were surprisingly large, with a wide variety of trees and azaleas and rhododendrons and an orchid house. But it was a cloudy day draining colour from the garden, so our overall impression was dull. It was a long climb back. Some of the houses were old stone structures, built in the 1920s. Fifty years before, they must have been handsome, but now they were dilapidated; they were surrounded by shanty town structures. Small boys played cricket on every available spot of open ground, flat or sloping.

An unexpected sound from a music shop was Bob Marley singing *Wake Up, Get Up*—not inappropriate with regional elections taking place the next day. Back up at the Chowrasta main street, we had a look inside the Planters Club. It opened in 1868 and used to be THE place to stay. It was a long, two-storey wooden building, painted a dull green. At the entrance, we stopped at a Members Only sign and asked the porter if we could come in. He called the manager who was most obliging.

He was disappointed that we did not want to rent a room, and sorry we could not come in for a drink at the bar because it was closed in accordance with government regulations that no alcohol could be served until after the election. However, he would be happy to rent us a VIP room where we could have a drink on the quiet. We thanked him for the generous offer and explained we really wanted just to take a look around inside his famous establishment. Suitably flattered, he summoned a houseboy to show us around. It was all a planters' club should be — silver trophies in display cabinets and hunting trophies on the walls. Peering through a glass door to an unlit room, Donald was surprised to see it was full of people enjoying a drink. He had found the bar. We left, happy in the knowledge that the spirit of the Tea-planter lives on.

Just up the road was a restaurant with an inviting display of chocolate Easter eggs and bunnies. But Donald was interested only in honey bananas, his favourite dish from the past. Alas, the menu did not have honey bananas, so we had a cup of tea anyway. We sat in a window that should have had a view of Kanchenjunga, but it was lost in the haze. We returned to the Windamere Hotel and Marie's Tearoom, in time for tea, carrot cake and shortbread. I talked with the architect overseeing the completion of a 10-room extension of the hotel. He came from Lucknow, and spoke knowledgably about the growing water shortage in the Delhi area. We had dinner at 7 p.m. by candlelight in the attractive old dining room. Apart from the three-course English meal, there was a strange-looking Tibetan dish, which I declined. Afterwards, we returned to our room, to sit by the fire, read and write, and early to bed.

Darjeeling to Kalimpong: Wednesday March 17

It was Election Day, and all was quiet—no speeches on loudhailers, no banners, no parades, and no open bars. Just as well. Our guide reported there had been a riot on the previous night and the leading candidate in Kalimpong had been arrested for having eight armed guards in his entourage; the limit was five. As usual, Donald was up at 6 a.m. We were packed, breakfasted and ready for the road when our guide, Binay, arrived at 8:45 a.m. The previous day he had spent going down to Siliguri where his mother had just undergone surgery to remove her gallbladder. I was impressed it had been a laparoscopic procedure. All had gone well.

Roshan set off on the same road he had taken us the previous day, but stayed on the Kalimpong road, instead of turning right to go down to Takdah. The road descended through forests at first, then tea gardens; many were idle because of a labour dispute between the tea-pickers and owners. Lower down in the Teesta valley, we entered teak forests. We stopped at a spectacular lookout spot from which we could see up the valley and see the great Teesta River, running brown between the high green banks of forest, and its junction with the clear waters of the Rangeet. At that junction was the sandbar where we had picnicked in 1944. Donald remembered that, when we set off in the car from Takdah, we were in mist and rain and so did not take butterfly nets. By the time we had descended into the valley, we had left the clouds behind, and the air was full of amazing butterflies. I remembered with him the frustration of driving through clouds of them without being able to catch one. At the lookout we found the couple we had met at Takdah, Richard and Imogen Parker. They were en route for Kalimpong, to inspect a school, but travelling slowly. Their Jeep was an original, built in 1948, with one careful driver and its original engine.

Further down, the road became steeper and steeper, eventually entering a double corkscrew-type section, like going down a multi-storey car park. We emerged close to river level, joining the main road from Siliguri, the main trade route for centuries from the plains of India up to Gangtok in Sikkim and on into Tibet. We crossed the Teesta on a new concrete bridge and stopped on the far bank at a restaurant for our mid-morning tea. Roshan had his breakfast— rice and curried potatoes. The establishment also was the base for a white-water rafting outfit. Their rubber rafts were stacked on the roadside. A plaque recorded that we were only 300 metres above sea-level—this was amazing, given the distance we were from the sea.

The branch road to Kalimpong started just up-river from the bridge. It climbed for twelve kilometres up the eastern side of the valley, again through teak plantations and tea gardens to the ridge where the town perched.

Kalimpong had been at the centre of the wool trade between Tibet and India, until the border was closed after the Chinese occupied Tibet in 1949. It consisted of a single main street on the crest of the ridge, flanked by a thin layer of dilapidated houses. A church dominated the northern end of the street. There were many police, because of the rioting between the GNLF and pro-Indian parties the day before and during the previous election. We stayed at the Himalayan Hotel, an historic place owned by the Macdonald family for 100 years. David Macdonald had been with the Younghusband expedition into Tibet in 1904, and had spent his life in Tibet, Sikkim and Bhutan. When he retired, he turned his family home into a hotel. There were twelve double rooms, a large lounge and dining area; the hotel was a veritable museum of Tibetan artifacts. The attractive two-storey stone buildings had oak ceilings, teak pillars and walnut and teak furniture. It was surrounded by a garden full of flowers. Two spectacular white and pink bauhinias competed for attention with a huge chestnut tree in extravagant flower. Even a monkey puzzle tree was in blossom. Azaleas bloomed; tree ferns and a stand of gigantic bamboo towered over beds of ixora, sweet peas and lillies. Unfortunately, haze obscured our view of Kanchenjunga.

We had an excellent lunch of chicken broth, chicken curry, potatoes, spinach, chickpeas, daal, rice, chapattis, and fruit salad—all of this merited a well-earned siesta. Refreshed, we drove to a Red Hat Buddhist monastery at the top of a nearby hill, surrounded by an army camp. It had been built in 1957 at the order of the chief of the sect, as their new headquarters, following expulsion from Tibet and a temporary sojourn in Bhutan. The central temple, a three-storey structure, was surrounded by a wide courtyard bounded by stone dwellings where the monks and trainees lived.

We went back to the hotel to have tea comfortably on the ground floor verandah, surrounded by flowers. Binay and Roshan were both interested in politics; they explained that the bad feeling locally was due to an influx of Bangladeshi immigrants, who were displacing the Gurkha people. This had led to call for an independent state for the Gurkhas. They said this had caused fighting the last year but, in this election, the GNLF had moderated its demand for independence to a call for increased local autonomy. The GNLF had a green flag with a Buddhist cross, the Communist government of West Bengal had a red flag with a hammer and sickle, a third party had an elephant motif and the fourth a weighing scale.

After dinner, we rejoined the world by watching BBC World Service on television. The main item on the news was the sacking of six people from the Olympic Committee, and reprimands for nine others for accepting bribes. I was bearing up well to the travel — stiff in the mornings but loosening up by being bounced around in transport during the day. The altitude was not a problem, and my digestion worked perfectly.

Kalimpong to Sikkim: Thursday March 18
Our first stop was a cactus nursery in Kalimpong. The owner reported happily he had 1,500 varieties of cactus, imported from around the world, and also exported. The variation in appearance was astonishing, and the way that brilliant flowers suddenly appeared from the most unlikely looking plants. We drove back down from the Kalimpong ridge to join the main road at Teesta Bazaar, and turned right to follow the river up the valley. It was low water, exposing areas of rock and gravel either side of the fast-flowing stream. Many people were out gathering building materials from the riverbed. We crossed three major landslides. During the monsoon season, the road must have been blocked for weeks.

At Rangpo, we stopped at the border to show our entry permits. Sikkim is now a part of India, but it was independent until 1975 and still had some autonomy. At Singtam, we left the Teesta valley and headed up a tributary towards Gangtok, the capital. The roadsides were attractive with flowering bushes, bougainvillea in brilliant pink, coral, purple, and yellow; poinsettias and hibiscus.

> Placards on the roadside exhorted drivers to drive carefully:
> Life is short. Don't make it shorter.
> Drive slow.
> Better be late, than be the late.
> Attention avoids accidents.
> If married, divorce speed.
> Speed thrills, but kills.

Blow Horn.
Arrive in Peace, not in Pieces.
Alert today, alive tomorrow.
Donate blood to the Blood Bank, not route NH 31.

and encouraged the legion of road repair people:
Excellence is never an accident.
Quality is our policy.
Inconvenience regretted (of road works):
Well done is better than well said.

Much of the time, the road was carved out of a cliffside, but sometimes ran across the valley floor. The village homes had walls of wooden board or wattle and mud, and roofs of thatch. The terraced fields were bare or grassed for feeding livestock, waiting for the rains to come when the rice planting could begin.

Gangtok was a disappointment. It was an unprepossessing mass of newish buildings spread over a hillside facing west; the roads were poorly kept and traffic was dense, dusty and dirty. Perhaps 30 years ago it would have been the fabled Shangri-La kingdom we were hoping for. Now it was an extension of India. Maybe Bhutan had taken note and been warned. We checked in at the Norkhill Hotel, said to have been a guest house for the VIP visitors of the Chogyal, the King. It was a long rectangular block, with the entrance at one end leading into a large reception-cum-lounge area; it had the feel of China or Tibet, rather than India. We had to go through the dining room to the far end of the building, to the stairs which led up to the bedrooms on either side of a long corridor.

At the front of the building was a carefully laid-out terraced garden. Beyond it the ground fell away to a large stadium in which a crowd of thousands was listening to the heavily amplified speech of the local Chief Minister. The speech went on for hours. Binay explained elections were just coming up. The Chief Minister was telling everyone what a good job he had been doing and, more to the point, handing out to those qualified a gift of money to buy a home. Many of the people were wearing Tibetan clothing, a colourful woollen wrap-around with a high collar, trousers, and knitted woolen headgear.

The Chinese-style lunch was tasteful and spicy. After a siesta, we had tea in the front garden. Happily for us, the Chief Minister had finished his speech, and the playing area of bare earth was occupied by youngsters playing cricket and football. We watched the sun go down, or rather disappear; it was smothered by the haze that was still blocking our view of Kanchenjunga. The owner of the shop in the hotel, ever hopeful, insisted that we inspect his goods. He certainly had beautiful Tankas, paintings of Buddhist deities, for up to £300. One thing that caught my eye was a silver medallion with the head of George V on one side with the words "George V Kaiser i Hind", and a hill fort on the other. The term "Kaiser i Hind" seemed dubious, so I did not buy it; however, I found out later that it was correct.

Sikkim: Friday March 19
At 9 a.m., we set off in our mini-van for the Phodang Monastery of the Black Hat sect. This turned out to be a 40-kilometre nightmare journey on a road that promised to disappear at any moment down the side of the mountain into the ravine below. Several sections were over parts that had been swept away by the last monsoon rains. The monastery was on a flat area on a shoulder of mountainside. The square main building in the centre was surrounded on three sides by single-storey shacks that housed the monks and schoolrooms for the students. The third side was bordered by rows of tall bamboo stakes carrying

dozens of prayer flags. As we began our inspection of the main building, monks were chanting their lessons, juniors in one room and seniors in another, all in saffron robes. When we came out again, classes were over and the juniors behaved like any group of youngsters getting out of class. They rolled over in the grass, laughed and talked — happy to have their pictures taken.

The Black Hat sect believes in an element of magic in their religion. We were shown a special room where the walls were decorated with many paintings of threatening Kali-like figures. We retraced our route back to the hotel for lunch. After lunch and a siesta, we were driven up to the top of the ridge at Gangtok to look at a Red Hat sect monastery. It was smaller than Phodang but very colourful. Next stop was a Tibetan handicrafts centre run for children who had no other schooling. By way of contrast, we went round a flower exhibition, with magnificent orchids on display.

Back at the hotel, I joined a meeting of the only Rotary Club in Sikkim. It had 18 members, very friendly. At their request, I gave a short talk on the Rotary Club of Kowloon, and the political situation of Hong Kong. Donald declined to attend. He had been a Rotarian in St. Lucia. I re-joined him for supper at 7 p.m. The meals were good but never on time. Always it was coming — "In 15 minutes, Sir". Back in our room we watched television — that was a mistake. The world was full of grief and disaster, from Kosovo onwards; even sport had been sullied by the rigged heavyweight fight between Lennox Lewis and Evander Holyfield. Lights were out by 9:30 p.m.

Sikkim to Kalimpong: Saturday 20th March
It was another hazy day. We were on the road at 9.00 am, with our first stop the Tibetan Centre for Religious Studies; it was housed in a handsome purpose-built Buddhist style building,

surrounded by trees, on a quiet hill-top. We saw a vast collection of Buddhist scrolls, Tankas, religious relics and Buddha images. I bought a small book on Tibetan medicine, in English which I hope will help me understand better the great tome I bought in Lhasa years ago. On top of the next hill on the same ridge, we walked round a large stupa, brilliantly white in the sunshine with a gold spire. On one side was the picture of the famous monk to whose memory the shrine is dedicated.

Driving down the hill, we paused at a cliff top where political executions used to take place. The offender was stuffed into a sack and thrown down the cliff. This barbaric act was still being carried out in post-Chogyal times in 1975, when there was a Chief Minister. We drove up the valley, crossed the river and went back along the opposite side to Rumtek Monastery, 23 kilometres and about an hour's drive. This was an important teaching centre for the Black Hat, Karmagupa sect. In 1940, the 16th head of the sect, Gyalwa Karmapa, had left Tibet and had come to Sikkim after some years in Bhutan. He founded the Rumtek Monastery in 1962. He is buried at Rumtek and he is remembered in a shrine, the Golden Room; it contains a gold chorten, a Buddhist shrine, situated on the second floor at the back of the main temple. Within the sect, there was a dispute over who should succeed him. One of the two vice-heads sold out to the Bhutanese and accepted a supposed Bhutanese reincarnation of the 16th head of the sect. In the end, he was discredited and left the priesthood to go into business.

From the car park, we walked up the hill to a cluster of dwellings; a lodging house for pilgrims; curio stalls; and a tea house where we stopped for our ritual mid-morning cup of sweet milky tea. The monastery was a substantial establishment. A two-storey cloistered building containing the monk's cells surrounded a large quadrangle, at the rear of which was the main temple. It was richly decorated inside by paintings on the walls and ceiling, Tankas, hangings of the five colours denoting earth, sky, water, fire and metal, and a thousand Buddha images. Photographs hung over the shrines dedicated to the Dalai Lama, Gyalwa Karmapa and to the young 17th reincarnation. Behind the temple was a flight of stairs leading up to another brilliantly painted building, the University for Buddhist Studies.

On the way back, we stopped on the roadside for a picnic lunch. Looking across the valley, we could just make out Gangtok through the haze. We were on a hillside of rice terraces, dry and waiting for the rains. Above us on the slope was a typical farmer's dwelling. The walls were made of wattle and daub, and the roof of corrugated iron. Alongside it were a wooden barn for animals and a hay stack. We watched as three people slowly climbed up the hill from a small patch of woodland, bent double under loads of wood. They were passed by other wood carriers on their way down.

The drive back was not pleasant. The minivan was beginning to show signs of strain. A grating sound that had concerned us the day before had been replaced by an ominous clunking; Donald believed it was something to do with a break drum. Roshan was driving too fast, all over the road, cutting corners and hooting his horn at anything on the road. Our original schedule had been to spend a second night at Gangtok, and to drive all the way down to Bagdogra airport the next morning in time to catch our plane for Delhi at 2:30 p.m. Having seen the state of the roads between Kalimpong and Gangtok, we negotiated by phone with the tour director in Darjeeling, at an added cost of half of what he wanted to extort, for a change in schedule.

We felt eminently justified in this when we came to the huge landslide on the road to Kalimpong that we had inched our way over on the way into Sikkim; it was completely blocked. A petrol tanker had come too near to the edge of the road; it had given way, leaving the tanker tilting helplessly over the drop to the Teesta River. In front of us, a long queue of vehicles was waiting, while bulldozers ploughed a new road out of the friable sand and shale slope, uphill from the stricken tanker. Eventually, they made a new "road" and we gingerly followed the other vehicles over it to safety.

We arrived at Kalimpong at 4 p.m., much relieved to be in one piece. Since the Himalayan Hotel was full, we checked in at the Silver Oak Hotel; it was run by the Elgin Hotel Group, who also ran the Norkhill in Gangtok and the New Elgin in Darjeeling. It was the same size and rectangular shape as the Norkhill but better laid out; the stairs to the upstairs bedrooms led up from the reception area. The garden had been laid out by the same person, who had created a profusion of colours, with azalea and bougainvillea, on the terrace and down the hillside.

After a reviving cup of tea, we set off to explore. The main street was crowded with people coming from a political rally; the loudspeaker was still blaring. I saw dozens of police, on duty to prevent trouble; and half a dozen back-packers. I walked to the far end of the main street up to a church. It was a Church of Scotland building, boarded-up and with grounds unkempt. Nearby was the graveyard, overgrown and uncared-for. One headstone was for a Rev. McFarlane who had died in 1986, in his forties, perhaps the last minister of the kirk. Next to it was the church house "donated by Mrs. Anderson." I could not help wondering how this town must have been 50 years earlier, with a thriving British community of resident tea planters, colonial officers, military, and merchants and missionaries; and in the summer, all the visitors came from the plains, prepared to make the arduous journey to Kalimpong to enjoy the cool, healthy air. I remembered being similarly affected by a Church of Scotland building in the hills of Zimbabwe. That one was still in use, with the graveyard immaculately maintained. In the grassy hollow between the church and graveyard in Kalimpong was the inevitable game of cricket.

Back at the hotel, Donald told me that he had found the telegraph office, and phoned home to talk to Jo. He had learned that their son Innes was in trouble with his finances, being £8,000 in debt. Why could Jo not have kept this to herself till Donald reached home? It made him very depressed.

We too had our own money problems; we did not have enough rupees for tips to Binay and Roshan. Donald and I were due to part company the following day, Sunday; although I had plenty of UK and HK money, there was nowhere to change it. Happily, Donald had traveller's cheques which the hotel agreed to cash.

Kalimpong back to Delhi: Sunday 21st March
The name Kalimpong has various derivations according to Donald's 'Lonely Planet' guide:
>Stronghold of the Minister of the King of Bhutan.
>From the name of a local plant.
>Black ridge.
>Place where we play. (In the Lepcha tribal dialect.)

The drive down the mountain from Kalimpong to the bazaar on the main road was now a familiar one. Once over the Teesta bridge, instead of turning right towards Darjeeling, we turned left, down the west bank of the river, covering new ground. We were told that, when the Teesta valley road was blocked, as it frequently was in the rainy season, vehicles had to detour up the Darjeeling Road to reach Siliguri. We soon found out where the problem lay. The road was carved out of very friable mountainside and in a constant state of repair and rebuilding at the site of landslips. There were encampments of wattle and daub shacks for the Nepali road-workers every few miles. There were hair-raising sections where there was nothing more between the minivan and the Teesta River than a foot of dirt road.

We stopped for our mid-morning cup of tea at a hamlet straddling a tributary of the Teesta. I took pictures of women carrying great bundles of firewood, and others working on the half dry riverbed collecting stones. After three hours of slow and careful driving, we came to a spectacular single-span bridge over the river; it was the only road access from Bengal to Bhutan and Assam. A few minutes later and we were on the plains. The Himalayas were behind us. A long, low railway bridge spanned the Teesta, now spread out over a wide bed on its suddenly leisurely onward progress to join the Ganges.

We drove through Siliguri, and the inevitable, large Indian Army camp, to reach Bagdogra airport at 12:30 p.m. Binnay helped us through the formalities; and we parted company with him and Roshan—both were happy with our thanks and their tips. Our Jet Airways plane left on time at 2:30 p.m. for the flight to Delhi. When we had reached cruising altitude, the pilot told us that we were just 200 metres higher than Mount Everest. At last we were above the dust haze and could see Kanchenjunga.

Further west, we could see Everest, and later, Annapurna.

At Delhi airport, we were met by Singh and driven to our base-camp, the Oberoi Maidens Hotel. For our final dinner of the trip, we chose the Curzon Room. This was the main dining room, a large room with a high ceiling, flooring of marble in black and white squares, a rather Dutch look, black and white photographs of old India arranged in blocks five rows high, making the upper ones difficult to examine, and a large painting of a hunting Cheetah. There were few other diners; all were smoking cigarettes, but all far enough away not to damage our health.

Back in our room, we did a final reckoning of the accounts. I owed Donald about £100, which he refused to accept then; he promised to send a final account after his return to England.

Delhi: Monday 22nd March
I slept well, with extra covers to keep warm. Donald kept warm with fewer covers and slept next to the open window. Cornwall, where he was then living, is colder than Hong Kong. We were up by 6.30 a.m., packing. I took off the elaborate wrapping from my marble table, and decided that the heavy wooden legs would have to go in my hand luggage, because the marble top alone was going to bring me over the weight limit for my suitcase. The guide turned up promptly at 9.00 a.m., accompanied by the same driver and Ambassador car that we had used before. We had arranged a morning tour of New Delhi, and time off to explore for ourselves in the afternoon. Our flights out of Delhi were not until after midnight.

The traffic was light going into the city. It seemed that the best time to travel was between 6 a.m. and 10 a.m. First stop was to see The Gateway of India, the huge memorial to the dead of the World Wars. The flat surfaces of the red sandstone were covered with the names of the units and the men who had been killed. A very smart honour guard of four soldiers stood on duty. I wonder if many of these Indian troops really knew for what reason they were fighting and dying in Europe and the Middle East; I think not. Next, we drove up the gentle rise of the Rajpath to the vastly handsome, self-confident buildings of the colonial administration, mirror images on each side of the road. At the head of the road the ornate iron gates of the former Viceregal Palace blocked the way. Inside were immaculately kept gardens, including large topiary elephants saluting each other across the driveway. The grandiosity of the whole lay-out was staggering. The land was bought from the Maharajah of Jaipur by the British government and the design of this area and the surrounding New Delhi was done by Sir Henry Lutyens.

Just five minutes away from this grandeur was number 11 Tughlaq Road. This had been our home for at least one winter. It was a handsome-looking single-storied, white, stone building, set back behind a wide lawn, with a driveway running in an arc from one gate to the pillared portico at the front of the house and out to a second gate. The gates were closed and a soldier with a gun was on guard. A government official lived there but was presently out of town. Tughlaq road was a broad avenue lined by mature trees. It must have been a pleasant place in which to live.

I remember learning how to ride a bicycle in the garden. On one occasion, at an early stage of that process, I crashed into my father while he was talking with the gardener. Donald and I walked round the corner into Aurangzeb Road, another handsome avenue, to number 24. We had lived on the second floor of the two-storey building, now largely hidden by a high front wall lined by tall bushes. Donald, being two years older, remembered a great deal more than I did about these locations. He led me up a mews road which brought us to the rear garden wall of No. 11. He recalled playing cricket there with his friends; I must have been too young to play. Sure enough, there was a small Indian boy right there, with a broken stump of a bat, playing cricket with his chums. Over the wall I could see the servants' quarters, separated from the house by the back lawn where there used to be tall trees hung with loofas. I was astonished to see that, in place of the vegetable garden, there were six cattle in a field, and cowpats drying on the wall. Perhaps more than anything else, this typified for me the change from the "Days of the Raj."

A DOCTOR'S LIFE IN HONG KONG

We drove round the grounds of the Gymkhana Club. This was the place, just a few minutes' bicycle ride from either house, where we used to spend much of our time. We both learned to swim in the indoor pool; and remembered with pleasure sitting on the lawn eating potato chips with tomato sauce.

Next stop was Humayun's Tomb. He was the second Mogul ruler, and father of Akbar. His wife gathered the money for the tomb over a period of nine years following his death. The tomb and surrounding gardens were set out in absolute symmetry, in the Mogul style that was to reach perfection 90 years later in the building of the Taj Mahal. Many other tombs of Mogul nobles were in the area; and a Hindu temple, an ornate, dazzling white — what a contrast.

Further south, at the edge of the city, we visited the Qutab Minar temple complex. The Qutab Minar tower was the highest in India, situated in the oldest of Delhi's seven cities. It dominates a complex of ruined red sandstone buildings, and contains remains of the palace and temples. The pillars were ornately carved, each one different from the other. The base is visible of what would have been an even bigger tower, but the ruler at the time ran out of money. As boys, Donald and I remembered coming to the Qutab Minar, then a pleasant drive into the countryside. On the bank outside the palace walls, we found fragments of the colourful glass bangles worn by the ladies of the court. Our mother told us the legend that, when the city was first built, it was on the banks of the Yamuna River; in its holy waters, the ladies of the court would bathe and say their prayers each day. When the river changed its course further east, the ladies could not do their religious duties because they could not leave the palace. Instead, the emperor built the tower so that they could still be in sight of the river when they said their prayers. As the river moved further away, the tower had to be built higher —

hence several more balconies.

If the guide had had his way, our next stop would have been the large carpet factory just down the road. With the skill of hardened tourists, we headed him off and had him drop us at Connaught Circle, at the bottom of a 25-floor building with a revolving restaurant on top, recommended by Donald's tour book. This turned out to be a great idea. We had a panoramic view of the city and were able to identify all the landmarks we had visited. At the same time, we enjoyed an excellent Indian meal and rehydrated ourselves after the rigours of a morning without a tea break.

Refreshed after an hour, and one complete revolution of the restaurant, we set off to walk around Connaught Circle. In the old days, this must have been a most elegant place. The colonnaded buildings still had a classical symmetry, but were mostly in ill repair and needed a coat of paint. It was still a great place to shop and to eat. There were many restaurants, but the only one with a queue outside was a Pizza Hut; it gave the American tourists something they knew and could trust. Nowhere could I see a shop selling curry powder, which was Judith's only request from our holiday.

We decided to take a taxi back to the hotel. The driver's first demand was for US$10, equivalent to 416 rupees; his next price was 350 rupees and, when this was refused, he agreed to use his taxi-meter, which may well have been rigged anyway. The concierge at the hotel had suggested 120 rupees would be a fair price, but the driver vehemently claimed that this was the price of a motorized tricycle—a vehicle which Donald said was dangerously unstable and into which he would not go. In the end, we reached the hotel in the taxi without mishap and at the price of about 200 rupees.

It was 4 p.m.—time for our usual swim and tea by the pool.

However we were both tired and had to pack before vacating the room at 5 p.m.

So we showered instead and went down to sit in the garden and take tea — and talk. Both of us were conscious that there was little time left to share thoughts and information. The last two weeks had been a wonderful brotherhood experience.

At 9 p.m., Ravi, the boss of the Delhi tour agency, arrived with the Sikh driver to take us to the airport. It was a harrowing drive through poorly lit streets, in competition with the hundreds of lorry drivers who were not allowed to enter Delhi until 9 p.m. There were many near misses and much blowing of horns. Ravi did his best to distract us with a spirited exposition of the Sikh faith; Gobind Singh, founder of modern Sikhism; the Golden Temple confrontation and how Indira Gandhi had behaved so badly. Finally, she was assassinated by her Sikh bodyguards. In essence, it appears that the Sikhs worship the knowledge in their prayer book, not the teachers or gurus or any divinity, like Buddhism but without the hierarchy.

We checked in at the Indira Gandhi International Airport. This involved much queuing, baggage checks, changing of rupees to dollars and filling in an embarkation card. Eventually we made it to the Sheraton VIP lounge courtesy of my Prestige Pass card, enjoyed a free drink, and some more talking. Donald left first, for his BA flight to London at 00.30 a.m.

Return to Hong Kong: Tuesday 23rd March 1999
I read *The Far Pavilions* by Kaye until it was time to proceed through immigration. It was just as well that I was in good time; there was a long queue disrupted at regular intervals by latecomers desperate to board their planes. I boarded the flight at 1 a.m. and sat there for another hour before it took off. Economy was cramped. The meal was chicken again. I had been eating not

much else for three weeks. I slept till we reached Hong Kong.

On the way out of the baggage collection area of Chek Lap Kok airport, I took pictures of a number of the tobacco advertisements for Judith — hopefully, they would soon be banned forever. Oscar Abenoja my Filipino helper was waiting to drive me home.

My Family

I come from a loving family. My parents were reserved, Victorian perhaps, but still loving. I regret that most of my adult life was spent away from them, and that they were never able to visit me and my family in Hong Kong.

I enjoyed the company of my elder brother Donald and his wife Jo, whenever we were in the same country, which was not often enough.

1960s Eleanore

Eleanore is nearly eight years younger than me, and nearly ten years younger than Donald, so again we spent much time apart. I have written some nice things about her in another chapter. She has written very generously about me.

Eleanore's early memories of John
The watercolour portrait of baby John shows him relaxed and self-confidently gazing at the viewer from blue, blue eyes framed by a halo of golden curls. Now the curls are no more.

I've always looked up to John, both physically and metaphorically. He is nearly eight years my senior after all.

I would wait impatiently at home with Mum for my dad and brothers to return from their round of golf. He was the only one who would summon the energy to play with me before lunch. French cricket, catch and tig were favourites. I ran away screaming, though, the time he was chasing me, threatening to slip a big juicy worm down my dress.

Other times he was my saviour when it came to worms. One year we rented Milton of Lesmurdie for a month. It was a lovely Victorian mansion in the Cabrach, about 10 miles south of Huntly. After breakfast we would all don our fishing gear and meander down to the nearby Post Office Burn to drown the odd worm and perhaps catch a few trout.

Without an apparent qualm, John would gently thread my hook under the skin of a wriggling worm. We would go our separate ways, hiding behind the reeds whilst casting upstream and letting the worm float down in the current. The first and only time I caught a fish I was terrified by its thrashing around, so desperate was it to escape. John was my saviour yet again, even if it did mean I had to trudge in tears the 100 yards between us. Thereafter I used a plastic worm.

JOHN MACKAY

John has always had an inquiring mind. He and Donald, our older brother, experimented with creating a water powered butter churn. It consisted of a jam jar of cream from the farm next door tied to the paddle wheel they'd made from odd bits of wood. They quickly lost interest in it having proved their invention worked.

Another summer we rented Belcorach, a farmhouse in Ballindalloch. John and our cousin Alistair caught an eel in the local burn and cut it up into chunks to see what would happen. I was spellbound in my horror. We were fascinated to find the bits still twitching hours later. John says he doesn't remember this incident.

I was snuggled up in bed with Mum and Dad having chota hazri (Hindustani for 'little breakfast' consisting of a cup of tea and a rich tea biscuit). It was around 7 a.m. when the doorbell rang. Dad returned from answering it, holding a telegram. Mum waved it away, trembling. She had grown up with telegrams bringing bad news of their loved ones in the First World War. She couldn't bring herself to open this one.

Yes, it was bad news.

John was on a cycling holiday in the Loire with a couple of school friends, celebrating leaving school. He had been run down by car and was in hospital with a broken leg. Dad spoke fluent French, so sorting out the logistics of getting him home wasn't going to be as complicated as it might have been. Within a week Dad returned with an exhausted but upbeat John sporting an impressive cast. As a consolation, John was given Vicky, a black and tan miniature dachshund pup. When he left to do his National Service in the RAF the following year, Vicky became very much Dad's shadow.

As Mum used to assert, it didn't take John long in the RAF to realise the services were not for him, but becoming a doctor was. Why not a dentist, Mum asked him. For John, the regular hours didn't compensate for patients not wanting to see you and being glad when they got away.

Our parents bought 13 Morningside Park in Edinburgh in 1953, the year of Queen Elizabeth's coronation, so that we could stay with him rather than digs for John and myself being a border at St Denis School for Girls.

It was during this time that we connected again, after being almost permanently separated for years.

He told it how it is. I asked him how my new trousers looked on me. Like a camel with two humps battling it out he replied. I was 14. My ego was sorely bruised. He was also pragmatic.

Our Edinburgh house was heated by the odd open or electric fire, central heating being a new luxury, not for us. When I complained of being cold, he told me to put more layers on. He followed his own advice and used to study in bed wrapped up in blankets and a quilt. When ready for sleep, he'd strip off his four top layers and put them under the quilt overnight so that they were not freezing when he had to put them on again.

He very much did his own thing, sometimes with questionable outcomes. Like the time we all went on holiday to Barra, the island in the Outer Hebrides where Whisky Galore was filmed. After a week of exploring the island's delights, including climbing the tallest mountain, Heaval (538m), he had had enough. Using the excuse that he wanted to redecorate the bathroom, he left on the midnight Caledonian MacBrayne ferry back to Oban and on to Edinburgh. We returned to find the bathroom an eye-boggling flamingo pink with black touches.

John was always canny with money, and generous too. One Edinburgh Christmas we agreed a spending limit on an individual's present, the equivalent of the price of a pound of best mince. He was the one who overspent.

He invited me to stay with him for a week in Jersey, all expenses paid, when he was working at the hospital in St Helier. It was a delightful contrast to my existence as a poorly paid secretary at the Department of Physical Chemistry in Cambridge when I was saving for my air fare to Montreal and a new life in Canada.

None of the family knew of his plans to go to Hong Kong until it was a done deal. I'm told that non-communication is a common consequence of being at boarding school.

Marriage to Judith has been a blessing. She is a very loving wife and loving mother to our two children, Andrew and Richard, managing to combine family life with a stellar career of her own. For years we have travelled the world together, with and without the boys. In recent years she has been a huge support for me.

She has written the following piece about me.

A DOCTOR'S LIFE IN HONG KONG

I have been very blessed in my marriage. My husband weathered, with equanimity, my transformation from the Yorkshire girl he married to a committed feminist and outspoken international health advocate.

When I first saw John in the City Hospital in Edinburgh in 1967, I knew immediately, on the spot, knew I was going to marry him, and what a truly inspired choice that was. My mother always used to say that the best thing I did in life was to marry John. John disconcerted her once by saying that the best thing he ever did was to marry me! We are compatible in more ways than one. We are both Rhesus negative. I was born in the Chinese Year of the Ram/Sheep/Goat—an animal that is most compatible with the Boar/Pig—John!

John is quieter than I am. I am a quick thinker and John is a slow thinker. But he is a deep thinker. I think we are well matched. John has been a calming and supportive influence in my life; I like to think that I have brightened John's life—he jokes that otherwise he could have become the classic 'dour Scot.'

He is not at all fazed by the fact that I am very much in the public eye. Many people ask him: "Are you Judith Mackay's husband?" He has given nothing but total and loyal support and is like a safe harbour when I return home weary from battles with the tobacco companies and non-stop travelling. He remains my best friend, my support, my oasis.

He is like my father—everyone likes him. He was always courteous and considerate with his patients, and when he retired, he was hailed as the only doctor in his group medical practice in Hong Kong against whom a complaint had never been made.

We decided to build our marriage on equality. Aligning with my feminist principles, we have always shared or split our assets 50-50. If we stayed together, then it was only fair. If it didn't work out, then it would make things easier. This meant that I was in a marriage by choice, not by financial necessity.

It has been a surprisingly easy and flexible arrangement. We have been through times when we both earned; when John was the sole wage earner and supported me through decades of working with tobacco control with no pay; other times when I was the sole wage earner, latterly with Vital Strategies and then the Global Center for Good Governance in Tobacco Control.

We have also learned how to handle disagreement and how to negotiate; John has an infallible ability to make me laugh if I veer towards getting intense, and can completely diffuse a situation.

The respect works both ways. John prefers to leave home earlier for appointments than I do, to the airport for example, and it makes him tense if we are late. So, I said to him 'Tell me what time you want to leave, and I will be ready.' I have NEVER missed that deadline.

The two boys are a delight. When they were small, just 18 months apart, they took a lot of looking-after. I was working long hours and remember coming home to read or tell them a bedtime story and falling asleep myself. We were fortunate to live in a place where domestic help was affordable.

As they grew, so did our activities. For many years our boat,

Aloha, was a floating playpen taking us to the beaches in Sai Kung to build sandcastles, paddle, learn to swim. Later we had a sailing dinghy and windsurfers and built even bigger sandcastles. At the United Services Recreation Club, we all swam, played squash and tennis together.

Once we had built our own swimming pool at Riftswood we enjoyed large birthday parties with the boys and their school friends.

Holidays back in the UK, in Lossiemouth in the north of Scotland and Saltburn-by-the-Sea in Yorkshire were always fun, on the beach or a golf course, spending time with their grandparents. More exotic trips were to ski resorts in Kashmir, Australia and New Zealand, or to beach resorts in Kota Kinabalu and Club Med resorts in Bali and Mauritius. Some of the best times were holidays with Donald and Jo and their three children in St. Lucia. One memorable visit for us all was our visit in 1976 to Beijing.

1974 Our boat, 'Aloha' a family boat kept at Hebe Haven

JOHN MACKAY

Over the years Judith and I have watched with pride how our little boys grew up, excelled at school and university, have meaningful and important jobs, and in their turn have become loving parents.

I look back with satisfaction at what Judith and I have done as parents and grandparents, and look forward to the happy days together yet to come.

Epilogue

Life in Hong Kong has always been a roller-coaster ride. When I arrived in 1963, it was booming as a manufacturing centre. The population was 3.5 million. Fortunes were being made and there was a buzz of prosperity in the air. This growth continued for 20 years and the population doubled. British Prime Minister Margaret Thatcher's visit to Beijing in 1983 brought home the reality of the 1997 "Handover"; there was hesitancy about the future and many left. Judith and I decided to stay, because of our belief in the future of Hong Kong and her important work on tobacco control in the region.

The 1997 reversion of sovereignty to China went smoothly. Recovery was dented by the Asian financial crisis but recovery took only two years. Hong Kong shed its manufacturing role to become a world financial centre.

In 2003, the SARS (Severe Acute Respiratory Syndrome) epidemic was terrifying at the start. Doctors did not know what caused it, how it spread or what was the treatment; hospital staff were dying. The World Health Organisation issued a Travel Advisory warning people not to come to Hong Kong. The streets were deserted. We stayed at home. Happily, the Coronavirus and the manner of spread was identified; strict tracing and isolation got on top of the infection. Four months later, it was all over. We emerged from isolation. A total of 1,755 people in Hong Kong had caught it, of whom 298 died. Hong Kong recovered again.

Despite the 2008 global financial crisis. Hong Kong continued to prosper. But, since 2014, social unrest has caused immense problems. The "Occupy Central with Love and Peace" movement was started by a trio of academics—Prof. Benny Tai, Prof. Chan Kin Man and retired priest Rev. Chu You Ming. The original peaceful sit-ins were transformed into a student-led Umbrella Demonstration for universal suffrage. Streets in Admiralty, Causeway Bay and Mongkok were blocked, which was an inconvenience. On the other hand, it was a bizarre pleasure to walk around the traffic-free streets, among the students quietly studying or sleeping in their tents. We admired the ingenuity of the slogans and messages stuck up on a "Lennon Wall". It ended quietly 79 days later, with 89 arrests and no concessions from the government.

The 2019 demonstrations against a proposed Extradition Law were very different—violent and well financed. What started as "peaceful demonstrations, legal or illegal" often became destructive riots. Two people were killed by rioters. No rioter was killed, a remarkable evidence of police restraint. PLA soldiers were never involved. I walked from Causeway Bay to Admiralty one day after a March protest in 2020 and saw boarded-up Chinese banks, shattered shopfronts and closed MTR stations. I did not feel threatened, the violence was directed against the government, the police and the Chinese government. "Five demands, not one less" was the mantra.

The June 2020 National Security Law brought the riots to an end: it was an act by the Beijing Government to rescue the situation. The aftermath has been a succession of prison sentences for the worst offenders who had actually broken the laws of Hong Kong and the departure overseas for others facing prison.

In January 2020, the Covid-19 epidemic reached Hong Kong, having been first reported the month before in Wuhan, central China. The first waves of infection were well controlled by public health measures. But the Omicron variant proved lethal to unvaccinated, immune-compromised and elderly people. I and my household took up the vaccines as soon as available, avoided crowds and reduced contact with friends to the minimum and watched sadly as any outdoor activity was forbidden apart from hill-walking, masked of course.

March 2022 was a low point, two years since the epidemic started. Two years since we had the freedom to go everywhere and do everything that we regarded as a normal life.

Since those dark days, life has turned around. Judith and I enjoyed three months in Britain, seeing family and friends, enjoying going maskless and without using the 'Leave Home Safe' application on our iPhones. When we returned to Hong Kong, we found a more optimistic atmosphere. The new Chief Executive, John Lee, and his team started loosening regulations. Major events like international conferences were held in November, and we attended the Seven-a-Side Rugby tournament again with the noisy crowd resplendent in costumes, cheering on their country's team. The winners were Australia for the first time in 35 years, over a Fijian side that had won on the last six occasions. I am optimistic about the future.

Looking back on my 60 years in Hong Kong, I wonder at the huge developments that have taken place here, and how they are reflected in me. I arrived with a suitcase and little else, apart from a good education and ambition to make good use of it. Hong Kong has given me that opportunity. I fulfilled my academic and professional ambitions and enjoyed the first 30 years in doing so.

A DOCTOR'S LIFE IN HONG KONG

For the last 30 years I have been able to indulge my wish to travel and lead an active, busy life. For 55 years Judith has been at my side. Wife, companion, friend, mother to our two children, life with her is a blessing.

Acknowledgements

Much credit for getting this book up and running goes to Mark O'Neil whose contributions, advice and research were invaluable. At the other end of the process, Graham Earnshaw and his team have done a superb job in putting together my words and pictures.

I wrote these memoirs primarily so that my family would have some lasting memory of my life, much of which was spent far from Scotland and my relatives living there. My parents spent much of their lives in India, and to my lasting regret left almost no record of their lives. I thank my sister Eleanore for sharing with me the only part of my father's memoir that we have.

My wife, Judith, has helped and encouraged me throughout the writing process.

About The Author

Dr. John Mackay was born in Scotland, the second son of his father, an officer in the Indian army, and his mother, both from Moray in Scotland. During World War II he and the family were in India. Ever since, he has loved to travel. Back in Scotland after the war he went to a public school, did National Service in the RAF, and entered Edinburgh University qualifying as a doctor in 1961. During university years his thirst for adventure took him on hitch-hiking trips in Europe and across North America. As a doctor he chose to do two years of further training, in Nassau in the Bahamas and in Britain, before settling in Hong Kong, for the first 30 years with a private group practice. He married Judith, a newly qualified doctor, in 1967; they have two sons and three grandchildren. Judith has built an international career as an advocate for a tobacco-free world. In the last 30 years he has travelled extensively with the goal of climbing the highest point in each country visited.

www.ingramcontent.com/pod-product-compliance
Lightning Source LLC
LaVergne TN
LVHW030317070526
838199LV00069B/6482